¡Mande!

A Memoir

Gail Henderson Dimitroff

To Pat,
With fond memories of
our growing-up days in
the 50's. Love,
Gail
2004

Silver Threads
San Diego, California

gaildimitroff@
cox..net

¡Mande! A Memoir

Becoming Whole: Writing Your Healing Story

For information, contact Silver Threads, 3738 Carmel View Road, San Diego, California 92130 (858-794-1597)

Silver Threads is an imprint of Silvercat Publications®

Publishers Cataloging in Publication Data

Dimitroff, Gail Henderson

Mande: a memoir / Gail Henderson Dimitroff. — San Diego, Calif : Silver Threads, 2004

p. ; cm.
ISBN 1-893067-02-5

1. Dimitroff, Gail Henderson. 2. Americans—Mexico—Biography. 3. Mexico—Social life and customs.
4. Assimilation (Sociology) 5. Women—Socialization.
6. Self-actualization (Psychology) 7. Women—Biography.
I. Title

F1210.D56.2004   2003114919
917.2/082--dc22   0403

printed in the United States of America

For Jeanne Marie

F oreword

M ande is a command form in Spanish. This polite form sig-
nals subservience, a desire to serve. "May I help you" or
"pardon me" or, more literally, "command me." I have not heard
the expression used in any country except Mexico, and it is a part
of Mexican consciousness that I could relate to as a young
woman. I still carry shades of it, even now.

I want to speak of the theme of liberation—the voice of a
woman growing up in a strange country, the lingering images of
colonialism, and the accompanying sense of self-contempt—
and of its antidote: grace, love, and self-knowledge.

Out of the struggle to visualize, call in, and squint into the
past, I have come to realize that soul force, the love of beauty,
and the power of joy can transform even painful events into rich
memories and create something of value.

Prologue

*L*ast night I was being hugged by an orangutan. Its strong, hairy arms entwined me in a tight embrace as he whispered, "Happy Birthday," in my ear. His rolling eyes seemed to hold some ancient secret I could not penetrate.

Upon waking, I found that the dream remained vivid. A brief search for meaning over morning coffee was followed by an "Aha!" Then, the fresh, bright images of the ape and the birthday message collided, causing an unstoppable and nostalgic cascade of memories. The dream had to be linked to my father and to Len.

I spent my first seven years in Chicago where Daddy worked for the Postal Telegraph, a service that sent telegraphs around the world. He'd read me the comics on Sunday morning, share stories of his glamorous work, and tell me that life was fine. He did public relations for the company, and his stunt with an ape gained him some fame as a public relations guru.

Once, he brought home two lion cubs in a small cage. He let me play with them. They were to play a part in one of his current publicity stunts. As a small child, I was puzzled by these events and unable to understand how such a large company fitted into the world of lions. They were soft and cuddly and had huge paws. They were learning to walk and play.

The most memorable of these promotional events involved a trip to the Lincoln Park Zoo in Chicago. My mother and I took the El downtown. I must have been about four years old, for I remember my mother's quick steps as we tripped through the park on a beautiful spring morning, and how I had to struggle to keep up with her.

It had sprinkled earlier, and the smell of rain still lingered along the sidewalk that wound through the park. All glistened fresh and clean—the smell of spring fragrant with blossoms. Chicago, refreshed by the passing storms of spring, enjoyed the thaw. With the Depression behind us and Roosevelt as president, new life was welling up. A profusion of lilies of the valley and lilacs lined the pathway.

"Where are we going?" I asked.

"We have to meet your father at the orangutan cage." She seemed breathless, yet she still hurried. Her new patent leather high-heeled shoes clicked on the pavement and made a cadence that challenged me to keep up. I took her hand and glanced up at her. She looked beautiful in a lilac dress that was covered with little flowers and a saucy hat with a tiny peek-a-boo veil. Something important was going to happen.

When we arrived at the specified location, we found the cage to be dark yet spacious. My father looked especially dapper that day, his hat a bit crooked. It reminded me of the hats that George Raft wore in the movies. Daddy directed a technical crew and ordered them to place spotlights at strategic locations around the cage. Ladies and gentlemen of the press jostled for good camera angles.

Bob Crosby and the Bob Cats gathered in front of the cage. I was slightly confused to see that the Bob Cats looked nothing like the feline beauties that Daddy had brought home for me to play with only a week before. These cats were singers who appeared with Bob at The Black Hawk Night Club.

In the corner of the cage hunched a huge orangutan—strong, proud, and severe. On this particular day in spring, however, a tense wariness came over him as the commotion outside his home increased. The closer we got to the nearly four-hundred-pound animal, the smaller I felt. And then the celebration began.

It was the orangutan's birthday. A large cake composed of edibles suitable for an ape sat in the middle of the cage. I could not tell exactly its ingredients and, except for the celery stalks that served as candles, it looked like an ordinary cake.

The Bob Cats wore Postal Telegraph uniforms, the kind worn by delivery boys and girls—neat navy-blue uniforms with metal buttons and perky pillbox hats. They gathered in front of the orangutan and sang, "Happy Birthday to you, Happy Birthday to YOU." At first the ape ignored them. And then he took the stage, apparently listening to the sassy, swinging songsters.

They sang with authority and made us believe he liked it. And then the ape took the cake, assumed an attitude of poise, kept us guessing for just a moment, and heaved it at us.

Candles flew, and what turned out to be a messy batch of gooey fruit and leaves hit the bars of the cage. Some, but not all, flew toward us. The tempestuous loner swung his limbs, beat his chest, and spat on the balladeers. The sharply tailored ladies and gentlemen who were there to witness the event stepped back nimbly, but not everyone missed being hit by the flying mess. A heart-stopping moment.

I looked up at my father who gave me an impish smile.

This was the event! The first singing telegram ever invented had been sung right there in the Lincoln Park Zoo. It said to the world, "Get ready for something different." In the marketplace of ideas, this turned out to be a successful venture. And there would be many more singing telegrams to come. The nation took to it and it soon became a popular way of sending greetings all through the War years, and even for a time thereafter. None of us that day could foresee the twists and turns that the communication industry would take in the future. His invention of the "Singing Telegram" catapulted my father to fame.

While World War II raged in the Pacific and Europe, Daddy built on his past success and made a name for himself as a fundraiser. He collected millions of dollars for the Red Cross and the War Bond effort. Three years after the War ended, a unique opportunity came his way. Bishop Charles F. Buddy from the Diocese of San Diego asked my father to raise money to match funds from the Religious of the Sacred Heart. The purpose was to build a Catholic college for women—and that is where my story will begin—but first, a little more about Dad.

Alfred Henderson, my father, accepted the challenge to secure contributions and pledges to begin construction. The campus was named "Alcala Park" after a Spanish city near Madrid. By 1949, bulldozing began. Within months, the lovely Spanish Renaissance buildings and courtyards of the college stood tall. One day, it would be transformed into the University of San Diego. Daddy could not have known at the time, but I would be one of the first students to attend the San Diego College for Women. In 1953, fresh out of high school, I won a full merit scholarship and completed a year and a half of study.

My parents saw to it that I had a Catholic education. The fixed values of the Church enmeshed me—and for years I felt secure, nestled in the crook of its arm. That is not to say that I did not, at times, rebel. I tasted my first flavor of dissent in high school. It was a dramatic incident beginning with Barbara, a classmate. She had been dating a sailor, got pregnant, and went to Tijuana for a quickie marriage. Dismayed, haunted, estranged people brought out compassion in me. The poor girl wanted to be married in the church and she asked me to come to her official wedding in the church rectory. When I agreed to go, the arm of the Church in the form of my homeroom teacher wrapped itself around me.

"If you go, you will be showing your approval of what she did," the nun said.

"I wouldn't miss it for the world," I replied and tried to recall my class in Apologetics. "What is not forbidden is permitted."

This memory would come back to me throughout my life. I have a natural antipathy to anything that does not allow freedom of thought. But more than that, it was a powerful taste of self-assertion, establishing that at my core, I was not a person who would always say to a loved one or to an institution, "¿Mande? Command me?" if I didn't believe something was right.

⚜

Why mention the orangutan? The dream itself revealed my unconventional childhood, and as I unraveled it, I came to the conclusion that I need to know the difference between a hug and a stranglehold. Still another reason—just as on that day at the zoo when I had a feeling something big was going to happen, I realized I'd had the same feeling the day I met Len.

Blinded by a dazzling smile, I was seduced by a young man's dream of success. The first time I met him, I found him exciting, irresistible, and handsome. In 1954, at the age of nineteen, I turned my back on a promising career in modeling, gave up my scholarship, and married him. My initial ignorance of what the marriage role would entail was matched only by my anxiety that I play it perfectly.

One and a half years after we were married, I left my home and sheltered life in San Diego, my five-month-old infant daughter in tow, to join my husband on his adventure into Mexico. It is a strange and penetrating experience, this journey to the past. I sit on the deck, sip my coffee, and once again find myself in the mercado in Monterrey where I learned to bargain, in the Ambassador Hotel's patio debating with a student, or in the Plaza Zaragoza listening to the bells on a Sunday morning. I see my baby, little Jeanne, whose pale beauty charmed all, and wonder if she has any memories of these images—she was only two and a half when we left Mexico. In my reverie, I can sometimes hear Len's voice droning in Spanish, repeating a lesson in anatomy, telling a joke with a fine Irish accent, or see him lifting Jeanne over his head.

Then, half-aware, some coldness creeps in as I reminisce and my spirit sags. I am aware of it and of the passing of days and long afternoons. Some of the battles I fought with myself and with Leonard could have turned out better.

From the moment I met him, I felt as if I had been sucked into an unfamiliar vortex of glamour, passion, joy, and despair. Perhaps it was my destiny. In retrospect, I see how unprepared I was for what would unfold. I can also see how our intentions created the vortex.

I was naïve at the very least, with a natural reserve. I was private, elusive. In contrast, he was warm, inexhaustible, charming, and expansive. Len was considered a good catch. I couldn't believe it when he showed an interest in me. He brought an abundance of vitality and joyous humor into my life. We told ourselves that we would abandon all other relationships and devote our lives to each other. And we did—at first.

But behind his gaze, I glimpsed dissatisfaction in his eyes. It was only a flash. I probed, learning that his creative spark had been hindered in some way. As the eldest of six children, he'd suffered from a lack of affection and needed it in a relationship. He was also discouraged with the banality of his life. The year we met, his creativity rekindled. He doodled away his excessive energy, and many of his scribbles would have been considered art. I often wondered why he wasn't interested in pursuing this. However, medicine was his passion. I still marvel at his unwavering sense of vocation.

I started with a complete acceptance of Leonard's vision. I have a blurred recollection of intimate chats, or unexpected and nimble brainstorming sessions about the future. His words lifted, animated, and beguiled me. We were different, but I learned to tune myself into his mood.

"You're calm and strong," he said, "and really understand me."

He said that I outstripped him intellectually; yet he surpassed anyone I had ever known in charm, wit, and physical beauty. I liked to be alone with my thoughts and my books, even though when pressed, I could do a strong public presentation. But then I needed to re-charge. Not Len. People energized him. Left alone for five minutes, he would whip up a party. Len thrived on voluble, intense interaction, and in the process defined himself. Moreover, with radiant self-assurance, he assumed that his presence was always welcome.

Now, as I am almost seventy years old and Leonard dead nearly five years, I see that as I became close to him, I accepted his ideas and attitudes, but the intimacy achieved by compromising what is vital was not real.

Yet, despite bitter experiences, nothing is regretted. My meeting with Leonard seems fated. Thinking of him now and of all that happened, I wonder if my dream of the orangutan has another meaning. Have the animal forces of dominance, which I allowed to gain a stranglehold on my life, been tamed? Are they now whispering a seventieth birthday greeting of congratulations?

I offer a lens to others—through which to view the past—in the hope that they might gauge their own balance of dependent submission and independent self-assertion, a balance that rocks destinies as it shifts.

Part 1

One

Never Forget
1955

A Saturday morning in May. The fragrance of sea lingered in the fading fog and mist that encircled Alcala Park. Everything was quiet. A silvery sun shone above. With Jeanne Marie in my arms, I hurried up the slight hill to the main entrance of the San Diego College for Women at Founders Hall. Reaching the top, I glanced across Mission Valley at the Presidio and steadied myself for a moment, aware that only a month earlier I would have been too weak to make it up the little incline. After a second wind and a deep breath, I fairly sailed into the vestibule. Situated to the right on the far side of the familiar partitioned door, sat a student worker. Today, she was the receptionist.

"May I help you?" she asked. She looked at me quizzically and then at Jeanne. Babies were not a common sight at the San Diego College for Women.

"Good morning. I have an appointment with Mother Danz. My name is Gail Burns."

"Didn't you used to work in the library?" she asked.

"Yes, that was last fall." I continued wistfully, "I worked in the rare books section."

"I remember you." She led me into the French Parlor.

I entered, sat down on a brocade divan, settled myself, and propped Jeanne on a little pillow. I had been careful to select her soft, flowing baptismal gown for the occasion.

Jeanne was supposed to have been born this week, the first week of May, but instead she showed up six weeks early on March twenty-third. During the past month, she had developed rapidly. By now, long eyelashes and fingernails appeared where none had been before. Her skin had become rosy instead of jaundiced. And after a return visit to Mercy Hospital following her delivery, an emergency "D&C," and a blood transfusion, I had finally regained my strength.

The delicate, dainty room we'd entered had been designed for discrete conversation and intimate meetings on chairs and sofas of slender proportion and easy curves. The furniture, inlaid with rare woods and mother of pearl, was light blue or cream in color and lavish with gilded trim. Mirrored walls filled the room with light and reflected the beauty of the pastel ceiling. Wall hangings of silk, tapestry, and an overall abundance of gilded ornaments created a sparkling, thoroughly French version of the Baroque. For one terrible moment, a pang of regret washed over me at having relinquished all of this.

The room was a piece of living history and appropriate for the Religious of *Sacre Coeur*. After all, it was the French Revolution that had given rise to the order— a group of courageous women who had taken pity on the daughters of the aristocrats and vowed to save them. They called themselves the *Madames of the Sacred Heart*.

A few select pieces of Chinese porcelain had made their ways into the sitting room. I greatly admired their thinness and the translucent finish. As I looked down at Jeanne Marie peacefully asleep in my arms, I noticed that her skin was like the porcelain. One of the more colorful vases caught my attention. Elegant and flawless in finish, its deep-blue enamel was heavily decorated in gold, unforgettable.

The light of spring filtered through the window, leaving a strange lucidity. From the hallway, I could hear the distant sound of students chatting. Wonderful things began to happen.

The atmosphere provoked a flow of memories—rendezvous with friends, consultations with teachers. It had been here, in this very room during 1953, that Bishop Buddy had awarded me my scholarship, and afterwards I had curtsied and kissed his ring. He had taken my hand and congratulated me.

"You have a vigor of mind," he had said and looked me in the eye. "Use it well."

It was here in this beautiful parlor that I had met with my advisor, Mother Danz, when I abandoned that scholarship. I had to tell her that I was too ill from the pregnancy to continue my studies. Her amiable nature and good will eased my discomfort, so embarrassed was I with self-consciousness. After all, my marriage and pregnancy were not topics of academic relevance, particularly in a Catholic girl's school. I found my situation extremely disquieting.

But today was different in that Jeanne would be presented on the altar to become forever *Une enfante de Sacre Coeur*, a child of the Sacred Heart.

A grilled gate partitioned the parlor from the entry hall. It squeaked on its hinge, and as I turned around, Mother Danz bustled toward me. I rose and curtsied, looking up at her thin, narrow face so neatly framed in the starched white ruff, emblematic of the order.

"*Bonjour, ma petite.*" She smiled at me. "And look at the darling baby. She is so tiny, still?"

"She's grown quite a bit, Mother."

Mother Danz inquired about my health, my husband Leonard, and my family. Then she explained the very private nature of the ceremony.

"So, our little one will be dedicated today. This is a special, personal ceremony, just for our girls. We began the practice shortly after our founding in Paris right after the Revolution, oh-so-many long years ago." When she spoke, I knew I was about to be included in a beautiful and sacred secret.

Jeanne wriggled in the long, white baptismal gown, opened one eye, then promptly closed it.

"What did you call her?"

"I gave her a French name, of course. Jeanne Marie after Joan of Arc."

"A strong name for a strong young lady." Madame smiled at me and then at the baby. "Well, let's go," she said and gestured for me to rise.

Mother Danz opened the gate and I followed her out of the parlor, past the foyer, and through the Spanish courtyard. Deep-orange and bright-pink bougainvillea climbed the stucco walls of the courtyard. In the center of the enclosed area, a fountain overflowed into a tiled basin. Splashing water, the scent of roses, white buildings shining in the sun—all made me feel as if I was in a castle in Spain hundreds of years ago. We proceeded to the far end of the garden and entered the vestibule of Founders Chapel.

Inside, the light was dim, but I knew the way. We paused momentarily at the Chapel door, just as we had done at General Assembly when I was a student. Today, however, I was no longer wearing the cap and gown of a scholar.

As I stood in front of the carved stone entry, I looked down the aisle toward the altar, which gleamed at the far end. Looking up at the golden façade, I realized that its degree of ornateness was unparalleled. Carved in wood and burnished in gold, it furnished a rich background for the altar. Vertical shafts and horizontal bands divided the altarpiece into panels with elaborately carved niches and figure sculpture. The dim light and the unadorned surfaces of the rest of the chapel only served to enhance the majesty of otherworldliness combined with magnificence.

My high-heels clicked on the rose-colored marble floor as we proceeded toward the altar. Slowly, we made our way through the pews and past the Stations of the Cross. Stained glass windows on both sides let in pools of light that made little jewel-like spots on the pink floor inlaid with dark bands of forest-green marble. I paused at the front pew and, leaning over, laid my bag on the plush green velvet cushion that covered the pew.

I hesitated before entering the sanctuary. Only twice had I been on the far side of the communion rail: once for my Confirmation and once for my marriage. Custom made me reluctant to go further, but Mother Danz led me on. As we approached the altar, my heart began to pound. I faltered at the base of the green marble steps that led up to a large alabaster altar. Six large candlesticks, three on each side, surrounded the tabernacle of gold.

"It's all right," said Mother Danz. She took my arm and led the way to the top step. There, she rearranged the candlesticks so that there was sufficient space for me to lay Jeanne Marie.

"Here?" I asked, looking at her for guidance.

Madame nodded. Carefully, I placed Jeanne Marie on the altar. *She is the essence of sweetness. I give her to you, to the Sacred Heart forever. Keep her safe.*

Mother Danz said gently, *"Toujours une enfante de Sacre Coeur."*

"Toujours," I whispered.

From the center panel, the compassionate eyes of the crucified Christ looked down on us with a glance that said He would accept my baby and protect her for all her life. At the base of the cross, the Virgin Mary, Mary Magdalene, and St. John the Beloved composed a triangular group. They looked down on us through a frame of painted crimson drapery as if from another dimension, and Madame and I were looking through a window to a safe, divine world. And now, Jeanne Marie and I, attending her on the altar, were a part of it all.

I had been in the chapel dozens of times before, but never had I really seen it. My breath caught in my throat. I could feel my heart race.

The most amazing thing was the way the powerful patterns, gilded figures, Mother Danz, Jeanne Marie, and I seemed to merge and become, for just one moment, whirls of light specked with gold. Tears came to my eyes.

I looked down at Jeanne and was amazed. Tiny arms waved in jerky circles toward the glittering gold above her head. The smoothly flowing silk of her gown cascaded down and over the alabaster stone. As I looked closer, I noticed that the slate-gray of her eyes were now blue, the same blue as the Chinese vase in the sitting room. I was shocked to see clear, cornflower blue staring back at me. Angel eyes of blue.

"Jeanne Marie, you are now and forever a child of the Sacred Heart."

I picked up the baby and held her close. She was so tiny, so precious. "I know she will come back here, Mother. I just know she will."

And then, Mother Danz turned to me and said what she had said so many times to me and to all of her students, "Never forget: nothing is too good for you girls."

Two

A Golden Opportunity

*B*rimming with excitement, and with my arms barely containing a squirming Jeanne, I rushed up the stairs into our apartment. The thrill of the ceremony was still fresh in my mind, and I wanted to tell my husband, Len, about the dedication.

He sat in a corner of the living room noiselessly blowing smoke rings. His first words had an edge that wilted my eagerness. "I need to talk with you." He stood and came toward me.

"What is it? Did something happen at work today?" I stood still and waited.

"Here, come sit down," he pointed to the couch.

I put Jeanne down next to me.

"The thing is," he paused, " I—well I've been offered a promotion at work."

I breathed a sigh of relief. I had imagined something terrible. With a promotion and raise, I could see us living plumply in our cozy apartment overlooking Mission Valley. Len edged closer. I could smell the freshness of his aftershave. He was handsome—so handsome that I sometimes felt plain beside him. I think he knew that.

"That's great." I felt relieved. Still, my mind raced. My eyes skimmed the living room: early American maple furniture, brass table lamp, chintz curtains. I had worked hard to get it all together before Jeanne was born. Now, I could make things even better. I imagined the improvements I would make with a little more money.

"The thing is," Len hesitated, "if I accept the promotion, I would have to commit to stay." He looked away.

"What did you say?" I felt a flutter in the pit of my stomach. My soaring spirits flagged suddenly and dropped.

"I said, 'no.'" He said it quickly and directly. "I want to be a doctor. I don't want to find myself here, ten years from now, at the San Diego County Health Department. All I can think about is medical school. I don't want to lead a life of mediocrity."

I nodded that I understood. He interpreted this as agreement, then leaned over and kissed me.

His next words raised real concern. "Have you ever thought of living in Mexico?"

"I used to go to Tijuana when I was a kid. We went there during World War Two."

"You went to Mexico during the War?"

"Yes, actually, we went to Tijuana to eat meat. It was tough, but it was meat. We couldn't get steak here. Everything was rationed. What are you getting at?"

"So you liked it there?" he insisted.

We stared at each other. I was puzzled. There was no cogent connection between this conversation and what he had told me just moments ago.

"It was an outing," I said, "nothing more."

"But you liked it?" He pressed on with his point.

Bewildered, I continued, "Once I had my picture taken sitting on a burro. I've got it around here somewhere. And, oh yes, we went into the Long Bar. I saw myself in the distorted mirrors. It was like a fun house."

"Well, I think we should go to Mexico." He emphasized the *we*, drawing it out slowly. Flashing his movie star smile, he continued, "I think I can get into medical school there."

Nothing could have forestalled my shock.

"Didn't you try that before?" I asked. I remembered some story he had told me about going south of the border. But that was before I knew him.

"Yes, but that was in Mexico City," he said. "The school was huge and I didn't speak a word of Spanish. Now, I do."

"I can understand that you're eager to avoid a humdrum life. But how about the job you were offered as a professional cartoonist?" I looked down at Jeanne as if the answer were there.

He shook his head sadly. "I don't want to be a cartoonist. Don't you understand? I have to be a doctor. I think I can make it in Monterrey," he persisted. "The school is small and it's easy to get in. Besides, I heard that there's a small group of American students. They report that things are okay."

Apparently, he had been thinking about this for some time.

"Remember Bill Saccoman?" Len went on, eager now.

"He's one of your mom's golf buddies, isn't he?"

"Yeah, that's the one. Well, Bill just got accepted to Loma Linda, just a few miles north of San Diego County."

"Didn't Bill become a Seventh Day Adventist?" I asked, baffled.

"Yes, and that probably helped get him in, but his wife is a Sabbie and she was on his case."

"A what?"

"A Sabbie. You know, Seventh Day Adventist. Bill told me that there's a group of Americans who didn't get into Loma Linda. They went down to Mexico. Actually, Monterrey. They're in school there and doing well. Many have families."

"Does this mean you have to become a Sabbie?" Len had a proud Irish soul. I wouldn't have married him if he had been anything but Catholic. His whole family was Catholic.

"No, it's just nice to know that some Americans are there already. They are doing well. This could be a golden opportunity. I mean for us."

Interrupting him, I said, "This is a big decision. How would we pay for it?"

A noise caught my attention. The front door swung in the fresh afternoon wind. It slammed shut. Jeanne, sensitive to the sound, jumped. I spoke to her quietly. I wondered what would become of us and of her—the fragile little figure beside me. I was unwilling to admit that I was afraid.

"Trust me," he said. "My boss said he will give me $50.00 a month. That's a start. I'll get more."

Looking out the window above the rooftops, I began to see the threads that made our life in San Diego slowly unravel. I felt excitement, but also trepidation. I didn't say what I wanted to say.

Len put his arm around me. "We'll be fine." His voice was soothing. Then he added, "How was the dedication at the chapel?"

I was so blindsided by the turn of events that I simply answered, "Fine."

❦

That weekend turned out to be one of the longest I had ever experienced. I soon realized that we would have to liquidate all our belongings, things we had just bought. Some of those possessions, like wedding gifts, could be stored. As we planned what had to be done, I withheld the news from my family.

❦

It was the end of July. I helped him pack the car with quiet determination. Finally, when the trunk, back seat, and floor could hold no more, we said our goodbyes. Len put the car in gear and drove alone out of San Diego in the direction of Arizona and on to Laredo, Texas. There, he would cross the border and the muddy Rio Grande and head southwest, at last arriving in Monterrey. From that point on, he'd only need a few weeks to find a house for us and enroll in Medical School.

ᚷ

I had been right in anticipating the reaction from my family.

"You're going where?" my grandfather roared. He rarely shouted—and never at me. But today, he did.

"To Monterrey, in Mexico," I stammered. I loved this old German grandpa more than anyone in the world. Except, of course, Len.

"Why, in God's name, would anyone in their right mind choose to go to that God-forsaken country? And Monterrey— Why there?" He threw up his hands, exasperated.

My grandmother stood behind his chair kneading a handkerchief in her hands. My mother cried. She sat on the couch and held Jeanne. From time to time, she looked down at the baby. Only my grandfather had spoken. In this world of women, my grandfather still ruled the roost.

"It's a center of technology," I went on. "It's the Pittsburgh of Mexico." Tears came to my eyes.

"Pittsburgh of Mexico!" He scoffed. "Pittsburgh of the U.S. is bad enough, and you are traipsing off to the one in Mexico?"

"Grandpa," I insisted, quoting Len, "it's a golden opportunity."

"And I suppose you'll be taking that little tyke with you," he nodded at Jeanne, "to Pittsburgh, Mexico." His asthma caught him off guard. He started to wheeze.

"Yes, of course."

"You're only nineteen," my mother sobbed. "You just got out of the hospital."

"I'll be twenty next week."

"Leonard wouldn't do anything to hurt Gail and Jeanne," my grandmother sighed. Like my mom, they were both utterly charmed by Len.

"Why isn't he traveling with you?" my grandfather demanded.

"He's gone to find us a house—to enroll in school—to make things easier." I wanted to cry, but I didn't. I had to show them that I was competent.

In the end, I got their reluctant blessing. As with most victories, this one came with a price. I left knowing how much my actions distressed my family. My grandfather, now old and fragile, would have preferred that I remain close to him. I knew I would miss him—miss them all. I didn't mention that I thought I was pregnant again.

Three

Gambler's Son

I told my mother not to worry; Frank would take me to the airport in Tijuana. Frank and Alice Denny had taken me in when Len left for Mexico. In those six weeks, I learned quickly enough that the Dennys were the subject of a great amount of gossip and criticism.

For one thing, the nature of their relationship was puzzling. It was said that they had left the East Coast quite suddenly under peculiar circumstances. Stories had it that their name "Denny" was fictitious—an alias. In addition, rumor held that the glamorous couple gambled obsessively. They had been on the run for several years until they arrived in San Diego where they set down roots. Gossip flourished. Moreover, Alice had a reputation for being a most audacious flirt, a habit that only fanned the fire of talk.

Alice was Len's mom and everyone said that he got his good looks from her. From the moment I met her, I knew she was an extraordinary woman. Beautiful, blonde, and sensual, she possessed the same vivacity and charm that I so loved in Len. With a voice both youthful and summery, she filled the moment with sunshine. Living within a whirlpool of excitement, she captivated everyone she met and seemed genuinely fond of people, often connecting with them immediately in an intimate way. She and Len were so much alike.

While Jeanne and I were guests in the Denny home, Alice seemed to take an intense interest in me. I was quite flattered. At first I felt like an intruder, but Frank's kindly attitude and Alice's warm regard made me feel at home. Frank, twelve years her junior, was handsome in a dark, Mediterranean way. Together they were striking. He was obviously mad about her.

Family and friends buzzed incessantly about them and the fact that I was a recipient of their hospitality. I felt increasingly uncomfortable with all the gossip. One of the advantages of going to Mexico would be permanent distance from the endless chatter.

As a frequent visitor to Caliente, the racetrack in Tijuana, Frank knew the Mexican roads well. Rumor had it that he'd made a killing down there. He made me a little nervous despite his appealing gentleness, but when he offered to take me to the airport, I agreed on the spot. On the day of our departure, he maneuvered the back roads. His nonchalance made me feel relaxed as we entered the airport terminal.

I'd never flown, and a case of nerves overshadowed my excitement. Jeanne squirmed in my arms as we checked the bags and went to the departure gate. I'd dressed her in a soft jersey jumper with rosebuds to match her complexion. I held her tightly as we approached the gate.

I thanked Frank who nodded reassuringly and pressed a ten-dollar bill into my hand.

"Just in case." He turned and walked away and I was on my own.

"*Pásale, Señora.*" The attendant at the gate waved me forward.

With more than a few butterflies tickling my insides, I boarded. The stewardess helped me as I struggled with the baby, bags, and a whole array of baby supplies. At a little before ten o'clock, we took off from Rodriguez Airfield. Images streaked by:

a control tower, a tree, a fence, a cardboard shanty. The adobe buildings seemed to vibrate in the warm atmosphere and wriggling vapor. I turned northward. Behind me, I saw the border town and the U.S. fade into the distance.

Banking over the ocean, the plane turned southeast. Before long, we were over the Sea of Cortez. The pressure or the drone of the propellers seemed to bother Jeanne. She shook her head and twisted and fidgeted. Soon, she screamed in pain. I picked her up and dug the pacifier from my pocket, but she would have none of it. Not knowing what else to do, I patted her back gently and said things my mother might have said to me. I told her we'd be there soon; we'd see Daddy. Too little to understand, she nevertheless relaxed a little and collapsed on my shoulder with her wet cheek against my neck.

The attendant offered what help she could, but there was not much that anyone could do, and what help she offered, I couldn't understand.

In front of us, a woman passenger close to my mother's age turned and spoke soft, soothing words. I couldn't understand the meaning, but it sounded right. She rose and stood next to me and stroked Jeanne's head. The woman crooned gentle, soft sounds. Jeanne's little blonde head turned upwards.

I looked up at the woman. Full of figure, she radiated feminine strength. Thick gray-black braids framed her face. As long as she hovered over us, I felt all right. Her large, brown eyes comforted me. I sighed, wishing I could speak with her, for she seemed to hold secrets that could soothe not only a child, but also a young mother. Gradually, Jeanne's frantic howling subsided. The woman patted my shoulder and returned to her seat while Jeanne drifted into a restless nap.

In the clear light below, the mountains of Northern Mexico stood out—rough contours fringed with bright sunlight. Between the plane and the earth, clouds billowed. I lost all sense of time in the beauty of the swirling shapes and pastel colors.

Thump. We hit some turbulence and the reverie dissolved. A bright flash startled me. I grabbed Jeanne and held her fast.

An elderly man across from me leaned over and said, "Sometimes thunderstorms flash light across the clouds for hundreds of miles. Nothing to worry about." His face crinkled with a reassuring smile.

"First time in an airplane," I responded.

The flash threw shadows in the cabin, and I reconsidered for a moment where I was going, what I was doing. *It isn't what I do. It isn't what Len does. It's what we do together.* The courage of my commitment gave me strength.

❦

Nearly two hours after taking off, the plane made a low arc and landed. A fast stream of words came over the loud speaker.

"Chihuahua," was followed by a flurry of words and, "Chihuahua." I couldn't understand the rest of the announcement, but I figured out that we were to stop at Chihuahua. Once on the ground, the stewardess gestured with her hands. She indicated that there was no need for us to leave the plane.

When the door opened, waves of heat penetrated—mincing, crushing, and vaporizing. Several of the passengers moved to exit, including the woman with the beautiful braids.

"*Vaya con Dios*," she whispered. The woman walked to the door, turned, waved, and nodded.

I was sorry to see her go. The elderly man also nodded a goodbye before he deplaned. A middle-aged gentleman took his place. Very dignified in a suit and tie, the new arrival was tall with angular, yet fine, features. How could anyone look so cool and composed in this heat?

The man settled into his seat and nodded, acknowledging our presence. The heat in the cabin was now intense, while outside my window, the surface of the airfield shimmered like a mirror. We took off. Soon, air currents caused the plane to rise and fall erratically. I began to feel slight nausea as well as pressure in my ears. Just as I had feared, Jeanne resumed her crying, which soon became a high-pitched wail. I murmured to her.

"We'll be in Monterrey in just a little while. Hush. Not much longer, my little love. Shhh."

Words had no effect. I felt helpless. I made small offerings—a bottle, a pacifier, a toy—all of which were rejected with a frantic wagging of the head or a push with her fragile hand. Her pretty little outfit was now soiled and smelled of sour milk. The screaming intensified as the plane continued to climb.

The attendant approached me. "*¿Que necessita?*" she asked.

I didn't understand the words, yet knew she meant well. Her pretty face leaned over me with a look of concern.

"*¿Jugo, jugo de naranja?*" The attendant persisted.

I shook my head in frustration. Gradually, the plane leveled off from its ascent and Jeanne eventually quieted.

Again, the stewardess approached me. This time she leaned over my seat and helped me settle the baby in the vacant place next to me. Fortunately, the plane was not full. All the time, the attendant murmured soft Spanish sayings.

"*Que chula, niña. Sí, sí, así.*"

Jeanne finally fell asleep. The same attendant came down the aisle again. This time she carried a tray.

"*¿Café?*" she asked.

I nodded.

"*¿Negro o con crema?*"

Negro. At last, I recognized a word; it was same as in Latin. I actually knew a word in Spanish and responded, "*Negro.*" It was the first time I had actually spoken Spanish. It felt good. *Maybe learning the language wouldn't be so hard. Just say it in Latin with a Spanish accent. It might work.*

My brief respite ended when Jeanne awoke again. The incessant pressure in her ears must have been frightful. Unable to express her pain in any other way, she wailed.

We'll be in Monterrey in just a little while. How much longer? How much longer?

"Soon, we'll see Daddy. He'll be there to meet us," I whispered and felt my heart pound at the thought of reconnecting with my husband, of seeing his face again.

The screaming intensified as we made our final descent to the airfield.

Through the window, I saw a mountain range. The Sierra Madre Oriental encircled the city below. Tall peaks seemed split apart, revealing a jagged, wild terrain. To the right of the airplane, I saw Saddle Mountain. Its bold outline caught my attention as we headed for the closed area of land, the valley below. The mountain was magnificent against the immense blue of the sky.

Across the aisle, the gentleman looked over my shoulder, out the window. "King Mountain," he said while he pointed to the saddle formation, "the symbol of Monterrey."

ॐ

People filled the big, brightly lit waiting room. Relatives of the passengers waved to loved ones with handkerchiefs. Family groups beckoned. Some were laughing, some crying. Len was nowhere to be seen. I felt an emptiness in the pit of my stomach. Although it was ungodly hot, I shivered. Once more, I scanned the crowd. He was nowhere. The ecstasy of anticipation deflated. *He couldn't have forgotten our arrival time—or worse—the day.*

The gentleman who had been sitting across from me on the plane observed what was happening and approached us.

"Is everything all right, *Señora*? May I offer you a ride to the city?"

"No, thank you. My husband will be here soon. There must have been a delay."

"Here, take my card. If you need assistance, *a sus ordenes.*" He bowed. The card read: *Rodrigo Hernandez, Instituto Cultural de los Estados Unidos.*

For that moment, he was a point of reassurance in a world of color and sounds unfamiliar to me. As he walked away, I felt a stab of urgency. Perhaps I should have accepted a ride. But to where? I didn't have an address, and Len had no phone. Putting the card in my pocket, I walked though the terminal where I found the exchange. The air was hot, clammy, and full of dust. Struggling with Jeanne, the bags, and my purse, I managed to pass the ten-dollar bill that Frank had given me through the opening. The sign read: *Rato de Cambio: 8 pesos / $1.00.* The attendant took the bill and handed me a bundle of pesos. I stuffed the pesos in my pocket and momentarily regained my optimism. I looked around to see if Len had come, but when I saw that he hadn't, I pushed through the crowd and checked every corner. There was heavy smoke and much noise.

Off to one side, I saw a sign that read: *Café. Perhaps Len was in there.* I entered and found a table in the tiny restaurant—air-conditioned and wonderfully quiet—a peaceful oasis where I could sort things out. Jeanne—tired, limp, and listless in my arms—began to quiet now that the engines no longer roared in her ears. She affectionately clung to me as I tried to fight off panic.

I scanned the customers. When the waiter came, I indicated to the woman across from me. She was drinking iced tea with thin slices of lemon.

"That," I said. The man understood.

I was a stranger in a foreign country with eighty pesos in my pocket. I kicked off my shoes and stretched my head back. Finally, Jeanne fell into a deep sleep, and I laid her down next to me. I felt myself fade into the surroundings of the café; I became drab and transparent. We waited. By four o'clock the café was comparatively deserted.

The sequence of the day's events, so packed with excitement and expectation, only inflated the disappointment. I imagined the worst and could visualize Len sprawled out on the highway as an ambulance streamed to his aid. My brain swirled with questions and worries. I knew I had given him the right time and the flight number.

My mind raced—stopped cold. A dim memory was followed by a flash of clarity. I recalled a similar circumstance less than a year ago when I was working at the Walker Scott department store. I'd gotten off work and Len was to pick me up. When he failed to show, I grew nervous. I reached into my pocket, found my last dime, and went to the phone booth on the corner of Fifth and Broadway. A chilling fog moved in from the sea. I was pregnant, and my feet were swollen. On the brink of tears, I called home.

A sleepy voice answered, "Oh my God, Hon, I fell asleep. I'll be right there."

When he picked me up, I noticed that his eyes were puffy, supporting his claim of emergence from deep sleep. He apologized profusely, squeezed my hand, and asked me to forgive him. Moved by his sincere remorse, I tried to forget the matter. But now it had resurfaced.

Len finally arrived at the airport just before sunset. It was impossible to mistake his gliding walk and nonchalant manner in the dusky light of evening. He stood in front of me with feet apart, hands in his pockets, shirt and trousers finely pressed, hair damp as if just from a shower, and eyes puffy.

"Good God, Len, where have you been?"

"You're here already!" He appeared entirely natural and open. A smile, childlike and disarming, immediately changed the mood to one of ease and warmth.

My mouth began to tremble, however, and I fought back tears.

"How long have you been waiting? They told me the plane would come at six."

"We arrived at three, right on time, just as I told you on the phone." *He was late. Would I ever be able to trust this man?*

Len smiled, then shrugged. "Well, you're here, now. And that's all that matters." As we got up from the table, he left to pay the bill and quickly returned.

Jeanne, now awake, tilted her eyes toward him. Recognition. She kicked her feet as if anxious to be on her way. In response, he picked up the baby and tossed her into the air. She giggled, clearly delighted to see her father once more.

We drove away from the airport toward the city. The sky turned a murky brown that was oddly luminescent. A light rain began to fall. With it, a knot inside me relaxed. I leaned back in the familiar seat of the old Packard and breathed deeply. I had been genuinely frightened, yet he seemed to have no understanding of our ordeal.

We passed a few cars on the road. Most were old, dilapidated. Frenzy, fatigue, and panic dissolved. I watched the plains, hills, gas stations, and signs slip away as we drove toward town.

Gushing with contagious enthusiasm, Len talked about his life. He talked easily and fluently. Listening to him, I became an investigator looking for a clue he would not want me to find. The story of calling the airport sounded false. He had left us stranded for three hours with no hint of his whereabouts. He couldn't admit the lie. Instead, he took my hand and gave it a gentle squeeze, just as he had done once before. I felt a maddening wave of doubt as we drove, not knowing what I wanted of him.

When he spoke, his words came alive—the hospital, the city, the *cantinas*, his new friends. But I wanted just this once to be the star of the moment. He was so busy being one, he didn't remember us.

Len slowed down as we came to the medical school, which looked very much like the one in the TV series, "Dr. Kildare." The large white building, classic in design and with a winding driveway, was fronted by a garden of red roses.

The summer shower became a downpour as we continued on about a quarter of a mile and then drove around a *glorieta* into *Colonia Vista Hermosa*. The rain's din continued for a few moments and then stopped, leaving pools of yellow light below the dim street lamps that lit this part of the *colonia*. A strange calm held me in quiet suspension. In that moment, I first set eyes on our house. It lay on the outskirts of the neighborhood surrounded by a panorama of wild mountains. The noise of the traffic barely reached here. Len stopped the car in front of a low duplex and helped us out. The road in front of our house was full of potholes, the curb across the street, choked with weeds. To me, the little house in front of me with its windows aglow and patio shimmering in the damp evening looked appealing. I could smell wet grass and shrubbery as I carried Jean into the house.

I knew little of Len's life since he'd arrived in Mexico. He filled me in on the details of the last month as we lay in bed that night. It all sounded rosy, but with his charm, his way of making everything wonderful and interesting, he could spin what I feared might be an illusion. Yet when he spoke of his studies, there was a deeper intention, direction, and sincerity.

Did I have a right to expect more? Should I overlook what happened?

Except for the dripping of rainwater from the roof, all was quiet outside. I listened to Len's breathing, squeezed my eyes shut, and resolved to give things a try.

Four

Open Your Eyes Wide

The next morning, I awoke to the aroma of roasting corn. A combination of warm air, sweet smells, and general curiosity roused me. Peeking through the shutters, I could see two construction workers across the street warming tortillas on a brazier.

Len leaned over me, turned off the light, and kissed me goodbye.

"I'll be back later, after class, and I'll show you around town," he whispered. "There's a jar of Nescafé in the kitchen."

It was warm outside. I regretted not going out, but there was so much to be done. In the dining room, on a chair near the sideboard, I located my bag and picked out something cool to put on. I found the Nescafé, boiled water, discovered a chipped cup, and made my first cup of Mexican coffee. Jeanne slept soundly, exhausted from the ordeal of the flight.

Thank God that Len had been able to bring the basics with him in the car. Here and there, I found familiar utensils, as well as some wedding gifts—dishes, pots and pans, linens—that we had been given just over a year ago. The crib and playpen were already in place.

At least he had done something. He hadn't completely forgotten us.

I took a closer look at the place. The oblong house was constructed of cement blocks, concrete, steel, and tile. The entry opened onto a large patio adjacent to the street. The living room was two small couches upholstered in fire-engine red and standing on flimsy black metal legs that offered seating. Just behind, a large Formica table and chairs created a dining area.

Sparse, but not bare, tidy, there was not much in the way of decoration with the exception of a glass vase and lamp—both wedding presents—which Len had set out. The lamp appeared predictably out of place with its early American flavor: a brass kettle for a base and kelly-green ruffled shade. Nevertheless, it provided a touch of home.

I walked to the back of the house and peered out the kitchen door to a tiny courtyard. Completely enclosed with a tall adobe wall, it promised a sense of privacy and security. Juxtaposed against the mountain peaks, the wall exaggerated the fractured mountain peaks, stark against a background of penetrating blue.

The yard turned out to be a square of oozing mud, however, without a blade of grass or plant in sight. As I turned to go back inside, I noticed that a washtub with a built-in scrubbing board stood to the right of the back door. *Surely, no one used those things anymore.*

The kitchen sink overlooked the plot of mud in back. A small, ancient refrigerator squatted in one corner and a two-burner gas stove with no oven in the other. I opened a door off the kitchen and discovered still another bedroom. An old mattress lay on the floor and a chamber pot sat on a low table next to a small window, suggesting that it had been used as maid's quarters.

Our bedroom was situated in the front of the house next to the living room. Large, square windows across the face of the entire house let in filtered light that cast gray shadows on the shining tile floor. Jeanne's room, safe and snug in back of ours, contained boxes marked "baby." The house was roomy, much larger than our apartment in San Diego. It would do. It would have to.

I was on my own and, in a moment of reflection, experienced again the deep hurt of the day before—that Len had forgotten us at the airport in a foreign country. The memory bruised and left me staring into space, stunned that Leonard could be so heartless. The more I thought about it, the more my confusion turned to anger. Rather than blow up, I tried to focus on the business of unpacking and arranging.

Jeanne awoke, curious, aware, and interested in her new surroundings. I put her down on the cool, tile floor and piled an assortment of toys within her grasp. She reached for a stuffed doll and handled it with tenderness, caressing the well-known embroidered face. Forgetting me at the airport was one thing, but forgetting this vulnerable baby . . . I seethed anew.

Orderliness proved an inadequate refuge. Though soft summertime heat of early morning poured in pleasantly, I rampaged through our baggage and threw clothes into drawers. I shot the energy of my rage into unpacking each item, reaching a point of anger, not only with Len, but also with myself for accepting the situation. I fumed at my own passivity. *Why hadn't I said more?*

I worked the rest of the morning, anger pelting me as if striking raw nerves. I couldn't stop it.

"Hallo, hallo," I heard a man's voice call from the front door. The day was warm and Len had left the door open.

I tried to breathe slowly as I rose.

"Hallo?"

The glare from the patio, intensely bright in the morning sunlight, made it difficult to see. I looked toward the front door, and, squinting, could just make out a silhouette of a man. He completely filled the doorframe. Drawing closer, I saw a robust gentleman probably in his mid-forties. He puffed vigorously on a cigar, came through the door, and approached me with his hand extended.

"I'm Señor Sanchez, the landlord. So glad to see you made the trip okay." He looked down at Jeanne. "*¿Y la niña? Que preciosa.*"

Shaking his hand, I said, "I am really delighted with the house." My words reflected politeness more than enthusiasm.

"Good. We want you to be happy here. I was always very happy in *Tejas*." He pronounced it the Spanish way. "As soon as those are finished," he pointed across the street to the construction area, "I will rent them out, also."

His snug three-piece suit stretched across his chest and belly. He sat down. The buttons on his vest strained. When he opened his jacket, I saw that he carried a gun strapped to his side. The Stetson was gray like his suit. Black embossed cowboy boots completed the picture of a man of business—peppy, efficient, and dynamic. Here was someone busy collecting property, people, and opportunity.

"Oh, have you lived in my country, then?"

"Yes, I went to school in Abilene. I went with Ick. You know Ick. He is your president?"

"Ick?" I had no idea what he meant. I couldn't imagine whom he might be speaking of.

"Sí, Dwight Eisenhower. In Military School we called him Ick, just like you do now. Ick, the president."

"Ike! Of course."

Señor Sanchez roared with laughter. His good-natured wit put me at ease and I laughed with him. His words bounced as he talked about the neighborhood and its inhabitants.

"A doctor lives over there." He indicated to the far side of the row of houses. "María Elena lives next to you. She has two daughters—teenagers—and she is raising her husband's kids, too. She will tell you they are her nephews, but they are his kids by one of the mistresses." He laughed with a quiet sense of amusement as if he were blind to anything except the humor.

After a moment he hurriedly added, "María Elena is an artist," then stood up and paced the room.

Taken aback by his frankness, the talk of illegitimate kids, the mistress of the husband, I interjected, "Would you like some coffee?" I felt the need to instill a proper theme to the conversation, and the offer of refreshment seemed safe.

Señor Sanchez politely refused the coffee and settled back on the red settee. It looked small and overly delicate supporting his ample bulk.

"Open your eyes wide and you will learn much about México." His wide, toothy grin suggested more to come.

I was curious. What else might there be in this gambit? More about Mexico and more about people? I was right. There was more to come.

"How did you get here? Did you fly?" he ran on without stopping.

"Yes, it was a beautiful flight. Over the Sea of Cortez. And then we stopped in Chihuahua."

"*Magnífico*, you came by air. Then your visa does not have a car marked on it. You could go out through Laredo and bring one back. This is good. No?"

"Excuse me? Bring back what car? We already have a car down here. Len drove in through Laredo."

"Yes, but you will need one for yourself." He leaned toward me and smiled. His hazel eyes glittered, then he drew long, and with obvious pleasure, on his cigar. The smoke billowed toward the ceiling.

I coughed and cleared my throat. His blunt suggestion confused me. "For now, I think one car will have to do." I coughed again. The smoke hovered like a rain cloud over our heads. I wasn't sure he was serious.

"Look, here's what we can do. You go to the border to Laredo and pick up a car, one like mine. See?" He pointed to his conspicuous green and white Cadillac. Large, flaring fins extended from the rear of his unmistakable car, which stretched in front of our place.

For a moment I mused. *What would happen if I blossomed forth suddenly with a new car? A Cadillac at that. Where would this lead?*

"As you have noticed, perhaps, María Elena drives a nice car." He pointed to the street in front of the next-door patio. "I helped her," he said proudly. In the bright morning light, an identical car to his flashy Caddy was parked directly in front of his. To make the situation more fascinating, there were two such cars in front of the house next door. Two brand-new splendid cars that bore the emblem of "General Motors." Altogether, including his own, the three new cars parked in front gave the impression of a car lot.

"You use the car as long as you stay in México. Poof! When you leave, it will stay here. Then, you can go out on a visa that has no car indicated on the paper. It's so easy." The undertone of his voice was smooth, confident.

I was stunned. I had never met anyone so to-the-point as Señor Sanchez.

"American cars cost twice as much as they do in *Tejas*, and they are a big expense for the average *Mexicano*. As you have noticed, perhaps, not many people drive new cars."

Indeed, the short drive last night proved the point. I had noticed. Yet his suggestion sounded like a deal that could prompt real trouble, probably more for me than for him.

"Did you ever mention this to Len? This opportunity?"

"No, it just came to me just now, as I look at you. It's a great idea. Think it over."

"Thank you for the offer, but I don't think—"

"Think it over." He stood to go.

By now, the house fronts were completely bathed in bright light, which brought out every detail—the mosaic pattern of the tile, the lush grass between the houses, the pools of mud left by the recent rain. I picked up Jeanne.

"Come, *por favor*." He steered me out of the living room through the patio toward the duplex next door. Thick foliage bounded our gardens. Off to one side on the patio near María Elena's car, I saw a young boy, probably three years old or thereabouts, riding a bicycle.

"*Hola*, Lalo." Señor Sanchez waved at the child. A young girl sat on the patio and attended him. In her lap, she held another boy at least a year younger than Lalo. The younger child glanced at us. Enormous green eyes seemed to smile in recognition as Señor Sanchez waved at him. "*Hola, Fico.*"

The door was slightly open. A young woman, seemingly a teenager, rushed past. She called over her shoulder while flashing astonishing green eyes, "*Mami, tengo que irme. Ya me voy.*"

She jumped in the first car, turned on the radio, and started the car.

With a grin and semi-salute, Señor Sanchez chuckled, "And that is Diana."

Diana focused her green stare on me. "I'll see you," she yelled, then shifted gears and screeched down the road. We could hear festive honking and she was soon out of sight.

The young woman holding Fico indicated for us to enter, "*Pásale, Señor.*"

The door was slightly ajar. Señor Sanchez pushed it open. "María Elena?"

We entered the living room. It was a mirror opposite to the one I had just left, except where books and magazines were plentiful in ours, here modern painting, molds, sculpted busts, and bold mobiles filled the room. Clean lines and brilliant colors contrasted with the heavy mission style furniture. Presently, María Elena came in.

"*Buenos días.*" And when she saw me, "*Bienvenidos.*" Wide, radiant eyes, so brown they were almost black, met my glance. "I am so very glad to meet you," she said and pressed my hand.

Then she looked at Jeanne and exploded in a torrent of Spanish.

"*Que linda, la niña. Que muñeca. Chula,*" her face, animating as she spoke, became even livelier. "She is so precious."

I was somewhat taken aback by the profuse stream of compliments, yet at the same time, pleased at the outpouring of welcome and attention.

The woman in front of me was stunningly attractive, but not beautiful—voluptuous with full lips and a broad face. With hair pulled back severely, she swished her ponytail as she moved.

"May I present María Elena, a native artist of Monterrey. *Muy Mejicana.*" He obviously meant this as a compliment as it was spoken with much pride.

"I want you to bring *La Señora* Gail to the cathedral next Sunday. I will be there. My whole family will. You will enjoy seeing it. Very old church, over four hundred years since the Spanish built it. Mass is at 11:00 A.M. I must go, now. I promised María Elena I would bring you to her house today. Remember to come on Sunday, the *Charros* will be there."

As Señor Sanchez edged toward the front door, María Elena accompanied him. Once there, they paused. He shook her hand, kissed her on both cheeks, and waved "goodbye" to me.

"Next Sunday, *Charros*. And keep your eyes open wide."

He drove away in his new Cadillac.

María Elena remained there, poised in the doorway. Her sensual body filled the space. I could see that she appeared to be a little past thirty, if that—an exotic-looking woman with very high cheekbones, a full mouth, and satiny warm complexion. Her skin-tight dress was of a brightly printed pattern. The abstract figures of bold colors splashed here and there made her whole form resemble a living Picasso painting since the fabric clung to her softly molded contours.

Swaying slightly on red high-heeled sandals, she said, "I am happy that Señor Sanchez—Allesandro—brought you over this morning." The warmth of her voice was captivating.

Her eyes appraised me and she asked, "Have you had your breakfast, yet?" Before I could answer, she called to a woman in the kitchen, presumably a servant. Another rapid stream of words followed. María Elena's voice had a low, mellow quality, but it also signaled authority.

"No," I replied, feeling frumpy next to her, "I just woke up a few minutes ago," I lied. "Just before Señor Sanchez arrived. Call me 'Gail.'" I noticed that she smelled of rose water.

María Elena indicated that we should sit down in the great, high-back carved chairs with leather seats. As we did so, she called, "Ana" to still another servant in the kitchen. Spanish words spilled out of her so fast I couldn't make out a word. This time, an older woman answered her. From my vantage point, I saw that the servant was sitting at a table where she made tortillas by hand. The woman slowly rose. In a moment, I could hear the whir of a blender.

"Petra," María Elena called through the door. The young woman from the patio came in, leaving the boys alone for a moment. Thick braids tumbled down each side of her head. She seemed like a child despite a white starched servant's apron. Pausing, uncertain for a moment, the girl looked to María Elena for direction.

"*¿Mande?*" the girl said.

Another torrent of Spanish followed. Then Petra went to the kitchen to retrieve a glass from the older servant. Apparently, each had specific duties.

Pleased with the process, María Elena smiled. Here was a woman brimming over with life. She had a bright light inside of her.

"This is delicious. You will love it." She passed the drink over to me, all the while talking incessantly, "Papaya, banana, orange, and a raw egg with some vanilla for flavor."

I took a sip and found out that she was right; it was delicious. María Elena stared at me and leaned in my direction. Raising her thickly fringed dark eyes to my face, she said, "You look like you should be painted." She said it approvingly and with command. "I think I should do it. Your aura has beautiful qualities and you have very good bones."

"You're a painter, then?" I replied, intrigued by the glamour of her.

"I love to paint, but mostly I sculpt; that is where I find myself."

"What is your medium?"

She frowned, momentarily puzzled by the word. Then she said, "Oh, yes, *acero*, steel. This is a city of steel, you know. I love to work it. When it congeals, it expresses tension, turning points. I love the shiny surface. But first, I make the mold. I have to trust myself to find freedom. I let go as I reach into the very center of the subject." When she spoke about her work, her dark eyes flashed.

"Did you do this?" I asked, pointing to a small piece. It was made of stainless steel about twelve inches tall. The piece was sinuous and twisted slightly like a flame fluttering in the air.

"Oh, yes," she said. "It is the model for a much bigger piece. You will see it at my exhibit next month."

I liked the instant way she included me, as if we were friends and had known each other for a long time.

Waving her hands around the room, she added, "This is all covering, just the outside. I want to show the inner life—what is essential. The core of existence." She spoke each word distinctly, enunciating each syllable. Her English was very good.

"And you see life as a flame—a flame of energy?"

"I see life as fire—eternal, but never still." Then she added, "It is my duty to speak my truth, Gail. It is about passion."

María Elena fixed a sharp gaze on me. "Of course, we will go to the cathedral on Sunday, but now, tell me about tonight. What are your plans?"

"Len promised to take me to see the city. I want to get to know the place."

"Of course you do. Leave your baby here with us. Petra will care for her. Besides, she can play with the little boys. I would be hurt if you refuse."

Abruptly, she turned her head toward the patio, toward the two little boys and Petra. Then she added, "I have two teenage daughters, and now I have my two little nephews to raise." She pointed to the outside where the boys capered on a patio identical to ours. "They are three and one." She spoke with genuine affection. "*Preciosos.*"

The two little boys peeped around the column of the patio. Two pairs of bright green eyes stared at us. The boys looked at each other, giggled, then looked back at us.

"Meanwhile, we have to find you a maid. You need one. Leonardo tells me you are expecting another baby."

I stared at her, too taken aback by it all to say anything. I was not used to such immediate familiarity.

After a moment, I remarked, "Yes, we're having another baby in March. Jeanne was born in March. She's five months old."

"I also was married when I was young. Diana is now almost fifteen. She is my oldest. I have another daughter, Cha Cha. You will meet her." She took a long breath and went on, "Marriage is like art. It forces you to look into yourself."

As she spoke, I got the sense that what she said was a fragment of a tale far from complete. Señor Sanchez had given me clues, but there had to be more.

"How do you mean?" I asked. "I'm just trying to balance my hopes and desires with Len's and then come up with some kind of mixture."

"Yes, in the beginning, so it is. Later, it is about going within. You have to find out who you are and then you have to decide."

"Decide what?" Puzzled and curious, I wanted to know what this more mature woman had learned.

She burst into a glorious smile. "Decide what kind of art you want to become." She put stress on the "you" and continued. "In other words, we have to turn ourselves into pieces of art."

"How do you do that?" Something stirred in my imagination as if I'd discovered a magical mirror that offered a surprising glimpse of who I could be.

"Have to find out what is essential. It is the same in Spanish, *esencial*," she said.

"But what does that mean?"

"How much you can love and how much you will be tolerant," she answered quickly and to the point. "*Sí, tolerancia.*" There was no doubt about it. Here was an extraordinary woman. Her black eyes glowed.

"So, marriage is about love and tolerance?" I pressed her.

"*¿Cómo no?* What else?" she asked.

She glanced at her watch. "Gail, I must go now." Laying her hand on my arm, she said, "We are destined to be friends. *Amistad*, is that not a beautiful word?" She said it with an innocence and childlike charm that utterly captivated me.

The thrashing about inside of me that I had felt since I landed in Mexico began to quiet.

"I will send Petra to pick up Juanita."

I muttered something about being honored, pleased. I had never had a conversation quite like this in my life. I rose. She took my hand and, together, we moved toward the door.

"*Hasta luego*," she said when we reached the patio. When we got to where the little boys played, María Elena reached down and patted each on the head saying, "*Mi rey.*"

I didn't know that the expression, a very common one, meant "my king," but I did know it was a term of endearment from the way she said it. The little boys lurched toward her. She laughed good-naturedly.

As she hurried to her car, I followed her movement with my eyes toward the brand-new car parked in front of her house. It was an exact replica of the one that Diana had just driven away. Both cars, green and white, had shining chrome trim and unmistakable Cadillac fins. Then, looking back at me, she called, "There's always so much to be done here. I have a French class at ten. Leonardo says you know some French. Join our class."

She jumped in her car, peeled the tires, and sped away.

The conversation with María Elena gave me a remarkable boost. More than anything, her sinuous metal sculpture that made such beautiful visual music allowed my earlier mood to play itself out. I knew that I needed to forgive and move on.

ও

There was a shape to the early evening. Amber light as clean and sharp as the outdoor air permeated the living room so thickly, I felt I could touch it. I sat on the floor gathering Jeanne's toys into a little pile. She had gone to María Elena's and I waited for Len, hoping not be disappointed again. I didn't hear his footsteps, but glancing up from my task, I saw the brown leather loafers with little tassels.

He came nearer, reached down, and pulled me to my feet. "Ready to go?"

"I'm keen to see the city." Despite everything, I was thrilled to see him and wanted the evening to be a success, even though it felt like an excursion along the brink of a danger zone.

Twilight lingered, giving us light to appreciate the sights. We first drove past the *Opispado*, the renown fifteenth-century bishop's residence, and then to the Technological Institute.

The "Tech," a well-known institution throughout Mexico and all of Latin America, turned out engineers that were highly esteemed. We got out of the car and entered the compound, which was clean and in splendid condition. Two pillars framed the Saddle Mountain, which, in the dim light, shone like distant mother-of-pearl. We paused long enough to wonder at the sunset.

"Let's move on. There's more to see," Len said.

We drove past *La Purísima*, a large, modern Roman Catholic Church.

"This church has been featured in *LIFE* magazine," Len said as we drove around the plaza for a better view.

Off to one side, a tourist had set up his camera for a night shot.

"The extraordinary design is unique for its time, at least that is what it said in the article."

The doors of the church were open, and as we passed by, I could see that the building had no internal support. Its rounded shape loomed like a very tall Quonset hut. Len went on. "Across the plaza from the church is the Pan-American School, and on the far side, opposite the church, the English Library."

We circled the plaza once more so that I could take it all in. The library loomed, just a little larger than our house in the *colonia*. Never mind the size, there were books inside that tiny library. Books in English.

We drove on toward the center of town. Like most large Mexican cities, the cathedral was the pivotal point for community activity. In front of the cathedral, a large plaza spread over a wide area. Saturday night and the plaza burst upon us abruptly. Surprised at the action all about me, I asked, "Is it always like this?"

"On Saturday it is," Len replied and parked the car.

Hand in hand, we crossed the street to get closer to the heart of things. I could feel the slow thumps of my heart. It was great to be together, again.

"Len, this is wonderful. You are a wizard, a fabulous tour guide."

Not above playing to this flattery, Len grinned. "There's more to see." He winked as we made our way to the plaza.

An informal procession was in progress around the perimeter walkway. Young men and boys in neat shirts and trousers walked in one direction, and in the other direction, passing them, were young women, mostly mere girls in gauzy pastel dresses or lacy blouses and colorful skirts.

"It's the custom. If you're single, you come here and walk and check out the scene."

Len nodded in the direction of the passing parade. The young men and women were of varying ages, anywhere from teenage to early twenties. Walking face to face, no gesture overtly signaled any response. Everyone knew the rules. Although eyes tried hard not to give a hint as to what they were feeling, there was clearly an exhilarated tone of sexual excitement as bodies passed each other in silence.

At the eastern corner of the plaza and across the street, the cathedral loomed over the procession. Even the shadow of this ancient church imposed a mental image, powerful, perpetual, and indelible in the fading light. We found a gap in the stream of people and angled our way to the center. Here, older couples, families, and maids tending children found refuge in a little area encircled by a picket fence covered with roses. Once in a while, we could hear someone from the perimeter break out in a fit of laughter.

Len smiled his sunshine smile, and in a provocative way whispered, "Do you want to walk? After all, they are just looking."

I blushed at the suggestion and then at my own reaction.

He quickly added, "I was just kidding with you."

We continued toward the center, away from the busy border. I felt as I had as a child when entering a new classroom. I paused, took a deep breath, and continued along the inner path until I found a bench and sat down. This was not Nice or Paris—the places that had always drawn my attention, the places of my dreams. I hadn't pinned any hopes at all on Mexico, yet this was the opportunity that life offered. In that moment, I sensed that Mexico would be a strong presence in my life. We sat in the reflected glow of the street lamps that had just come on.

"How do you like the city so far?" Len asked pleasantly.

Hesitating, I said, "Well—" my mind drifted. I was thinking of my high-school boyfriend—a bright lad, intellectual, poetic. He bore a resemblance to the youth and innocence of the boys I saw in the square. "I've never seen anything like this before."

As we watched the evening walk, this ritual of chaste separation, I wondered how long this tradition had been part of the culture, a custom that divided heart and body. I knew that passion is deeply rooted in the Mexican people. Perhaps this women-in-one-direction-men-in-the-other tradition was a compromise, a way to make peace with the church, and at the same time, stir up emotions.

"The lights in the plaza go out at nine-thirty each night," Len said. "Let's move on."

We approached the large fountain at the very center of the plaza. Here, families gathered on benches. To one side, children played on swings.

Len took my hand and led me to a low stucco wall. We sat down. He spoke realistically with none of his customary flippancy and told me things I should have known but didn't. "When I was in college, I had—to put it mildly—an undistinguished record. I got bad grades. I spent a lot of time on booze and the coed circuit. Now, it's different."

"How is it different?" I wanted to understand him.

"It took me a long time to realize that I could actually do what I wanted. Instead of worrying about it, I'm just going to finish medical school. I couldn't do it without you."

I wanted to be his Girl Friday. "Now that you're here and actually in school, there's no splitting of the attention. You can focus. I know you can do it."

"It's not going to be easy," he went on. "At first, until I really learn Spanish, I'll have to memorize everything."

"Well, we have to begin somewhere." We got up from the bench, turned toward the street, and joined the collective promenade. I looked over the ancient plaza. Only then did I notice an outer ring of activity, a parallel procession.

A motorcade was in progress. A spinning, swirling, energetic motorcade encircled the plaza. This parade occurred at a dizzying speed, erupting as it did in the streets that bounded the square. Cars going one way, driven by young men, and in the other direction, driven by young women, swirled around the plaza, mimicking the traditional walk. Youngsters flirted through the passing car windows, re-passing each other again at a dizzying speed—bright-eyed adolescents in a pandemonium that, at second glance, turned out to have an orderly, undirected, and unmanaged precision.

On the far side of the plaza across the street, through the blur of moving vehicles, arches lined a lovely arcade. Shop lights aglow, I could make out a curio shop, a restaurant, travel agency, and a string of shops whose names I couldn't read. We started across the street.

Without warning, a green and white Cadillac careened around the corner nearest to the cathedral. The horn honked. We jumped back. A carload of girls leaned through the windows. They giggled and waved greetings to both those on the walkway and to others in cars. And the driver? It was the green-eyed Diana, my neighbor. She persisted, round and round. No one stopped.

"C'mon, let's get out of here," Len laughed. He turned and took my arm; we walked, bodies touching, our feet in unison.

As we cut through the lane of people, I had a sense that an innocent, yet confrontational, mood underscored the entire ritual. The plaza—a small island surrounded by streams of people, cars, and light—seethed with activity.

I supposed it was inevitable that some of the night's flirtations might escalate to something more significant, but overall, the Church and its ancient power to mold people's hearts and minds would have its way.

As for Diana, it would appear that she had been given a long leash. I had no doubt that María Elena knew what she was doing with her daughter and her joyful sense of freedom. Diana made another pass. She saw us and waved in recognition.

"*¡Hola!*" she screamed.

I waved back.

I took Len's arm and strolled toward the car, feeling as if my heart would crack wide open. I wanted to give him my love with no conditions. I looked into his eyes and saw how he thrived in this atmosphere. We made our retreat down to the road that led to the river. As we drove home, the smokestacks of the steel mills stood out against the darkening sky. Just to be alive together was enough. Wasn't it?

Five

Leader of the Pack

"*Lechuga, lechuga muy fresca.*" A man's haunting voice caroled through the streets. Drifting in and out of sleep, I listened to the melody, especially to the words, which were beginning to hold meaning for me.

"*Masa, tortillas a mano.*" This time a woman's voice—shrill, more energetic—sounded the call. Drowsiness lingered, but every word was comprehensible.

"*Papaya. Papaya de la mañana.*" Voices blended a morning chorus of street life. Every day, just after sunrise, the sounds of the hawkers rippled through the *colonia*. There were new names for everything, as well as names for new things. A second chorus repeated the words.

"*Lechuga, masa, tortillas, papaya.*"

Savoring the moment, I lingered under the covers and watched the sunlight push through the slats on the shutters, but the street sounds soon roused me out of bed. There was a new language to be learned. I wanted to try some of the words and expressions that I had memorized out of the phrase book. I threw on a skirt and blouse and located a supply of coins that I kept on the table next to the bedroom window. Then, I flung open the shutters.

In the street, sales were underway. Maids from other houses were out on the curb making deals, asking questions, and sampling produce.

"*Aquí.*" I called to a man with a basket of fruit balanced on his head.

He was a small, wiry man. I waved him over. He looked up with a big toothless smile, came over to my window, and held the basket up for me to see. Using phrases that I had memorized, I plunged into a dialogue very similar to one that I had read in the book. For a few moments, we bantered back and forth, with me gaining in confidence as the vendor accommodated my shaky Spanish. The window came up to my waist. I leaned through it and forward to better see his wares. I looked down into the basket of produce and pointed to some choice items, luscious-looking fruits, better than I had seen in the *supermercado.*

In no time, I managed to negotiate a deal. The vendor, a seemingly good-natured man, enthusiastically passed me a handful of bananas, a papaya, and a couple of mangoes. Through the window came the purchases, and with them the pervasive, pungent smell of fresh fruit.

"*¿Cuanto cuesta?*" I had practiced the day before with Jeanne as my audience. The man understood. I felt more confident.

"*Uno ochenta pesos.*" I handed him two pesos. However, he didn't have change, and I turned my back to reach for some smaller coins. Out of the corner of my eye, I saw a leg swing over the edge and through the window. He was trying to climb in.

"*¡No, Señor, no!*" Astonished, I shoved him out and slammed one of the shutters. With my other hand, I slapped the coins into his palm. "*Adiós.*" I pushed him away.

"*Muchas gracias, Señora.*" He chuckled innocently and crossed the patio to the doctor's house to the left.

There, watching the humiliating scene, stood the lady of the house. Three small children held to her skirts, and the littlest one, a girl, sucked her thumb as she peered from behind her mother.

"*¡Que hombre!*" The *señora* shook her head as she gestured at the man. The doctor's wife, my neighbor, appeared to be a few years older than I. Her eyes met mine, and I noted a formal sympathy. I felt abashed and annoyed by the whole business. I was a self-conscious stranger in a strange place. Had I done something to encourage the man? Was there some outlandish meaning to the phrases that I used that could possibly account for the unexpected event?

"*Sí, que hombre.*" I felt overcome with a sense of impropriety and confused. I didn't know if the vendor's behavior was an attempt at sexual foraging, or if it was a simple joke, or both. Badly shaken, I locked both the shutters and slammed shut the window.

A street man had just tried to climb in my window. What was he thinking?

I didn't understand why or how this had happened. The same could be said of Señor Sanchez and of his offer to purchase a Cadillac for me to drive while here in Mexico. My initial irritation was now turning into grim curiosity.

I had taken risks, tried new things. Simply coming to Mexico was a risk, but I was still very much rooted to my practical world. I wanted to sustain myself, one day to the next, responsibly. Was I feeling fragile because I didn't know what to expect? Suppose I had agreed to Señor Sanchez and his plan. What did I have to lose? To drive a new Cadillac? It would be fun and certainly pleasurable. But for me, the deal was out of the question. The risk was not the only drawback. There was my sense of right and wrong. What would happen if I were to indulge in that kind of behavior—a plan that had to be illegal? The casual attitude that I saw here confounded and frustrated me. A street man had just tried to climb through my window. Obviously, I needed to learn more.

I made a mental note to call on the lady of the house next door, the lady who had witnessed the scene. She appeared genuine and kind. Perhaps I could ask her some questions about what had just happened. Too ashamed of my ineptitude, I didn't tell

Len about the incident. I vowed it wouldn't stop me from future forays into Mexican culture. On the contrary, I set up housekeeping, learned to use the washboard, cared for Jeanne, and did what I could to support and encourage my husband, all the while immersing myself in the world about me.

In the days that followed, María Elena turned out to be a good friend, expressing her hospitality in a myriad of ways. She was shrewd, tough, compassionate, and big-hearted—an artist through and through, who poured churning emotions into sinuous steel figures. I came to trust her as she walked me through those precarious and confusing first weeks of my life in Monterrey. She laughed uproariously when I told her about the fruit vendor.

"Not to worry," she said.

María Elena radiated a desire to accept people as they are. She quickly altered my view about needing a maid. She didn't point out that I was wrong; she pointed out what was right.

"You need someone to come, do the housework, and especially do laundry by hand in the stone tub in the back yard. It is far cheaper than the purchase of a washing machine. And tell Señor Sanchez to plant some grass back there for you."

I knew I would take her advice but didn't look forward to dealing with another person in my home, especially another person whose ideas about boundaries and conduct would differ drastically from my own.

⚘

We were happy enough as a newly-wed couple. Once, during a dinner out and over the din of the restaurant, Len again emphasized how good it was to make a new start. Yes, it would be a challenging struggle, but he assured me that it would all work out. My mind was eagerly open and swelled with optimism. I couldn't have known how much of myself I had given up since leaving home.

"How much better than to be alone." He seemed to mean it.

Yet, he had changed. A kind of realignment had come over him, and once that happened, I also had to reposition myself around him. Certain things were happening in my immediate world that put the whole adventure in new light. Since our arrival, Len had whole-heartedly plunged into student life, and that included membership in the pack—a group of students who routinely met to go over the course of study. I first became aware of the pack when one evening Len came home and brought with him two Americans.

"Mario, Bill, this is my wife, Gail. She's a great girl, completely unselfish."

Just what I always wanted: to be praised for not being myself. I reached out and shook hands, "Stay for dinner so I can get to know you."

Bill, a tall, wiry Texan, clasped my hand. "Glad to meet ya."

He wore a big cowboy hat and had a handle-bar mustache. His hands were jingling change in his pockets when I asked him to sit down.

During our makeshift dinner, I learned that the men were from the States, and both were married.

"So, Bill, your wife is in Texas?"

"Yes," he replied. "Galveston's not that far away, and I can go home once a month, or so. We own a lab, and while I'm here, she will run it. That way, we keep an income and the business. During the summer and vacations, I'll go home to work."

"So, you plan to keep the lab, even after school?" I pressed on.

"I'm interested in pathology. And this way, I'll have a head start."

"There's a really good pathologist on the faculty, here," Len added.

"We call him *El Pato*," Bill said, "because he looks like a duck. But he's a good teacher, very demanding."

I turned to the other man. He was tall, broad shouldered, a little on the chubby side.

"What about you, Mario?"

"My wife's still in Germany, but she's coming to the States this Christmas. I'll go back to L.A. and get her." His voice was low, husky. Mario leaned forward. "We were just married last year when I was in the Army. I served in Germany and I met her there. She's great. Speaks pretty good English, too." His voice lifted when he spoke of his wife and I liked him for that.

So it was that Bill and Mario were the primary members of the gang. Very soon, more students came along. There was no denying the joy of the gang that developed from the common struggle, and with Len as the leader, there was no shortage of fun, jokes, and good humor. The gang was always hungry and usually poked fun of events in class on a particular day—how one of them had presented, how well they were doing, the next day's assignment.

I fed them, provided coffee, and for the most part stayed out of the way. I felt like I was part of a worthy cause. Each had a story, each had a good reason for their striving, and I wanted to support them. Fortunately, I was not a good cook and had not mastered the preparation of even a simple meal. Most of my dinners were notable failures. As it turned out, this ineptitude proved to be good luck as the gang ate less and less at our house. Still, I wouldn't have changed my life for anyone's at that moment.

I wanted to occupy my days and we needed money. If I were to work, I would need a maid. In that regard, Paula's arrival was a lucky break. She came with good recommendations, having worked for a friend of María Elena's in another *colonia*. Paula was middle-aged and mentioned to me that her only relative was a son who now lived in Tampico, the port city three-hundred kilometers from Monterrey. There was something appealing about Paula. She had a maternal face with large dark eyes and thick, curly, brown hair that smelled like peppermint. Another good point was that Paula was used to Americans, having worked in one of the small tourist hotels in the center of town.

Most of all, she was a good worker. *"Cien pesos,"* she replied when I asked her how much she wanted for a monthly stipend. For one-hundred pesos, roughly $10.00, she would stay with us all week and live in the back room. It was her custom to go home on Saturday and return on Monday morning.

I hired her immediately. Doing laundry by hand was back-breaking, and I needed someone to help in a way that I had never needed before. Who would have believed that my organized brain could be so out-of-control? Intermittent water and electric outages were common, all part of a day in *Colonia Vista Hermosa*. Paula could handle it.

As I got to know her better, I saw that she truly loved children. Her matter-of-fact approach to life and to the chores that she undertook was heartening. Tending children, cooking, house-keeping—all these were the stock and trade of a good *criada*. She was that and more. She was warm, kindly, and generous with Jeanne, and I never worried when I left her with Paula.

Besides, I wanted to learn how to get along in this country. The picture of the vendor swinging his leg through the window had left an indelible imprint, and I had no doubt that such liberties would not have been taken if Paula had been doing the bargaining that morning. She was patient with my Spanish, and became a good-natured, lively, walking dictionary.

"¿Cómo se dice en Español?" I would point to an object and ask? And in this way, I learned. My Latin background helped. Of all the romance languages, Spanish is the closest to the old Latin, which I had studied for four years. This little epiphany increased my Spanish vocabulary on the spot.

Six

Juggling on a Sunday Morning

It was the appointed day, the Sunday to visit the cathedral. I woke early, made a run to the bakery, and on my return, put a pot of stew on the stove where it could simmer slowly all day.

We had agreed that Len would play with Jeanne and pay some bills while I was away. Sitting at the dining room table, I savored the last drop of morning coffee and the delicious quietness of the moment, then reminded Len that the rent was due. He nodded.

"Do you think Señor Sanchez was serious about the Cadillac?" I nibbled on a *pan dulce*, fresh from the bakery that morning.

"Don't know. Sanchez never made any such offer to me," Len mocked. "You must have encouraged him somehow."

"What do you mean encouraged him? Are you crazy?"

"Well, he never said anything like that to me." He pulled out the checkbook and wrote a check.

"I can't believe you'd think I want to be a smuggler."

My exasperation was interrupted when I heard a car slam on the brakes and stop in front of the house. Within seconds, a crowd invaded the living room: Bill, Mario, and three Mexicans, all medical students. One of them, Raphael, I disliked immediately. He carried a large wicker jug of cheap rum, swaggered in, and stared at me with a strange, almost defiant, glance.

Len said, "Raphael—we call him Ralph—is from San Diego; he was born there." Len glanced in my direction as he introduced the newcomer.

"Yes, but my family is from Monterrey," Ralph said with pride. He was good-looking enough with long, blond hair, big cheekbones, and light-blue eyes. But he gave the overall impression of a pompous rogue.

A pickup truck screeched to a halt in front of the house. Two young men jumped out of the back and pointed to our door. The truck peeled away.

"Leonardo?" one of the men called out. He held up a bottle of *tequila*. The other, a lad of about seventeen with curly, dark hair and black eyes, had a serape flung over one shoulder. In his hand, he carried *Testut's Anatomy*.

Len went to the door and waved them in. "A*qúi, hombres.*"

As the gang—inspired by Len's hearty welcome—invaded the house, I sensed the power of the bond that held them together. Some people believe that collecting friends is equal to a successful life. If that were true, Len was already a huge success. A continuous vortex swirled around him. He was the undisputed center.

"The guys are here to help me study," Len said with his usual impish humor. He smiled at me casually with a glance that implied, "Didn't you know they would be here? Surely you did." He pulled up chairs to form a large circle in the living room and plopped Jeanne in the middle. She giggled and kicked her feet. "That's my girl. Daddy's little girl!" He blew her a kiss and Jeanne squealed. Len went to the kitchen to get shot glasses while the others settled in.

Len joked, he fibbed, he cajoled, he mesmerized, and he turned everyone into a player in his little drama. I knew better than to criticize, for I had learned that at any hint of disapproval, the gang quickly closed ranks. Within minutes, they were slamming down shots of rum or tequila and discussing the brachial plexus, apparently the next day's assignment. I picked up Jeanne, and as I did so, she wriggled to see what was happening in the rambunctious circle of men. I took her to my room.

"Do you want to come with Mamá this morning? Yes? Let's get ready." I distracted her with a toy, yet she turned and squirmed in the direction of her father's voice. I couldn't leave the baby at home with the gang. The enormous jug of rum only reinforced my concern. I snatched Jeanne's lacy pink dress with matching bonnet, an outfit perfect for High Mass at the cathedral. María Elena would be honking the horn in a few minutes, so I rushed to get ready.

"I'll be taking Jeanne with me," I called out to the living room. No one answered. I kept going through the motions, feeling extraneous and infuriated by the condescension of Len and the gang.

My navy-blue crepe with lace collar was clean and pressed. I had not had the chance to wear it since we had arrived in Mexico barely a week ago. Luckily, I could still fit into it, since I was only two months pregnant and very thin. This would be the right time to pull it out, the neat little dress that I had once worn to tea dances at college.

As I laid out my clothes, I bristled with irritation and resentment. *Just like a group of men to have their plans, no matter how they affect anyone else.* Then I recovered myself and got down to the task at hand.

I dressed quickly and piled my hair on top of my head, securing it with long hairpins as Jeanne watched. I made a game of it and danced around her to hold her attention. As I danced around, she mimicked some of my movements. I noticed how joyously her eyes opened when her gestures and exclamations were reinforced.

"Matching navy-blue pumps and a white *mantilla*." I held them up for her to see. They completed the outfit and we were ready. Jeanne looked adorable with strands of blonde hair poking out from her lacey bonnet, which framed her tiny, delicate face.

One last look in the kitchen. With Jeanne on my hip, I lifted the cover on the bubbling pot of stew, sniffed, and with one quick swirl of a spoon, replaced the cover. *Good planning on my part. It would be ready when we returned.*

Quickly, I checked for odds and ends that I would need to take with me, now that the plan had changed, and as I dashed around the room, I argued silently with myself. *Why hadn't Len mentioned this latest intrusion to me this morning? He had ample opportunity. So this was what "unselfish" meant to him. He could be inconsiderate and I wouldn't mind.*

Knuckles rapped on the front door. Someone opened it. I heard Len mutter something and then he called to me.

"Cha Cha's here."

Cha Cha, María Elena's youngest, not beautiful as the green-eyed Diana, was a bright, eager girl and bold for her age.

"Gail? Gail, are you ready?" Her voice was excited, cheerful. Her jet eyes sparkled.

Relieved to hear her cheery voice, it broke the tension of my irritation, at least for the moment.

"Yes, I'm ready, Cha Cha." I picked up Jeanne and stamped out of the house. "Jeanne is going with us."

"*Que bueno.* May I hold her?" she asked, genuinely delighted at the turn of events.

"Let's get to the car, first. Cha Cha, bring the *carrito* also." I held Jeanne tightly as Cha Cha grabbed my bag with one hand and the *carrito* with the other. We piled all the baby supplies in the trunk. I got in and immediately breathed easier once in the car. It was good to be with María Elena and her girls as they chatted animatedly in rapid-fire Spanish. Cha Cha talked incessantly with Jeanne. María Elena revved the engine, hit the gas, and screeched around the corner. Soon, we were in the center of town.

Seven

Silver in the Sun

A vast band of red, purple, and yellow flowers meandered along one side of the large *Plaza Zaragoza*. In the center, sparkling water cascaded from a tiered fountain the size of a carousel where, off to the side, a child bent to play. I glimpsed from a woman's hat, to a shadow cast by a tree, then to a clutch of children. The luxuriant scene was shockingly slow-moving in contrast to the brisk pace of the previous Saturday night.

"There is *El Palacio de Gobierno*," María Elena pointed to an elegant European-style government building at the opposite side of the square.

The plaza covered many acres, and I saw that the area where Len and I had gone to see the flirtatious promenade was only the small inner portion of the entire *Plaza Zaragoza*. An arcade of shops, offices, and hotels lined one side of the large square. María Elena drove around the smaller plaza until she found a space very near the cathedral and parked the car in the shade of a massive, sprawling tree. It's delicate branches hung over the curb and dangled into the street. It was just a little before eleven.

Wisps of clouds crossed a pale-blue September sky—a bold background for the ancient cathedral. The tall structure faced east, and the clear morning light accentuated a richly carved baroque façade. Yellow stones and crumbling yellow stucco enhanced the appearance of antiquity while the building itself commanded attention and respect as is so often the case with architecture that has endured many centuries.

The place had its own somber personality as if porous atoms of adobe had soaked up a storehouse of memories. There must have been weddings, baptisms, and funerals, not to mention the residue of the atrocities of the revolution, all absorbed by the thick adobe walls. A church of memories.

"It is just over four-hundred years old," María Elena announced. She turned and indicated the small plaza within the larger *Plaza Zaragoza.* "They are partners, the cathedral and the plaza. The kids meet in the plaza and they marry in the church." Teasing Diana, she looked directly at her, pointed her finger sternly, and said, "Remember that."

We all laughed. Cha Cha shook her head in agreement and Diana shrugged her shoulders.

The sound of horses' hooves on the pavement caught my attention as a group of riders came from the street behind the cathedral out onto the square. The riders, all men, were dressed in the style of refined Mexican cowboys. The lead horse, a gold palomino, pranced as the rider deftly maneuvered the horse through deliberate, formal steps. Red tassels from the elaborate bridle swayed with the rhythm. Immediately behind the lead rider rode Señor Sanchez dressed in black with silver trimming on his jacket and down the side of his pant legs. His black suede sombrero was enormous, at least as large as my umbrella at home. It flapped slightly as he put his horse through the paces. The ensemble of riders followed suit, equally resplendent with horses decked out in silver trappings.

Jeanne stared in fascination, and the longer she watched, the more mesmerized she became. A sprightly pinto mare—and at least a couple of grays and roans, quarter horses, like those I had seen in rodeos in California—trotted down the center of the street. The lead horse whinnied and swished his tail.

Señor Sanchez rode past and slid his hand down and over one of the silver revolvers holstered at his sides. A huge, silver buckle at his waist and silver studs on his shirt gleamed and reflected the sunshine. His horse, a black mare, trotted neatly. Like her rider, she was caparisoned in silver. There was silver on the bridle and the saddle and silver trim on the blanket under the saddle. Slowly, with grand pride, Señor Sanchez dismounted and tied his horse, as did the others, to the hitching post in front of the cathedral. The heat was intense.

I got the sense from the way they rode, and from the way they looked at one another, that they were friends, a community of men who had repeated this ritual frequently. With a hint of a swagger, the group of men made their way up the steps of the cathedral. Their manner and familiarity reminded me of the gang.

"*Los charros,*" María Elena acknowledged.

"*Estan muy bonitos,*" I responded, proud of my Spanish.

Jeanne was spellbound. She pointed to the horses and to the men. I was glad that I had brought her with me after all.

"*¡Juanita, mira los caballos!*" Cha Cha was as excited as Jeanne.

Several people in passing commented on Jeanne. "*Que bonita, la niña. Que chula la niña.*" Jeanne's dark-blue eyes were big and wide open. She smiled back, unabashedly open to praise. We moved onward with the crowd.

The tawny façade of the church was a hodgepodge of styles. Columns did not match and a cornice seemed out of place. Carvings were of varying types and motifs. No doubt that it had been a work in process for decades, if not centuries. Moving with the current of people, we climbed the well-worn stone steps and went into the vestibule just as the bells tolled eleven times. The church was a well of cool darkness. Not yet full, it was easy to find a place in a pew close to the front. Footsteps of latecomers from the square echoed as they came in from several side portals, as well as from the main entry in back. The coolness was delicious, a relief from the fierce heat of the morning. Mass began. I felt at home.

"*In nominee patri et fili et spiritu sancti.*"

The Latin that I had heard since childhood was comforting and understandable. It droned on and Jeanne dozed in my arms. How tender she looked napping, with a touch of violet above her eyes. A cool stone smell permeated the space. Such a good smell, the smell of mass on summer mornings.

The texture of the walls was rough and porous, handmade blocks of adobe transformed long ago by native hands into a place of Christian worship. In contrast to the roughness of the walls, a gilt altar shone and glittered, lit by tiers of tall candles in silver candelabras.

To the right, a side altar to the Virgin Mary stood in the shadows. At that stage of my life, nothing was more visually moving than the representation of the Virgin with her gentle gestures of protection. Under her feet was the insignia, *Regina Coelae,* "Queen of Heaven." Flowers were abundant and every votive candle at her feet was lit and flickering from a slight breeze through the open doors. Here, I felt welcome—a child come home. The church was the same. For twenty years, it had been my parent and my refuge.

The priest intoned the collect, and then it was time for the gospel. We rose. I could see Señor Sanchez ten feet in front of us. He stood proud in his black and silver outfit, surrounded by family—a pretty woman, apparently his wife; an elderly man; several older women all wearing black *mantillas*; and half a dozen children of various ages. They were strategically placed in a second row pew, easy to see and easy to be seen.

The bishop, prominent in the group of clerics at the altar, climbed to the pulpit.

White silk vestments shot through with silver threads contrasted with the dark mahogany lectern where he towered above us. As he leaned a little forward, toward the faithful, his chasuble sleeves, heavy with silvery lace, spilled over the ledge of the carved rail. In clear, sharp Spanish, he read the gospel of the day, and then he proceeded to deliver the sermon. We were close enough to clearly see the bishop, and I found his presence inspiring, though intense. I struggled to grasp the meaning. However, I could not make sense of it until María Elena leaned toward me and whispered a translation in my ear.

The bishop spoke to the theme of "selflessness." He was an elegant man, tall and light of skin. His eyes were clear and penetrating, like green glass. His features had a sharpness that seemed appropriate to a city surrounded by the sharp, craggy Sierra Madres.

He preached about giving. "There were many ways to give—to the family, to the community, to those in need." The bishop gestured to the Mexican cowboys who had come that morning in all their finery. "Thanks to men like these who have come today in all their trapping, we are able to maintain our traditions. There is beauty in ritual and beauty in tradition. And there is beauty in comradeship."

María Elena did her best to summarize the high points. The bishop said, "Founded four-hundred years in the past, Monterrey remained a poor city with only a handful of inhabitants. Then technology intervened. And so did cattle. Now, Monterrey was the second city in all of Mexico. Thanks to the generosity of the people, we have become great and now prosper. Prayer is also a technology, and so is devotion." The bishop paused and looked slowly around the ancient sacristy.

María Elena paused for a while as the bishop detailed the different forms that devotion could take. As he spoke, I began to catch some of the words, but I relied on María Elena for the sense of it. She continued, "To nurture the family is a duty and a virtue."

I winced when he said those words, still flustered with interior hubbub from the morning.

María Elena's soft, husky voice uttered the English words in my ear. The bishop's voice commanded, "These duties are free choices." His voice increased in tempo and volume. "Devotion is crisscrossed with the footprints of God and His Holy Mother. Jesus loves us as a Mother."

This statement surprised me. I had never heard it said that Jesus loved us this way. It was a new concept. As I listened, I found myself in an intensely impressionable state, wide open to the message from the pulpit. Worry had enveloped me since I had come to Mexico, and now it all seemed so selfish and superficial.

Sitting close by, a stylish woman listened intently. She daubed her eyes with a handkerchief and, from time to time, looked over at the Virgin. What secrets did the Virgin have to bear?

"It is always better to give than to receive. Live a life of grace. Those who rode today on the streets from the silver cities have enriched us all in many ways. We salute you." The bishop concluded his sermon. "Begin where you are. Begin today!" The bishop's voice thundered throughout the cathedral. His glistening vestments shone with the silver threads picking up the light from the windows above and from the candles behind.

As Mass droned on, I contemplated the bishop's words. Life with Len was not what I had expected, not what I had hoped for. Small rebukes, reproof, and blame in different shapes and forms came to my mind. Sacrifice and selflessness are important for a meaningful life; and so are devotion and grace. That was what the bishop had said. I felt his words in my heart. I deeply and passionately wanted to be a good wife, loving and supportive. I recommitted to "for better or for worse." Even so, I was afraid and shivered until, at last, some movement in front shook me out of my reverie.

Many of the congregations were standing and forming lines to take Holy Eucharist. A continuous parade of men, women, and children proceeded to the communion rail. Each knelt and waited a turn.

A choir of young boys sang, *"Panis Angelica,"* which means "Bread of Angels." The dominant response for me was one of ethereal repetition and trance. The chant had a way of putting to rest those portions of my brain that fixed on trivial matters—disagreements, disappointment, and offenses.

"Panis Angelica." Every syllable muted the ticking of reality.

I didn't mind the length of the service. In fact, I savored the coolness within the church and the familiarity of the liturgy, a way of being that I understood. Mercifully, Jeanne slept peacefully throughout the entire service.

Mass drew to a close as the celebrant turned to the congregation with *"Pax Vobiscum."* The bells tolled the endless stroke of noon.

I wanted nothing more that Sunday morning than to have peace in my heart. Despite my good intentions, I was not eager to leave the place and go home. I could have lingered in the cathedral for hours. I had come home.

As the bishop withdrew, Señor Sanchez stood up, looked around, then surveyed his family. He gestured to them and skillfully shepherded his flock down the aisle and toward the main door in back. The older children followed his example and guided the younger ones. Finally, at the landing above the steps, the little entourage hovered remaining there to greet friends as the congregation flowed past them into the bright Sunday light.

Meanwhile, we, in the central aisle, were caught in a stream of people also coursing toward the exit. Swept along, I accidentally brushed against a man. He stopped, and then he turned toward me.

"Dispénseme Señora," he said, and then his eyes lit up in recognition. It was the man from the plane.

"Señor Hernandez?"

"Yes, how nice to see you again, *Señora.* Everything worked out for you, then?"

"*Mami*, can we go to Sanborne's?" Cha Cha intervened as her voice carryied over the crowd. She pleaded with María Elena and tugged at her mother's hands. Cha Cha looked at me. "They have the best ice cream you will ever have."

"She's right. And it's very close to my office," Señor Hernandez said. "You are a friend of María Elena?" He looked back at them pushing through the crowd.

"Yes, I am," I answered quietly for we were still in church.

"I hope to see you again. A *sus ordenes*." He moved ahead of us as I waited for María Elena.

I intended to be home by two, but we lingered. Others from the congregation remained as we watched the *charros* mount up and ride their horses back down the street and around the cathedral.

"María Elena, thank you for bringing me here. Today will be remembered." I considered myself lucky to have friends, to be surrounded with approval and acceptance.

"I am so glad you liked it," she said. "Now let's go to Sanborne's."

María Elena and Diana led the way across the plaza while Cha Cha helped me push the stroller, the *carrito*, which we'd thrown into the car at the last minute. With Jeanne wide awake, we crossed the broad street and, after a brief walk, arrived at what looked like a coffee shop.

Cha Cha opened the door. A wall of frigid air hit us full-on as we entered. The restaurant was filled with families and young people out for the afternoon, and we stood by the door until a waiter spotted us and waved us past tables with mothers, proud fathers, grandparents—all with babies and toddlers, in and out of strollers and high chairs. I took note of the way that Mexican families cared for their little ones with joyous patience.

We reached our booth, settled in, and Cha Cha promptly handed me *la carta*. The list of ice cream indicated various exotic flavors: *mango, piña, fresa*, so much to choose from.

Soon, dishes of pastel-colored ice cream arrived.

"Cha Cha, you're right. This is the best ice cream in the world." I gave Jeanne a taste and she leaned forward wanting more. Passers-by remarked on Jeanne and spoke to her and to me.

"*Que chula, la niña.*" Jeanne's fair skin seemed to glow pinker with all the attention. With every compliment, her blue eyes sparkled.

I experienced a feeling of anguish and wished that Len were with us.

We left the hubbub of Sanborne's behind us and strolled past the flowers, winding paths, and bubbling fountain in the *plaza* in the direction of the car. Once again, in the shadow of the cathedral, I thought of the bishop's sermon and of its deeper meaning for me and for my family. I had a sense of the layered quality that life can sometimes have as I moved through the large plaza.

I'll never forget the scene at the cathedral—the bright heat, the rich color, and the silver shining in the sun.

Many things can be happening at once, and only later do the connections become evident and sometimes clear. On the ride home, I recalled Mother Danz in San Diego telling me, "Never forget; nothing is too good for you girls"—a mandate that conflicted with how I was living and what I had to do. A quality of peace in the cathedral had comforted me, and there I had felt at home. I was a part of it; my next child would be born here in this bright and colorful country. *I'm falling in love with México.*

༝

We arrived home close to three. Jeanne was now in a deep sleep. I held her carefully, progressing with cautious steps on the slippery tile. I crossed the patio and gently worked open the door. Between the pillars of the porch, my eye caught the shadow of an overturned, empty bottle of rum, which pointed to the street like a marker. Our car was gone. I went into the house and discovered a note on the table. It read:

We finished the stew. Went over to Ralph's. He plays the piano like a pro. Now, he needs a place to store it. I told him he could keep it here. See you tonight.
                    Love,
                    Len

The abruptness of the letter devastated me. It looked like a band of banshees had freewheeled through my house. The place was in shambles. As I set about to clean the mess that the gang had left behind, the garish scene only aggravated me more. There was no getting away from it. I had to face the brutal reality: the playful vices of a boy were unappealing in a grown man. I could feel a subtle decay infiltrate my consciousness. It could drive me away from Len.

Eight

Nothing to Forgive

That night was so intensely hot that I welcomed the brash wind, even though it buffeted the squat, square windows and blew gray dust under my door. I kicked an empty bottle of tequila and told myself that compassion was a disease.

As I passed through the kitchen, I glanced to my right in the direction of the piano and noticed a serape on the bench. The studious young man had forgotten it. Fingering the geometric design, I studied the tightly woven pattern—good wool, faded colors, worn spots. I knew the French word for vocation, *metier*. It literally means "a loom." I smoothed and folded the rough fabric and considered Len's passion for his vocation. The edges caught my attention; some were frayed, some rotten. The loom had created a frail web, more frail than I had ever imagined. In my imperfect innocence, I had become thoroughly entangled in it.

Nights like this were to become the norm as I discovered a side of my husband that I had never seen before. Agitated and irritable at home, he took any opportunity to leave and tore out of the house with fantastic energy. In return, I found things to be upset about—his disinterest in family, his obsession about work, money concerns. All the while, I wanted to accept Len the way he was, not tie him down. But insistent, intimate yearnings plagued my lonely nights.

The monotony of my isolation was broken by two things: my insatiable reading—I'd devour anything I could find in English, mostly magazines—and María Elena's parties. I'd lie in bed and listen to whispers of conversation, the clinking of glasses, and uproarious laughter.

Late one evening, I lay in bed listening to the dying sounds of the party next door. Even after I heard the cheerful hum of voices end, the sound of cars drive away, and María Elena's laughter subside, I could not sleep. Instead, I wondered if Len would be drawn home, drawn to his family, drawn to me.

That night I tossed and turned and tried to find some comfort. I fluffed my pillow in an attempt to force myself asleep. I glanced at the bedside clock. 12:48 A.M. Tires screeched. At once, my heart fluttered since I thought it might be Len. I tilted the shutters open, peeked through, and noticed two carloads of *charros*. They pulled up in front of María Elena's verandah. A group of men poured out and car doors slammed.

A high and pale silver moon, just past full, hovered above in no hurry to sink behind the mountain tops. Very quietly, the *charros* arranged themselves in a semi-circle on the verandah. Dressed in full regalia with silver trim from head to toe, they assembled their instruments. One man carried a trumpet; the rest had guitars strapped to shoulders. Fingers began to strum.

Pancho, María Elena's husband, stood in front of the group, and faced her front door. With a sweeping gesture, he motioned to the group. The rhythm picked up, the trumpet sounded, and the *mariachis* broke out in a pleading love song.

"*Querida, querida, lo siento.*" Even I could understand that. "Darling, darling, I'm sorry."

María Elena came to the door and stood there, facing the group. When she saw Pancho, her eyes softened with a look that said, "There's nothing to forgive." She nodded in satisfaction with seemingly no anger in her, not a shred. I wondered at that.

Pancho hung his head a little and worry lines wrinkled his broad forehead. María Elena opened her arms fully and smiled at her wayward husband. We hadn't seen him in days. Pancho approached cautiously and then fell into her embrace. She pulled him toward her into the house and shut the door. Romantic songs continued long into the night from the musicians outside.

The moonlight serenade provoked all kinds of thoughts in me. Where was my husband? I was losing my optimism about the direction our lives were taking. The growing distance between us left me feeling lonelier than ever.

Why did he have such an emotional effect on me, stirring me to such depths? Why, despite his irritating ways, did a glimpse of him leave me yearning?

Other people admired Len's passion and felt great empathy for him, enjoying his breezy, carefree spirit without seeing his obsession. Perhaps María Elena was right; the best chance for a happy marriage lay in the tolerant willingness to accept things.

Outside, on the verandah between the houses, moonlight silvered the shining philodendron leaves while the *mariachis* cooed love songs. The longing behind their words only stirred me more. I knew about anger and didn't want it to strangle me. Still, I couldn't shake it loose. I remembered the anger between my parents and the damage it did. I knew I had cause to be angry, but I didn't want it to poison Len or me the way my parents' anger had poisoned them and their love for each other. One thing became very clear that night: the man I married was not the man I had fallen in love with.

Did it matter?

Nine

Libre

One of the invitations I received that fall was from the Cultural Institute of the United States. There was to be a small exhibit of María Elena's paintings and sculpture, and I was invited to the opening. Eager to go, I also wanted to learn what the institute had to offer.

When I arrived, a spectacular series of watercolors demanded my attention—images of the rugged terrain of the Sierra Madre Oriental that surrounded the city. One painting titled "*Quiero*," which means, "I love," depicted a single cliff jutting out into the sky with a blue so intense it made me think of the local turquoise. The shape of the cliff distinctly resembled the profile of a long-nosed, defiant-jawed, rock woman. With her eye veiled slightly by a wisp of cloud, she looked out over the valley with a sense of tenderness and longing. Overhead, a crimson sun shone. Looking closely, I could see hidden within the sphere the shape of a heart, a burning sense of center. The piece communicated imprisoned splendor with its flow of color, outrageous brightness, and dark rock formations.

"Of course, she is better known as a sculptress." Señor Hernandez had come up behind me. I was so absorbed by the image that I had not noticed him there.

"Would you like a glass of champagne?" He asked.

"Why, yes, thank you." *Was it only a month ago that I had seen him on the plane to Monterrey?*

For the first time, we could actually talk. I was enjoying myself. This was the first festive event I had been to since my wedding, which now seemed eons ago. Señor Hernandez asked me why I had come to Mexico. I told him that my husband, Len, had great zeal in his desire to be a doctor, and Mexico offered a unique opportunity. It would be good for Len. I realized that I'd never seen him happier, and that, as a result, I wanted to help him. Odd that the things we tell strangers reveal ourselves to ourselves.

"And where is he—your husband—this evening?" Señor Hernandez handed me a tall glass of champagne.

I told him about myself and my life since I had come to Monterrey. I explained about the Green Cross, and how Len was kept busy there in the evenings and at school during the day. It would all be worth it in the end. I wanted the best for our family. I was looking for work. He listened attentively.

"Come to work here. Please do. You would be of great value to us."

I was stunned. "But you hardly know me."

"I know you speak English and speak it beautifully." He went on to explain, "There are some local journalists who need to practice English. Each of them wants a private teacher. They already speak English, but they want to improve pronunciation and vocabulary. You do not have an accent and you are very easy to understand."

He said that I could take as many or as few students as I wished, and that the pay would be ten pesos for an hour's lesson. That was almost two dollars an hour, more than some local doctors or lawyers made, and clearly more money than I had ever made in my life.

"Think it over." He guided me to a larger room. There, in the center, stood a tall, stainless-steel spire. It looked like a smooth flame twisting to a pointed flare at the top. "The title is *Life*," he said as we joined a group of admirers. One of the group, an intense young man, approached us. Scribbles and sketches covered the notebook in his hand.

"Juan, let me introduce you to Señora Gail Burns. I hope she will become one of our teachers."

"*Encantado, Profesora.*" He shook my hand. "I need very much to practice English for my work. It is necessary."

The three of us walked around the room and admired María Elena's work.

"I find it powerful and free," I said.

Juan added to his notes. "May I quote you for the paper tomorrow? You are very easy to understand."

Señor Hernandez gave me an approving I-told-you-so look.

What happened next occurred so quickly, so dramatically, that I don't know who or what I noticed first. María Elena burst into the salon, swooping down upon us. The two girls, her husband, and enthusiastic partisans followed. With high-heeled silver sandals clicking, she made a beeline toward the center of the room, to the sculpture of steel. Simultaneously, someone switched on an overhead spotlight, which shone down upon the flowing strand. The tip of the spire caught the light, which spilled down over its congealing, flowing form, and gave the impression of turning inside out, of wrestling with its very nature.

Dressed in a purple linen sheath dress, and with hair piled high, María Elena balanced herself on feet shoulder-width apart. She tossed her head, raised her hand, and pointed to her central piece of work. "I would like to introduce my fiery being, '*La Vida.*'"

Bulbs suddenly exploded. Two members of the press with cameras flashing caught her gesture in a kind of salute. We all raised our glasses to the artist.

"*Brava.*" The enthusiastic group toasted María Elena. "*Brava.*"

"Say something about the piece," one reporter pushed forward, microphone in hand.

"It is about radiance, creativity, purpose, generosity, warmth, the sun. We are all sons and daughters of the sun."

"What do you mean?" the reporter pressed on.

"Look at the flame—fire, vitality, and love streaming." She smiled at the piece, then at the group, and added, "Fill your space with fire."

The room exploded in applause. Raving fans swamped María Elena.

Energy welled up in me. I didn't want to stay in my little box. I wanted to be more, forged in the fire. I wanted to be a daughter of the sun—radiant, luminous, and expansive. As the evening wound down, I realized that I was not alone in being touched by the work. The shining piece in the center of the room was like a point in a whirlpool, constantly pulling in a sense of wonder.

Later, as I was leaving, Señor Hernandez approached me again. "I hope you will choose to join us here."

That night at home, the idea of my going to work at the *Instituto Cultural de los Estados Unidos* persisted. *The work would not be hard.* I ran the script in my mind. *I could devise lessons using paragraphs from the weekly* TIME *and* LIFE *magazines—small reading assignments followed with questions and a dialogue. It would work. I could tailor the lessons for the students' individual needs and interests.*

The money would be a godsend, living as we were on less than two-hundred dollars a month. I had sold our furniture before leaving the States, and with the two-thousand dollars, opened an account in a Mexican Bank. I was haunted by the fear that our little nest egg would evaporate too soon. The thought of a steady stream of income shored up my confidence. The tight feeling in my chest relaxed. I liked Señor Hernandez. He was kind and helpful.

I had not had many choices in my life. Things happened and I was expected to go along, and for the most part, I did. When I graduated from high school, I was offered two scholarships: one at the San Diego College for Women and one at the Catholic University of America, in Washington D.C. I had wanted desperately to go to Washington and told my parents.

"Are you crazy? What would you do in Washington? How would you get there?" When it came to matters of education, my family was not a big support. No one in our family had ever gone to college. To be sure, just staying in a Catholic High School had been difficult. My tuition had been waived the last year when my father's business failed.

"Why don't you wake up and find work," my mother had shouted in exasperation. "I don't know what you are thinking of."

My vision faltered.

Shortly after that encounter, I chose the offer from the San Diego College for Women, a liberal arts college in San Diego. It was a fine school, after all, and I had a full scholarship. The Sacred Heart noticed my potential.

I began to see a relationship between knowledge and consciousness. As a student, I realized that I needed time to be free, to think, and to form my own ideas. The Mesdames nurtured that tendency.

I also found work then at Mercy Hospital, first doing billing in the pharmacy, and then I ran a small X-ray unit used to screen employees for TB. My mother seemed pleased that I had come to my senses. That was the summer she introduced me to Len.

When I met him, I was afraid for myself. There was so much liveliness in him. He was bold and flirtatious. I wanted to be with him, to be where he was. And now I was there. My tenacity and passion for learning had been transferred to my feeling for Len. There are strange ends and beginnings in these things.

That night, it never occurred to me to consult Len. All I knew was that I had to make a choice and take a course of action. I felt a swell of determination. I reached for a pen, found some note-paper, and wrote:

> *Dear Señor Hernandez;*
> *Thank you for your kind offer. I shall be delighted to accept a position as a teacher at the institute.*
> *Sincerely, Gail Burns*

ॐ

And so I began my career as a teacher. I decided to take three students, all of them journalists. It was easy to individualize the assignments. One student, Juan Luís, covered international politics for a local newspaper, so I selected short passages on Current Events or International Affairs from the most recent *Time* magazine. Journalese grammar and vocabulary were colloquial, and thus easy to convert into dialogue—perfect for his need. This approach proved to be so successful that I began to use the same method for my two other students. I met with them individually, quite early in the morning at the Ambassador Hotel, and sipped coffee as we talked. The days were still warm and we sat outside on the brightly tiled patio. I began each session by asking a leading question from the first lines of the assigned article. We then proceeded through the main points while practicing phrases from the reading.

With teaching came new status. In Mexico, there was genuine appreciation for knowledge and learning. One year of college set me apart to a great extent. The students always addressed me as "*Profesora.*"

I was able to use my skill as a scholar. Books, libraries, and classrooms triggered a deep sense of pleasure and fulfillment. Having three young newspapermen as students turned out to be a delightful assignment. They were bright and confronting, yet respectful, and I found the work interesting.

Current events forced me to focus on the present and the future, and thus, get beyond the hold of the past. Reading, and really thinking deeply, became a transformational event for me. In retrospect, I was educating myself. I was learning to bridge the two cultures, Mexican and American, in my commitment to become a teacher. The students' conversations challenged my comfort zone and made me think in new ways.

"It is U.S. owned fruit companies that are to be feared more than Communism," Juan Luís stated after a review of an article, "The Communist Menace." He described unspeakable conditions in the large plantations run and owned by U.S. Fruit. "It is they who have prevented development," he insisted. "My family owns a small, independent sugar plantation south of Monterrey. I invite you and your husband to visit and to see a *granja* at work."

We eventually did visit, and found a beautiful farm surrounded by a lush, growing area southeast of Monterrey. Only an hour's drive away from the city, the tropical terrain was a verdant paradise in contrast to the arid city we lived in. The ranch was tidy, carefully cared for by people who deeply loved the land. The Mexicans definitely could—and should—run their own farms.

It was through the students—our interactions and lively conversations—that a whole new world began to open for me. That fall, I had many others request me as a tutor, and I helped Señor Hernandez update and improve the English Language Program.

"What is it that makes the class work so well for you?" he inquired in his formal, polite way.

"I believe it's because we are using living examples, articles that report life as it is happening." I offered him one of the *Time* magazines. "Here, for example, is a story of President Eisenhower taking a vacation and playing golf. The style of writing is journalistic—reads fast and incorporates current jargon. It's appealing in that way."

"Do you have any other recommendations?" Señor Hernandez pressed on.

I nodded. "Yes. It is important to stay with the text. When I studied philosophy, my teacher emphasized *explicación du text* and I was quite good at it. When we stay within the range of the sentence, we can pull out the meaning, and after all, that's what it's all about, isn't it?"

"Absolutely!" His own English was soothing and fluent. "Anything else?"

"Yes. And I think this is the most important thing of all. The students have questions. Those questions must drive the lesson. It's their own curiosity that brings energy. But this means that the teacher must be willing to go with it."

"How do you mean?"

"Well, for one thing, even though I may plan something, I have to be ready to change directions when necessary." I laughed. "In a way, it's like jazz."

"You mean you play off each other." He nodded. "I know some very fine Spanish philosophers who would agree with that."

"It's just what I have found to work," I said. "I realize that it may go against convention, but it really does work."

In the end, he gave in to my way of thinking. He accepted the idea that changeability of daily life filled the space; discovery and learning are one thing.

༝

Before meeting with my students, I dropped Len at the Medical School around seven A.M. on my way to town. Pleased with the arrangement, he got to his favorite café in time to go over notes with some of the gang. I liked the fact that I was often back home when Jeanne was just waking. One day, I found her in the laundry basket. Paula was carrying her from room to room, combining chores and taking Jeanne, who was having a great time and going along for the ride while Paula sang.

On the way home from teaching, I passed by the English Library and found it to be irresistible. I soon became a regular.

Where previously I had only magazines and a handful of books to read, now I had a wide selection of novels and poetry. I discovered Henry James, Emily Dickinson, and Walt Whitman—good companions for a quiet evening. Sometimes, I shared a short piece with my students.

Henry James's *The American* fascinated me. I found common threads between the European way of life as contrasted to the American hero in the novel. Sometimes, I could see hints of me in the main character, Christopher Newman, dreaming of better worlds and traveling in strange lands—romantic longings beside American practicality.

I was beginning to draw out from the Mexican culture a tenuous thread of comprehension, yet I wasn't close to weaving a whole pattern. Hungry to know more of the day-to-day culture in my new home, I lapped up experience. The pure vitality around me clashed with the boundaries of propriety, however. The memory of the fruit seller incident remained a constant irritant. Perhaps my naïve eye couldn't behold or interpret meanings and customs. Clearly, I needed feedback.

I hoped my neighbor on the far side, the woman who had witnessed my blunder, would help me. In the sultry afternoon stillness, I made my way through the hedge of privet to her door. When I knocked, she invited me to enter, rest, and chat. The Señora had a graceful and appealing hesitancy about her. I confessed my embarrassment and humiliation over the incident. She responded as if she were whispering secrets and did her best to explain how I should deal with street vendors, which was to meet them in the street or have them display their wares on the patio.

I tried to smile graciously as she assured me the incident was nothing. I wouldn't need to make a stand for my dignity. She and her doctor husband seemed to live quiet, conventional lives, unlike María Elena, my flamboyant neighbor to the right. Despite their differences, however, I could count on both of my neighbors for a little guidance when it was in order.

I made my way through the privet hedge back to our verandah that afternoon, thinking I might be able to handle Mexico's cultural peculiarities, but that my greatest challenge would arise from the knots and whorls of my life with Len, unraveling as they did with such frightening chaos. Very different energies such as his and mine tangle in unexpected ways. I struggled to wear an outer mantel of "unselfish" calm, but it was a garment lined with doubt.

Ten

Wild Boys

Midmorning class with my new student had gone well. I had enough time on the way home to dash into the English library and pick up a Henry James novel. As I pulled up in front of our house, boisterous, noisy, and wild banging of the piano poured into the street. It had to be Ralph. He was playing the piano that had been sitting in our dining room, abandoned and untouched for several weeks. He turned his head to look over his shoulder as I entered the house.

"Hope you don't mind. Len dropped me off. Said I could practice. Do you like Bach?"

"Yes, very much." I found Bach's contrapuntal maneuvers enticing and satisfying. But I found Ralph's presence annoying. Bach gave a balance that one could anticipate, but Ralph radiated a ferocity that tilted toward chaos.

He played well and he knew it. Strong, precise notes and harmonies sounding against one another resonated throughout the house. He pounded the keys loudly and the instrument shuddered, fitfully. The music disturbed me—the way he played it, the way he hammered at it.

In the kitchen, Paula kneaded *masa* for *tortillas*. No morning song for her today as the piano music thundered through the

91

house. Even Jeanne was uncharacteristically somber. Paula handed her a lump of dough. Jeanne squeezed it and squealed in surprise as the *masa* oozed between her fingers.

"Len's gone for the others. He'll be back soon," Ralph called out as he played.

"Back? It's midweek. What about class?"

"*Huelga*, didn't you know? There is a *huelga.* A strike!"

"What strike?" The only strikes I had ever heard about were those led by John L. Lewis and the coal miners in the States. "Are the mills on strike?"

"No, the students. We're supporting the Communists. They demand more services for the poor."

"What do you mean?" I asked. "I thought that Mexico already had socialized medicine. Isn't that what *Seguro Social* is all about? I've never heard of students going on strike. Besides, government services are extensive, aren't they?"

"Well, it's different here. Students go on strike all the time." His fingers flew up and down the keyboard. "As for services, they are extensive in a way, but in remote areas many people go without—or they use a *cúrandero*, a shaman." As he talked, Ralph didn't miss a beat and the music became more furious. "Bach fugue in B minor," he added.

I heard a car stop in front of the house. Len rushed in with Mario and yelled over the music, "Sounds great, Ralph." He looked at me. "You heard? *¡Huelga!*"

"No class today," Mario said. " Maybe no class for days."

"Weeks," Ralph added with melodrama.

"Let's go, then. We've been invited to Saltillo."

Glancing in my direction, Len countered my confusion. "Profesor Montemayor's the mayor and we're invited for the afternoon." Len called to the kitchen, "*Ándale*, Paula!"

"*¿Mande?*" she responded.

Len rushed to the back of the house and gave instructions.

"*Sí, Señor.*" Paula ran to Jeanne's room, reached for the diapers, and threw an abundant supply into a bag along with bottles, small flannel blankets, a handful of toys, and some warm clothes. "*Hace frío, allá, Señora.*" She handed me a sweater.

Flustered by the news bursting around me, I asked, "Where are we going?"

"Our anatomy teacher, Professor Montemayor, has invited us to come up for a barbecue. He's the Mayor of Saltillo," Len said. "It's in the mountains—in the neighboring state of Coahuila. We'll take two cars."

Just then, Bill and Luís appeared at the door. I could see another car in the street. "Looks like the gang's all here," Len said. "I'd just as soon leave town." He whisked Jeanne up in his arms and twirled her around.

"When I was in Mexico City, there was a strike and the government set up machine guns in the square. Someone put a large bundle of firecrackers under the box that a policeman was standing on. He was directing traffic. The box blew up right under him just as I came around the rotunda. I'm sure the poor guy was badly injured—maybe he died."

I gasped. "In that case, I'd just as soon leave the city, also. Saltillo? Isn't that the famous silver city? The bishop mentioned the road to the silver towns."

He nodded.

"Len, will there be a chance we can take a walk, get away together up there?"

"Sure, take the stroller. Let's just get out of here."

Paula helped me put the stroller and bags in the trunk of the car. "*Regresamos tarde,* Paula. *Adiós,*" I yelled as we pulled away.

She stood on the little patio in front of our house, waved "goodbye," and as we turned the corner, I could see her begin to mop the patio tiles while singing at the top of her lungs.

Within half an hour, our little caravan of two cars was outside of the city. Sharp, gray-colored patches of clear sky offered respite from the blazing brightness of the city. As we headed west, the curved line of road began to ascend over barren uplands, winding its way between rocky corridors. We accelerated. The old Packard's cylinders fired. The car roared with power as it passed a series of old, broken-down cars, all the while steaming and hissing as the engine heated up from the steady climb.

"This is one hell of a road." Len peered over the edge. "Don't they build guard rails in this country?"

"We're lucky that it's paved," Ralph said.

The drive, a long and frightening one with sharp drop-offs, revealed a forsaken world with forlorn colors and shapes—ashen and isolated to my way of thinking.

Already, after only two months in Monterrey, I realized that Mexico had a different time frame. No one ever arrived on time. Parties that began at two o'clock really began at five. There had to be a *siesta* between one and three in the afternoon. Everything closed down. Was there time for Len and me? I hoped that the afternoon in Saltillo would give us a chance to be alone together. Perhaps we could go for a walk in the plaza, visit the silver stalls, and stroll together in the town. Both anxious and eager, I thought maybe it wouldn't happen.

A procession of barefoot Indians ambled along the way with shoulders slumped. Their feet scuffed below baggy, white pants and their bright, rainbow-striped serapes draped over shabby shirts. The lead man, tall and lithe, had skin the color of walnuts. Donkeys, laden with wares, slowly trudged behind them down a narrow path by the side of the road—a harsh place, full of thistles and weeds. There was a sense of timelessness about the little group retracing the steps of ancient ones, who had brought silver and woven goods down from the mountains to barter. I chafed at the relentless poverty reflected in wrinkled, strained faces. I couldn't reconcile the severe beauty of the mountains with the obvious human lack in front of me. Len, engaged in conversation with Ralph concerning cranial articulations, didn't notice. So, I kept my thoughts about the Indians to myself.

The afternoon sun was a giant orange in the rearview mirror. We accelerated. Moments later, the car entered a narrow passage and eventually broke out on the high plateau toward the still-higher mountains. Sharply sloping rocks came alive. Time-weathered stone emerged as an ancient woman with spindly thin arms beckoning us forward to Saltillo. Lost in reverie by the sight, the old feeling of misgivings returned. I felt the baby kick. I should have been happy, but I felt only worry. A baby deserved to be the center of attention, the core of the hub. I doubted that would happen.

Against the background of the pale-gray sky, the antique-yellow sandstone towers and adobe walls of Saltillo lay ahead. The air was glaringly and blindingly clear in the mountains.

⚜

Bazaars and shops lined the plaza. Even from the street I noticed the lovely woven shawls—*rebozos*—that Saltillo was famous for, along with colored blankets and serapes—red, green, yellow, blue stripes, geometrical patterns—like those that the Indians on the path had worn. An atmosphere of sixteenth-century Mexico permeated the little town.

We drove along the main road, which was lined with buildings whose façades were still gouged, here and there, with bullet holes—remnants from a not-too-distant war. Continuing on, past the cathedral and past the shops, we came upon a large, square house. Wooden columns supported its flat roof. It was plain from the outside. No windows faced the street. I was learning that in Mexico you can't tell from the exterior when you are entering a beautiful home; there may be a simple adobe façade, no decoration of any kind, but inside, something quite wonderful.

Len pointed excitedly at the house ahead of us and said, "That's it—the house of Dr. Montemayor."

Before we could get out of the car, Dr. Montemayor burst through the double doors of the hacienda. The big, broad-shouldered man, seemingly fiery and dynamic, approached us with a smile and shouted a welcome in Spanish. He had a gravelly, throaty voice and a booming laugh. He wore a revolver at his side, and, unlike that of Señor Sanchez, this one did not appear to be decorative. The pale sun was still high, but a cold wind whipped around us. In the distance, the strata of the mountain slopes revealed in their grays and browns, their hints of crimson and blue, a likely abundance of metals.

"*Hola*," Dr. Montemayor cried. "Everything is ready for you."

I love the way Mexican men embrace in the streets with nobility and pride. Dr. Montemayor greeted his students in this familiar manner.

I gathered Jeanne up into my arms and followed Dr. Montemayor and the others into a large inner courtyard. It was a chilly afternoon. Servants scurried here and there with covered bowls and baskets of tortillas. Doors and grilled windows from many rooms opened into the inner court consisting of hard-packed dirt, sparse as the land outside, except for clusters of clay pots filled with succulents and other lovely plants. In the center, a tiered, stone fountain bubbled gently. I loved the feeling of protection, of safety.

Dr. Montemayor spoke enthusiastically about the strike as he showed us into a sitting room. Local rugs, pottery, and family pictures covered thick adobe walls. Heavy red velour covering the windows fed a lust for color. Sumptuous pillows, scattered in convenient places, were covered with hand-woven native tapestry. Dark, heavy furniture carved from wood carried a feeling of permanence, of history. A brooding intensity saturated the crowded room, adding to this heavy, warm, and enclosed atmosphere.

Within moments, Señora Montemayor, the doctor's wife, arrived. She had a beautiful face, straight patrician nose, brown velvety eyes, and smooth, golden skin. A dark-blue dress made of wool clung to her elegant body. She wore a brightly colored *rebozo* over her shoulders and a comb of tortoise shell in her glistening black hair. Taking her place on the sofa, she arranged the pillows and indicated for me to join her. I held Jeanne in my arms and struggled to discuss our trip. Señora spoke no English. I smiled nervously at her as she spoke in a soft, reassuring voice.

After a few minutes, the men moved to the far end of the room where an array of shot glasses and a bottle of mescal—a strong, local drink—stood in the center of a low, square table. Inside the bottle, a dried *guisante* hovered near the bottom.

"For flavor!" Dr. Montemayor pointed to the creamy white worm, which bobbed in the bottle as he poured the drinks.

I was left alone with Señora Montemayor. I had been in Mexico long enough to learn that we were meant to spend our time together discussing children and domestic matters. Fortunately, she did most of the talking. I nodded at what I thought were appropriate moments. We did, however, form a relationship. It was based not so much on what was said, but more on the mood—appreciative, dreamy, contemplative. I loved the peace, the gentleness, the hospitality. There were many layers to Mexican life—inner secrets that I wanted to penetrate.

The men talked about the communists, and Dr. Montemayor seemed especially interested in Len's comments. Why was it that all eyes were on Len—even the señora's? At a glance and with a slight flush, she caught herself and demurely looked away. He had an extraordinary magnetism for women.

Len commented that it was a privilege to see Saltillo, drink mescal, and catch up on studies. He offered a toast, *"Por todo mal, mescal, por todo bien, tambien."* (For everything bad, mescal, for everything good, also mescal.)

The response: booming laughter. Señora Montemayor smiled at me with a smile that said, "Boys will be boys." I didn't smile. I couldn't help but think of the men drinking and of the dangerous road that we had to drive that night.

ॐ

The señora offered me Coca-Cola or coffee. She was a good-looking woman, full figured. Her dark eyes sparkled when she called her children. *"¡Vén! Vén aquí. Ándale."*

Her brood scrambled into the room. There were five: three girls and two boys. The eldest, Camilla, resembled her father with light, chestnut-brown hair and lively, hazel eyes. The youngest, a baby boy, was practically a newborn. His eldest sister held him and crooned softly.

The other children politely shook hands with me and looked at Jeanne. Her golden hair and fair complexion never failed to draw attention.

"Qué chula, la niña. Preciosa," whispered one of the little girls.

Jeanne, with her soft, angelic face, enchanted the children and La Señora. Jeanne was diminutive, and even at seven months, chatty, gregarious, and electric-eyed. She reached out to the children with her tiny hands. A magically smooth moment of happiness settled over us.

One of the servants, a young girl with long dark braids, offered to take Jeanne. I handed her over to the young woman, who immediately began to coo and chatter in Spanish. Jeanne responded—receptive, open, and eager. The children had their own space in a secluded nook. Toys, books, and a thick rug made the ideal spot for play.

Finally, Dr. Montemayor gave the word. We passed through the courtyard to the dining room. A fringed red cloth covered a long table. Accented by colored candles, bone china and heavy antique silver set the places. By now, a sharp wind was blowing and, although the shutters were shut, little whirls of dust seeped through to the sill.

An old woman, *La Viejita*, sat at the head of the table. She was introduced as the Montemayor matriarch. An aura of authority shimmered around this old woman. Thin, arched eyebrows formed points above her wide-awake black eyes, suggesting verve and tough-mindedness. She told us when she was introduced that her family had lived in the *hacienda* for over one-hundred years, during both the revolution and the Mexican-American War. Her story and expression revealed a critical mind and indomitable spirit.

The meal started pleasantly. Servants watched *La Viejita* for cues and followed her every command. Various dishes had been laid on the sideboard, copper trays shining among bottles of local wine.

"This is turkey *mole*, and this is *cabrito*, baby kid," the doctor pointed to the unfamiliar dishes. I know it is close to your Thanksgiving time. *Mole* is a traditional Mexican way of cooking turkey. It is made with chocolate. However, *cabrito* is considered a great delicacy for our people. I hope you will enjoy it."

Exotic smells and the aroma of roasted goat filled the room. Besides the meat, there were flour *tortillas*, freshly made and steaming hot; spicy *frijoles*; and rice with plenty of garlic. Turkey *mole*, as it turned out, was a kind of stew, which was served over rice with fantastically hot peppers as a side dish. The meal commenced and Len again became the center of attraction—joking, encouraging, and making light of difficulties.

Dr. Montemayor said, "México is like a drug. It will enmesh you if you don't take care."

I felt revived. The day was proving that good company and good food conquered homesickness. Moreover, I felt like a pampered guest, almost a celebrity. Doctor Montemayor's favorable comments about Len and his progress gave me a sense of security and of progress.

"Len is doing very well in our school, *Señora*," Dr. Montemayor said good-naturedly. "I understand that you are teaching at the *Instituto*."

While I spoke a little of my work and the students, I could feel Len's eyes riveted on me. Had I made another mistake? I became self-conscious. Was I talking too much? I could feel my cheeks flush red. Maybe young wives were to be seen and not heard. I didn't know what was expected.

La Viejita intervened. She hadn't spoken to anyone except the servants during the meal, and then only to issue orders in Spanish, like an old but proud field *comandante*.

"And the communists, *jovencita*?" Her dark eyes flashed in my direction. "What do you think of this latest incident?" It was as much a command as a question. Her English was perfect.

"I don't know much about communists except what I learned in school." I blurted it out, hardly thinking.

"You studied communism in school? Where was that?" She leaned forward on her elbow. Her black eyes held my attention.

"I attended a Catholic Girls School, Our Lady of the Rosary, in San Diego. We watched live television in our Religion class—clips of the Korean War and later, the House Un-American Activities Committee."

"Did they tell you what 'American' might mean?" the old woman pressed on. She seemed to be enjoying the conversation—or was she teasing me? She was elegant and, at the same time, intimidating in her high-necked, black dress with jet buttons reaching to the neckline, almost martial in style.

"No, the argument went the other way. We focused on communism." My face grew hot, yet I went on. "We learned that it was aligned with the anti-Christ, and that anyone related to the red menace was evil."

"Aha, probably right," she thundered. "*¡Anti-Christ, seguro!*" By now, the old woman stared around the table and her jet eyes shone in the candlelight. She scanned the guests. "These communists remind me of the Zapatistas," she hissed the sibilant sounds. "The *Zapatistas* strung up my father from a lamp post in the plaza. He, too, was mayor." She eyed her son with pride. She threw another demanding glance my way. "So, you studied Communism in Religion Class? What a novel idea!"

Dr. Montemayor, not ruffled by her comments, went on. "Yes, many of our family have been involved in politics here in Saltillo. The area surrounding the city is rich in natural resources, especially silver. At one time, this little town was the seat of government for all of Northern México."

"That must have included what is now Texas, Colorado, New Mexico," Ralph added. Then he asked, "Just how far did that jurisdiction go?"

"At least as far as the North Pole!" said *La Viejita*. She chuckled, and there was a hint of self-importance. Turning to me, she pressed on, "So, Gail, what do you want from México? Everyone wants something."

"This experience in Mexico is what I want. We've come here with friendship and a desire to learn. I—"

"And to drink," Len interrupted. Everyone laughed. And the glasses were filled from a pitcher of beer.

Though angry and humiliated, I understood. He had to turn the attention back around to him. He had to be the center of everything.

The talk went on. At one point, I finally whispered to Len, "Do you think we can get away for a while to see the town or go for a walk?"

"I'll check with the gang after we eat," he said, not missing a word of the conversation. "Dr. Montemayor, how long do you think the strike will last?"

"*¿Quién sabe?*" He shrugged as if it were not terribly important.

After dinner, we adjourned once again to the sitting room. Story-telling, jokes, and drinking absorbed the rest of the day with the men's boisterous constellation at the far end of the large room. I kept waiting for Len to make his excuse and invite me out for a walk. The drone from the far end, with its twin distraction of tequila and peanuts, swelled until the chatter was so loud it overcame our women's conversation about children. It was then that I realized that there would be no walk, no visit to town.

"Come, come," the doctor said, "frankly, I don't give a damn if the communists hold a strike. It gives me more time to work on my political agenda here." He looked at Luís. "How's your brother?" He took a swig of mescal. "In case the rest of you don't know it, Jorge, the brother of Luís, graduated last year with high honors."

Luís beamed proudly. "He's doing well, Doctor. At present, he is serving his six months of social service in the South, in the Yucatan."

"In the Yucatan?" I asked the old woman. "Isn't it pretty wild down there?"

"One could say it's very interesting," *La viejita* said. "The people practice their ancient religion, very mystical with *curanderos* and magic. Many people don't speak Spanish at all. The need for health care is great." She went on, "It's a chance to share and merge the cultures. We are all *Mexicanos*."

I loved the expression in her eyes—brooding, fiery, and deep.

The ladies of the house and I sipped coffee at the far end of the room, relaxed, quiet and cozy beside a large open fireplace. Jeanne played contentedly with the children. *La Señora* held her newborn, covered herself and the infant modestly, unbuttoned her dress and began to nurse the baby.

I was stunned and a little embarrassed. Such a thing would never have happened at home, particularly in mixed company. Nursing a baby in front of a group of men, of students, was unheard of. No one was breast-fed in the fifty's. It was a thing of the past. But not here. Yet, no one seemed to notice the lovely Madonna-like image, modestly draped, rocking the baby who made little sucking sounds.

Dr. Montemayor's voice carried. "Someday, you fellows will be posted somewhere in the countryside to complete your duty to the Mexican government."

"Do we have a choice where we'll be sent?" Ralph asked.

"Some, but it is always a rural area. The Yucatan is a nice place to go. It's very beautiful, but the drawback is that the Indians there do not speak much Spanish. They still hold on to their ancient Mayan dialects of Southern México."

The fire cracked gently. A large grandfather clock in the far corner chimed ten.

A faint glow from the fire spread over the room and brought out with a kind of clarity the distinction between the two ends of the room. One, where we—the women and children—sat close to the fire, *La Viejita* watching the fire and the children; the other, where men drank and engaged in the discussion of student life and politics.

"Our position is no different," Ralph said. "As visitors in this country, we, too, will owe six months of service—upon completion, of course." He got up, and then sat down in another chair. The topic of social service seemed to agitate him, and this surprised me for Ralph was usually stoical. "As for the communists, they will do all they can to boost their way of thinking. At the very least, they want better care for the poor."

'The poor—they really are the crux of the matter. And as for the communists, I'll remain deaf and dumb. The journalists can handle all that." Len glanced my way. He, too, seemed uneasy. "For my part, I just want to study medicine," Len swigged his drink and settled back in the chair.

"I know where they'll send you," Len leaned toward Ralph, "to *Oaxaca*. You know what they say about the men in *Oaxaca*." Len whispered something low under his breath, held his hands about two feet apart as if he were measuring something, then tousled Ralph's hair. "You'll fit right in."

The men exchanged knowing looks, laughed, and passed the bottle again. I felt a smoldering discontent.

§

It was after midnight. Len had too much to drink, so it was Luís who drove us home. Near the horizon, the rising crescent of a new moon peeped over the jagged peaks. Len, Jeanne, and Ralph all dozed in the back of the car

"See that road over there?" Luís pointed to a split in the road. "I come from a small village up there in the mountains. Very pretty."

"Where did you learn to speak English so well, Luís?" His English was fluent and he used the kind of colloquial expressions one did not pick up in school.

"I worked in a gas station on the outskirts of our village. Many tourists from Texas passed that way, and so I learned. So did my brother. How about you, Gail—where were you born?"

"In Chicago. We lived with my grandparents until I was seven, and then we came West." It was pleasant to chat about our lives and families. I felt at ease. "I went to California during World War II. My Dad was a fundraiser."

"What does that mean—*fundraiser*?" Luís asked.

"My father found ways to get people to give money to certain causes, like the American Red Cross and War Bonds. He was very good at it and raised millions of dollars. He helped to build a beautiful college in San Diego."

Moonlight made shadows come alive in the starkness of the mountain passes. There were steep ravines, and the road twisted dangerously. I peeked over the edge of the road and when I saw the sheer drop, I felt a flutter in my stomach.

"And did your family know México?" His hand on the wheel was steady. It was chilly in the car, but Luís wanted to remain clear–headed, so we kept the heat on very low. What he said and what he did didn't matter. I felt safe with him. I looked at Luís and I realized that for the last weeks, he had seemed strange—even distant to me. Small, wiry, tawny-skinned, and lean, he very much resembled an Indian. As we spoke and shared stories, I decided that I liked Luís the best of all of Len's friends. Besides, he was my age.

"No," I said. "I'm the first one to live here. But in my growing up years, my great uncles told me stories of the West. I must have at least fifteen great uncles. Some of them were born in Germany, and in their teens, they rode the rails. They went all over the United States, and when they returned, they told us about the high mountains, the desert, and the great rivers."

A broken cluster of mountains rose ahead in the distance. "They told me that many young men rode the rails; they took work where they could find it, and saw the country that way. These young men got to be called 'Wild Boys.'"

"That's a great name, Gail. Wild boys. I like it."

"I like it, too. They were wonderful people—not afraid. And they loved adventure."

The road dipped slightly and saw-toothed mountains appeared on the horizon. Presently, we emerged into open, flat country. And I thought of home, of my family, and especially of my grandfather, who was one of the Wild Boys.

I wanted to go home. Somehow I would get there for Christmas.

Eleven

So Fresh, So Alive

*E*ven the icy blackness of pre-dawn did not cool my enthusiasm. For days, I had practiced Spanish phrases. The *mercado* would provide the opportunity to put my hours of practice to the test. We planned to go to the outdoor market before Paula left for her day off.

The street was empty and silent. I shivered as I sat in the car waiting for her. At last, she appeared in the doorway, grinned, and held up three *bolsas*, large hemp bags that would carry our purchases. She threw the bags in the backseat and climbed in next to me. I had twenty-four pesos, the equivalent of three dollars in my pocket.

Somewhere behind our house, a coyote howled. The sound connected with something deep and primal.

"*Vámanos*," I said.

I turned the key in the ignition. The coyote howled again. I turned on the windshield wipers to clear off the residue of insects, now dry and crunchy from the night before. Switching on the radio, I found a Texas station. A male voice urged me to love Jesus. I changed to a local station. Paula nodded in favor as a Mexican love song throbbed, "*Adiós mi amor, mi amor, mi amor.*"

We drove out of *Vista Hermosa* toward the river road. It took at least ten minutes to get to the broad highway, which stretched along the bank. On the far side of the river lay the *Colonia Independencia*. Its cardboard shacks and unpainted huts were all part of a district, which—despite rusty cars, mangy dogs, and miserable hovels—thrived and expanded. Most of the servants came from the *colonia*.

A gravel slope led down to the river on the right where, at this time of year, only a small stream trickled. Here and there, a man scampered up the gravel to the road and dashed across to the *mercado*, which lay at the far side. I slowed down. Dim shapes swept across the road ahead, only to vanish into mere shadows. It was dangerous. A Coca-Cola truck swerved in front of me then turned abruptly. Paula pointed to follow.

"*Aqúi, estamos aqúi,*" she gathered the bags. Paula was witty, vivacious, and highly practical. There was a distinct bond of sympathy between us.

I parked the car next to the Coca-Cola truck. Once in the parking area that was matted with flattened grasses, I parked and noticed a young man. His profile faced toward the mountains. As he walked, he held my attention. In the early light, his face so beautiful, I found myself staring. Skin, the color of ivory and eyes, almond-shaped—the youth wore traditional clothes of the Indians from the local hills: white tunic and pants, and a serape over his shoulder. A feather was fixed to a colorful woven headband, which held coarse black hair in place. His graceful walk impressed me. A kind of poetry happened in him.

"*Es un Indio de allá.*" Paula pointed to the hills below the nearest range of mountains coppering in the morning light. The Indian disappeared into the crowd ahead.

We turned and walked to the edge of the *mercado*. It spread for several acres in a curious kind of order. Complex patches of color, unusual scents, and exotic sounds blended. The pitch of the bazaar picked up, signaling business. We could hear the hawkers.

"Tortillas, tortillas a mano." "Papas." "Chicharones." "Mango."
The sounds floated on the chilly breeze and mingled into a morning song.

Both eager and hesitant, I knew that this was no practice run. This was the real thing. I had reason for concern. After all, my Spanish was limited to less than one good paragraph. I wondered how I would perform in a one-on-one bargaining session.

If it had not been for Paula, I wouldn't have had the nerve to try and would have chosen to sleep in this morning. Although Paula had been with me for only two weeks, it was she who encouraged me to go to the *mercado*. She made it clear that it had much to offer. We would have much more to choose from as compared to the *supermercado*.

A cool breeze tickled my skin. I shivered. A hot cup of hot coffee would be nice, but that would be later. First, I had things to do.

Left and right, merchants set up their stalls. Paula pointed to a twisting corridor. I followed her direction and we surveyed the huge variety of fruits and vegetables. The produce was displayed in artistic patterns on serapes on the ground or on rough boards, which served as makeshift stands. The scents of ripened fruits and vegetables permeated the gradually warming air. Attractions included edible cactus, many kinds of chili, and handmade tortillas.

The sun rose higher over the tips of the mountains. Here and there were threads of tangerine in the sky. Slowly, the light began to fill the bazaar. There were *zapatos*, shoes with rubber tire soles, silver jewelry, belts, buckles, baskets, and bags—all in neat rows, piles, or hanging from makeshift holders.

I came here to learn, to see, to experience. I moved on and into the area where the farmers unloaded their goods. Crates of chickens blocked our path, and their cackles and squawks followed us even as we turned and found a new corridor. Hurrying men, bent on catching early shoppers, jostled my elbows as they rushed to set up shop. There was fellowship, a closeness in the way the *mercado* brought us all together—shoppers, maids, tradesmen, and farmers.

Paula and I returned to the produce area. Root vegetables with strange-sounding names caught my eye, along with the usual potatoes, onions, carrots, and fall vegetables for a good pot roast dinner—the only dish I knew how to make.

We never paid the first amount demanded for anything. As we surveyed the items, Paula stood on one side and nodded to me when she thought the price low enough. I'd glance at her, watch for the sign and utter, *"¡Sí!"* Then, the vendor put handfuls of potatoes or onions into the bags, the *bolsas* that we had brought with us.

"Carne," I said. I wanted to buy a hunk of meat, and Paula led me through the maze closer to the center. A cluster of more permanent structures stood toward the center of the square. Protected with corrugated tin roofs, these stalls had glass fronts like a butcher shop at home. Men in white aprons stood behind counters and cut meat. At still another stall, a man dressed in a white smock laid out whole fish in freshly chipped ice.

"Todos muy frescos," he called to me across the counter. He beamed. His broad smile revealed great, white teeth. His wares compelled me to stop and look.

"¿Qué es esto?" I pointed to a reddish fish.

"Juachinango," he replied.

"Sí, Juachinango," Paula chimed in. *"Es muy rico."*

I had no idea what "watchshenango" meant. I had trouble just catching the sound. I shook my head. Cooking fish exceeded the skill of my limited culinary repertoire. "No," I said, and then restated, *"Carne."* And so we passed by the fishmonger until we found the butcher that Paula recommended. Once there at the meat counter, I noticed that potential buyers had the habit of feeling the meat to see if it was tender. Paula did the honors. She pinched the meat between her fingers and smiled in approval.

"*Sí, es muy suave,*" she said.

I motioned to the butcher that I wanted to buy the meat and negotiated a price.

"*Dos kilos,*" I said.

The butcher took down the large piece and went to work. The knife shimmered as he cut the meat. He wrapped it in white paper and tied it with string. We added the bundle to our collection in the bags.

Finally, when we had enough and the bags bulged with groceries, we headed back to the car. I stood in the parking area with my back to the river and the vehicles that whizzed along the road. I relaxed in the sun. One last look. It had been fun—more than enjoyable. The morning had been more than a shopping spree; it was an initiation.

Paula arranged our purchases in the trunk of the car. I turned on the radio and found songs of love, songs of loss, songs of passion.

Heavy traffic stirred on the road. I backed out and drove home feeling exhilarated. The sounds and momentum of the morning had a keen effect on me. I was rapidly learning not only the language, but also the ways of the place and the people. All that was lacking was a hot cup of coffee. I could almost smell it.

When we arrived home, I parked the car and together, we collected our purchases—so fresh, so alive. I picked up a branch of bananas that would not fit in the bag. As we neared the front door, a terrible stench assaulted us. I went in ahead, leaving Paula to bring in the bags. The smell grew stronger as I walked into the kitchen. Two large kerosene cans boiled and bubbled on the little stovetop. The peculiar odor puzzled me. I smelled bleach, a hint of kerosene, and something else. It was acrid. It burned my nostrils and hurt my head.

"Hi," Len called to me. "Where've you been?"

"We went to the *mercado,* the big outdoor one by the river." I sought his eyes in hope of explanation of the stench.

"Skulls," he said.

Twelve

Nobody's Funeral

"We got two skulls today. Good ones. No one claimed the bodies at the morgue. Indians. Probably accident victims." Len absolutely beamed and the corners of his mouth turned up. "Don't worry about the mess. We're almost done."

Len pointed to the old kerosene cans on the stove. At the far side of the kitchen, I could see Mario, his thick shoulders and broad back directly in front of me. Like some ancient warlock stirring a cauldron, he leaned over the can and poked at the mess.

"My God," I said.

"You know we'd never get a skull in the States," Mario turned his head toward me. "Len sweet-talked the woman at the morgue into it yesterday. I picked up the skulls this morning. Hope you're not squeamish, Gail."

Len turned to his friend and pointed to the can. "Mario, yours looks clean. What a honey! You can put it out on the wall in the back. It can dry out there. With the sun as strong as it is, it'll be as white as paper in a week or so. Mine's not quite done."

Mario removed his skull with a sturdy stick. He surveyed it, walked out the kitchen door to the thick adobe wall that surrounded the pool of mud that was our tiny backyard. He reached high, placed the skull on the top, and stepped back. "I'll call mine Louie, after Louie Prima. Do you remember, 'Sing Sing Sing?'"

"I sure do." Len hummed the Louie Prima standard and did a little dance step. "Great music. Maybe I should call mine Keely Smith in honor of his songbird." They both laughed.

Leaning forward over the bubbling can, Len waited until the last bits of flesh bubbled away into the stinky brine.

"A female, around thirty years old," Len said. "Hello, Keely."

I could imagine limpid brown eyes and coarse black hair, possibly in thick braids. Now all this bony, human composition would be a learning tool for two gringos so that they could grasp anatomy. I understood the logic. Still, something seemed wrong. It offended me to have human remains in my kitchen. It distorted the brightness of the morning.

"I'll take yours now," Mario said as Len stepped out of the way. "C'mon, Keely." Mario gently placed the second skull on the adobe wall next to its companion just as Paula walked through the door into the kitchen. She dropped the bags and stared. Fear flashed across her face. I met her gaze.

"*Madre de Dios, no se puede mirar. Esto es malo.*" She blessed herself. She looked at me, then at Len. She read my mind and said, "*¿Dónde está la niña?*"

I pointed to the bedroom and nodded. She immediately went in, and with the baby in her arms, hurried out the door to fresh air.

"Upset you a little, huh?" Len asked.

My voice went up a notch. "I'll say."

I didn't want to present obstacles, and yet an uncomfortable sensation of hostility came over me.

The wall blocked off almost the entire mountain behind, but what it left for a view had been spectacular. Now, heightened by the silhouettes of two skulls, it looked like some bizarre picture by Salvador Dali. Two soul-disturbing skulls huddled together, as if for warmth, against the scraps of clouds.

"Well, what do you think?" Len asked.

I drew back into myself. "I shall never forget this to the end of my life."

I looked out toward the top of the mountain from the window over the kitchen sink. Two skulls bleaching in the intense sun of early fall greeted me. I recalled the beautiful native that I had seen only an hour ago and his fine face.

The hollow, staring skulls challenged me as I stood at the sink. I wondered if I would ever be able to cook in the kitchen again, but I knew I had to, even though the idea repulsed me. I fought to over-come the nausea, which engulfed me in a sickening revulsion.

"It's hard for me to get my mind around this." I swallowed hard. I wanted to maintain a distance from the horrible sight, the terrible stench. I had trouble breathing. I couldn't say anything. I couldn't even think, except to wonder if even God knew how this came to be.

"Do you have any idea how lucky we are? We could never do this in the States. It would be impossible."

I could only stare.

"I'm going to annotate all the articulations in Indian ink, right on the skull."

"Annotate what?"

"All the articulations in the cranium! There must be dozens. I'll really learn 'em that way."

I had to say or do something. "Clean this up as soon as possi-ble. I can't have a baby in this filth."

"I will," he muttered. His eyebrows knitted in a frown, puz-zled at my lack of enthusiasm.

I retreated back toward the living room with fresh air and light. I found the baby in Paula's arms and took Jeanne from her, then went outside. All the while, Paula muttered under her breath. She dragged a chair from the living room and followed me outdoors to the verandah with it. I sat down. She handed me a blanket, which I wrapped around Jeanne. I sat outdoors in the frosty sunlight for some time. The slightest hint of wind blew.

As I sat there, it continued to blow, freshening the scene, spreading waves of clean, clear air. I stroked Jeanne's forehead with the tips of my fingers. At that moment, I had a vivid picture of my family and the house I grew up in. I wanted the same qualities in a home: cleanliness, cooperation, attention to food, the rearing of children. Home added up to security and safety.

Living with Len meant chaos. There was a casual lifting of normal rules. All this led to choices for some purpose—a higher purpose for him and for me. At least, that was how he presented it.

Higher purpose or no, I flinched whenever I recalled the gruesome sight in the kitchen. I was no coward. I had looked, even though it made me shudder. I also felt a sense of desecration for the horrible mutilation of those two human beings. For Len and Mario, there was only a satisfaction—a rare opportunity for learning.

Len and Mario got rid of the cans and the liquid. Paula and I were finally able to put the produce away. Still fresh and nicely colored, I hung the branch of bananas on a nail in the corner.

Paula went into her room and shut the door. That afternoon, she left for her weekend off. When she left, I knew she wouldn't return. She didn't.

⚕

In the days that followed, I contemplated the jarring, vacant-eyed skulls perched outside my window. An awareness began to roost in me, a new intimacy with death. How easily Louie and Keely caught my attention. I began to get used to them in a way that I supposed medical students get used to dealing with death very early in their careers. I never succeeded, however, in developing the sense of humor around the subject so typical of the students. Rather, I developed a darker awareness—one that fractured the optimistic outlook of my youth.

The skulls conveyed the fragile nature of life. They no longer appeared horrible. I became accustomed to their presence. Not

surprisingly, in their powerless state they began to exert a strange
kind of power over me, and I felt an obligation to look at them,
although they never sought my gaze.

On All Souls Day, I lit a candle and ate supper with Louie and
Keely as is the custom in Mexico on the Day of the Dead. Who
else was there, except me, to pay the last respects? I found a book
of poems by T. S. Eliot at the library and selected a passage to
read my friends.

And what the dead had no speech for, when living,
They can tell you, being dead: the communication
Of the dead is tongued with fire beyond the language
*   of the living.*
Here the intersection of the timeless moment . . .
                                        — Four Quartets

Thirteen

Limits of the Heart

"I see it is going to be quite difficult to get you to leave early." I cornered Len as he scrambled to get his bag and notes, eager to leave for his last meeting of the semester.

"Just this one clinic left, the one with Dr. Montemayor. I'll get back as soon as it's over, and then we can get going. Mario will be ready then, also."

It was all planned. We were actually going home to California for Christmas, and the house bustled with excitement. I was packed and had paid the maid. Since Paula left, I'd had a series of servants, most of whom lasted a week or two in our house, and then left. I was never sure if it was my ineptitude with the language and culture or the sight of the skulls that made them leave.

Mario was traveling with us. With three drivers, we could drive straight through. Our happiness at having the semester and a successful six months behind us was to be short-lived, however.

Probably nothing was quite so helpful to Len as his friendship with the gang, and that fact was born out when Luís showed up at the door. I was surprised to see him because I thought that he, like the other students, would be on their way home by now.

"Something's happened. Sit down."

"What's going on?" I asked.

"It happened at school this morning," Luís said. "We went into the cardiac ward. Dr. Montemayor gave a brief introduction before we started rounds. We usually don't get to go into the wards, but he wanted us to have some firsthand evidence of what he wanted us to learn. Dr. Montemayor said, 'People with heart lesions do not have a normal life expectancy. Of course, some beat the odds, but others die young. The valves become damaged—congestive heart failure, the result. Personally, I think someday someone is going to invent an artificial valve. For now, we just treat these people as best we can. Let's see the first patient.'

"Len, along with Mario and me, were told to practice listening to a patient's heart. We took turns to see if we could find any abnormality.

"Len said, 'I'm not sure,' and he pressed the stethoscope to the man's chest, 'but, I think the man has a heart murmur.'

"Dr. Montemayor said, 'Listen to your own chest to be sure and then compare.' So, Len did as directed.

"He said 'It's hard to tell. They sound alike.' Len pressed the stethoscope to his chest and then to the patient's chest. Once more, Len listened to his own heartbeat.

"Then, Dr. Montemayor handed me the stethoscope. 'Luís, your turn.' It was like an exam. I was nervous. I listened and said, 'The man has a heart murmur. Clearly, he does.' There was no doubt.

"Dr. Montemayor grabbed the stethoscope from me and listened, first to the patient, and then to Len's heart, and back to the patient.

"He said, 'Correct diagnosis!' and congratulated me. As he listened to Len's chest, Dr. Montemayor became very quiet and asked, 'Has any one ever told you that you have a heart murmur, Len?'

"He said, 'No, and I was in the U.S. Army during the war. The Army Air Force. I passed the physical with flying colors.'

"Montemayor quipped, 'They must have needed you very badly.' "

When Luís told me that Len had been diagnosed with a double mitral valve lesion, my blood froze and my throat went dry.

"Many people live long, productive lives," Luís said. I knew he was trying to make me feel better.

Hours later, when Len came home and when we had time to talk about what happened, I couldn't wait to ask, "What is it?" as my voice cracked. "What does this mean, Len? Is it serious?"

He tossed around some technical jargon and finally, "It means that I have two leaks in the heart valve." Smiling benignly, he paused and thought for a moment. "Probably caused by rheumatic fever when I was a kid. Strep infections sometimes go that way."

"What does it mean for your life? Your health? Medical School?" I pressed on, trying not to panic.

"Some people think that I don't have a normal life expectancy, that's all. We'll talk about it on the drive to California. We'll have lots of time on the way home. Don't forget, I have the luck of the Irish."

Fourteen

Starry Vision

*W*e didn't talk about it. We headed out north to the border, with Mario in the front seat next to Len, Jeanne and I in the back. Desert wastelands, once an ancient ocean, surrounded the road on all sides. Frightened as I was to admit it, I was afraid of losing my husband, this man who seemed so healthy, so vibrant. I was young, short on life experience, and as I surveyed the fading landscape, now gray and forlorn in the pale winter sunshine, I felt hopelessly inadequate. And it was in that state that I thought of my grandfather. He lived in the back of my mind. He was my hero. I heard a whisper, *never be afraid that life will take things from you. Live a fearless life and you will feel full. Always build your future—build. But make sure it is yours.* Was it the wind? Tumbleweeds tossed by the chilly wind rolled aimlessly like wandering Mexican nature spirits—spirits of chaos.

From time to time, the road curved sharply and we could see the remains of a modern tanker or a dilapidated truck turned upside down, or on its side. Burnt-out wrecks, rusty with time, punctuated the curving path to Laredo.

The cumulative effect of the pregnancy, the months in Monterrey, and the knowledge of Len's heart condition had left me in a whirl of fear, desperation, and grief. Just the thought of the visit home was a tonic, even though my confidence in the future was crumbling.

It was the first day of the trip and the ride was especially tedious until we got to Texas. Once over the border, the highway would be more trustworthy. Cactus, endless sandy hills, ruins, and junk along the way made me say, "Not much to see here." No one commented. To the left, masses of mountains continued. Behind them to the south, the morning's bustle in Monterrey would soon begin without us.

During the long drive, I experienced spikes of panic. *What if Len died? What would I do?* Upon the crests of the distant mountains, snow glittered. December trees, burnished by the winter sunrise, stood cold and bare in the misty desert. Eighteen hours to go. Occasional gusts of icy air surprised us as we drove late into the night, stopping only when necessary to buy gasoline or a snack. The road wound through the chipped stones and pearly gray surfaces. Low over the horizon to the right, I saw the Big Dipper. Under the dark, nocturnal sky, the twinkling stars showed me the way. I found the pointer star, and it was easy to determine *west*. The starry vision gave me an orientation, and I knew where lay San Diego.

"Hush, hush," I comforted Jeanne who awakened from a bump in the road, and tried to ignore my own spasm of anxiety.

After sunrise, we stopped every hour or so. Len bought Dr. Pepper and potato chips. He offered me a bottle, saying, "This stuff really keeps you awake."

When we got to El Paso, Mario paid for hamburgers and shakes, and I agreed, with the help of the last of the Dr. Pepper, to drive the last leg of the trip.

We arrived in San Diego County at dawn. As we drove on along the edge of the Coastal Mountains, a stretch of hazy blue split the cliffs far ahead. It took me a second to realize that it was the sea. I rolled down the window and inclined my head to the familiar tangy, brisk aroma. No longer fatigued, I breathed air that carried a hint of sea breeze. I pressed down on the accelerator. I was home.

When we arrived at the home of Len's parents, the Dennys, we noticed a car filled with people waiting out in front: Mario's family. Just as we stopped, a young woman burst out of the other car, ran to Mario, and embraced him. Clinging to each other, they wept. Moments later, Mario retrieved his belongings from our car and piled into the car with his wife and parents.

"See you in a few weeks," Mario called out the window as they drove off.

Len waved them off. "I just want to hit the sack." He lifted Jeanne out of the car and carried her toward the apartment.

Alice called from the balcony, "Len, Jeannie."

It was Frank who stayed behind to carry the bags and help me.

When I stood up, I felt my legs buckle and had to cling to the car door. My whole body was shaking as if a current of electricity coursed through the nerve ends. I finally made it into the apartment and Jeanne, now wide-awake, was ready to play. I knew there would be no sleep for me. Jeanne looked at everyone's face and then back at me with questions. At last, she spied the Christmas tree. She pointed to the tiny tree glistening with colored lights, tinsel, and shiny orbs.

"*Mira, Mamá.*" She had a delicious glow about her, ready for the day.

Alice reached for two cups from a cupboard, then stopped at a sudden thought.

"Are you going straight to bed, Len?"

"Yes," he said matter-of-factly.

She looked at me, and before she could say anything, I said, "I'll have a cup of coffee, strong and black."

For a long moment, I saw nothing except Jeanne's face, entranced by the magic of the Christmas tree, the lights, and the decorations. Then, I moved my eyes to the coffee. Not the Nescafé we had in Mexico, but the real stuff—fresh-brewed heaven. I sat back and surveyed the scene—Alice, Frank, Jeanne, the tree. It was as if I were seeing the whole year in a flash. As I drank, I sat for a moment with closed eyes, feeling the hot liquid in my throat and savoring the taste. It was delicious, and yet I felt the tremble in my limbs. I'd quit school and placed all my eggs in Len's basket. I couldn't imagine where I'd be without him, yet a burden weighed down on me that I'd never known before.

⚜

Alice and Frank Denny filled me in on the news. Important changes were taking place in San Diego. Healthcare was expanding, new homes popped up everywhere, and my college was thriving. I thought Len should explore opportunities in the States—in California, particularly—where people were now flocking by the hundreds.

His heart condition haunted me. I thought we should consider careers that were less demanding physically than what Len had chosen to do. At a deep level, I knew that if we returned to Monterrey, there would be hard times ahead.

Len would have nothing to do with any other plan, though. It had to be Mexico and medicine.

"What's the matter with you? Can't you live on beans and rice for a couple of years?" He joked, trying to use his charm to defuse the situation. His question only fed my general list of concerns and had a powerfully deflating effect on me.

We decided to remain at Alice and Frank's charming new apartment during the holidays, giving us plenty of time to discuss plans and ideas about the future. One of the most imprudent suggestions came from Len's mother. While we were in Mexico, Alice had embarked on a project to start up a carpet store with an older gentleman who had come under her sway. Alice was a beautiful woman—blonde, curvaceous, seductive. Mr. Johnson, a man in his mid-fifties, had a large vacant store, and he wanted to take advantage of the boom in the housing market. He needed an experienced store manager who could also sell. That was Alice. Her knack for positioning herself as opportunities arose seemed like absolute genius at first. Frank's enigmatic silence led her on. He never voiced any concern to what looked like hair-brained ideas, only one of many dubious business ventures.

"We'll call it 'Sunshine Carpet'—'Sunshine,' for Alice," Mr. Johnson said when I met him and heard of his plans. Alice hugged him and then turned to Len.

"Len, you can help get the store ready. If the business interests you, it can be a fallback position. You know—I'll give you a piece of it."

It wasn't what she said; it was how she said it that intrigued me. I could see moves that reminded me of Len. There was an immediate intimacy about Alice. She could get under the skin with a shifting unknown, yet attractive, power that was coated with a bewildering innocence. I decided to keep an arm's length away from her. Later that night, sensing my reticence, she found me and invited me to go into her bedroom so we could talk privately.

She faced me and said, "Gail, I want to show you something. When you see these things, you may be shocked, but I want to be honest with you. Now, you're family." Reaching into the closet, she pulled out a large box tied with blue satin ribbon. Alice sat on the bed, drew me close to her, then placed the box between us and slowly untied the bow and opened the box. Like a child sharing secret treasures from her toy box, she fingered a picture, then drew it out. It was Frank. He was wearing a roman collar.

She spoke as if she were telling me a bedtime story in a soft, appealing voice. "Gail," she cooed, "Frankie is a priest. It would be unkind to postpone this talk any longer." Seeing the question in my eyes, she went on, "No, we are not married. Someday, Frank may want to go back to God." She lowered her eyes like a bewildered child.

"Let me show you something else." She rummaged in the box, finally withdrawing a manila folder. She opened it slowly and carefully as if it were a relic. "All the secrets are here," and handed me a clipping from the Oswego, New York newspaper. *Mother of Six runs off with Parish Priest.* "That was nine years ago. We have to keep it quiet, even here. Len was in the army when I left." Blue magnetic eyes held my attention. I wanted to look away, but I couldn't.

"Here's my 'Sonny.'" She retrieved a picture of Len. He was dressed in an aviator outfit with a leather helmet and goggles. He looked like Errol Flynn, very handsome, very sexy. Then, she found one of him as a baby—golden curls and dimples. The resemblance to Jeanne was remarkable.

Next, she picked up a picture of a dark-haired beautiful woman. She must have been close to Len's age. "This is Virginia. She went to Mexico City with Len. You know, the first time he went to school down there."

"Virginia? I didn't know he went there with someone. He never said anything, except that school in Mexico didn't work out," I said.

Why hadn't Len told me?

I felt a surge of rage. It was all I could do to keep from smashing the picture in her hands.

"All they did was party. But that won't happen now that he has you. Virginia wanted to marry him in the worst way. Sonny never wanted to get married, until he met you. Then, everything changed."

I moved closer, fascinated by the story. "He never said much about Mexico City," I said. As she talked, I withdrew into an inner core of myself to reappraise my life with Len.

She went on. "When he met you, he was bowled over. 'Met this girl,' he told me. 'She's real smart and very pretty. Lots of the docs have an eye on her, but I'm going to marry her.' That's what he said." Shoving the box aside, Alice put her arm around me.

With eyes wide and imploring, she half whispered, "Now this thing about Len's heart. Don't you worry about it. Nothing's going to happen to Sonny. Nothing! If he goes, I go. Besides, he has you, now."

I wanted to scream at her to shut up but fell silent instead, broadsided by such a tell-all event. Cautious, discrete, I let people in slowly.

Alice's story about her and Frank was not totally unexpected. I'd heard the gossip from others in the family. Somehow with the telling, the details, I felt trapped into the transgression with them. The episode pointed up for me the embarrassment of our differences. If there had been scandal in my own family, I'd never heard about it. I hadn't expected to be brought into Alice's confidence, at least not this way. Now, her words bore into my head. They were all too real.

The only moment I loved about that day was when Len came home. Something in the sound of his footsteps gave me such a rush of anticipation that I hardly knew what to do or say when he entered the room.

ॐ

Len actually took his mother's advice. For the few weeks that we were in San Diego, he spent his time painting walls, moving large rolls of carpet, and generally exhausting himself. In counter measure, he only strengthened his resolve to return to Monterrey. Meanwhile, the deal at Sunshine Carpet had already begun to unravel. It would appear that Mrs. Johnson was not sure that pretty Alice was the right person to mange her husband or his store.

Fifteen

Mirrors and Memories

The sun had gone way south. The days were short; the nights, long. I had been working steadily to nourish old family ties and pacify new ones. I tried not to be bothersome, but it soon became evident that Alice was bored, if not irritated, with our intrusion into her secure harbor. I wanted to turn off the pressure, forget Sunshine Carpet, slip into a nice, comfortable place, and escape the squabbling, the selfish stupidity, the noise. I just wanted rest.

One late afternoon, a few days before Christmas, I found myself alone. Len had taken Jeanne to visit old friends from the hospital. I headed out of Kensington, over the Adams Avenue Bridge to Normal Heights and the home of my grandparents. I was not really keen on relinquishing the familiar and comfortable state of my childhood. Perhaps I was working against myself in that regard by holding too tightly to the past.

I did not have to ring or knock or anything, for the door was open as it had been on so many other occasions. I turned the handle of the door, went in, and found him in the living room. Grandpa sat in his usual chair by the window. His gaze drifted toward me. He looked up. "Hi, Kid."

I stared at him, too surprised to say anything. He didn't look, act, or sound like the man I remembered from only a few months before. He folded his paper, put it down, and looked at me curiously. Nonny came out of the kitchen, wiping her hands on her apron.

"You look good." She hugged me. "Visit for a while, and then we'll have dinner."

"How long will you be here?" My grandfather looked at me. His thin face was clean-shaven with a touch of the familiar talcum, giving him a smooth, clean look.

"Three weeks." I noticed how thin and frail he looked as he rolled a cigarette between his fingers.

When he was in Chicago, he wore spats on his shoes. I could remember as a little child going for after-dinner walks with him. On the way home, we'd stop at the tavern, the one with straw on the floor by the corner of our street. He'd have a beer and I'd eat a large, salted pretzel. Everyone knew him. They called him Skipper. On the way home, he'd show me his blackjack and brass knuckles. "Just in case," he'd say and add, "don't tell Nonny where we went."

When I asked him why, he didn't give a straight answer. He told me that she'd throw dishes at him if he went to the tavern, especially if he took me along. That was thirteen years ago. Somehow, to a child of six, those evenings provided ultimate adventure.

"They won't let me smoke tobacco anymore, so I use this. 'Green Mountain,' they call it." He picked up a package that looked like tobacco, except that it was green and sweet-smelling.

"Can you believe you can actually buy this crap in a tobacco shop?" He carefully picked out what looked liked weeds. He laid it on the paper, deftly rolling with one hand. Then, he licked one side and pressed the paper together until it stuck. He lit his cigarette. A cough and a series of wheezes followed.

I looked through the smoke at the picture window behind him. The glass showed the reflection of a large smoke spiral, not unlike the appearance of a ghost at Halloween in a haunted house.

My eyes roamed slowly about the room. The wingback chairs and the burgundy- colored curtains gave the room a touch of elegance. From various mirrors, memories stared back at me. One predominated: that of him sitting in his chair, smoking, reading his paper, and talking back to the newscast. The Allies had bombed Berlin, and we had to close all the curtains and keep the doors closed at night. "We just wanted to make our Christmas tree ornaments," he yelled in fury. He was, after all, a German.

Now, I took in the handsome room full of books, the old radio, and his oil paintings on the wall. Grandpa was someone I loved very much. Every moment spent with him had seemed exactly right. He was dependable as heartwood.

We walked together through the kitchen where Nonny was preparing dinner, always an event. Nonny didn't just cook; she was a Cook. But she didn't teach me anything. Her kitchen remained off-limits.

I followed my grandfather outdoors in the mild San Diego winter weather. Along the side of the garage, Spencer sweet peas of all colors abundantly covered the wall. The fragrance was the same voluptuous sweetness that had been there every year for as long as we had lived in the house. We had spent a good bit of time here, sitting under the pepper tree or puttering in the garden. Walking further, he showed me the old victory garden, which, together, we had so carefully tended during the war years, only now it was greatly diminished in size. Nevertheless, he had managed to keep the little canals for water irrigation open.

The sweet fragrance mingled strangely with the smell of Green Mountain. How I missed this place, envied the lifestyle—peaceful, steady, quiet, satisfied.

Grandpa wheezed. I felt an emotional wrenching, even more painful than when I'd learned of Len's heart condition. It must have shown on my face.

"Emphysema. That son-of-a-bitch doctor said there's not much to be done."

Hearing him curse, I felt better. He hadn't changed. He still had the sound of a Wild Boy.

"I miss you, Grandpa. Wish we were closer."

The garden was still vibrant with rows of beans, spinach, and winter squash. Leaning on the pole at the end of a row and swaying slightly, he mentioned the War Years.

"Remember 1944? Chickens and the rabbits?" he asked.

I nodded. "Remember how Nonny tried to convince me that eggplant was some kind of war meat?"

"You gotta' do what you gotta' do," he smiled.

"Well, she got me to eat it, but it left me very confused."

"The yard's too much for me, now." He seemed delicate and resigned. He let go of the pole and moved on.

I felt a crushing melancholy. The best of times became inexplicably clear. I could easily imagine the rows of rabbit hutches and chicken coops in the far corner of the yard. From this little plot, he had raised the crops that kept us well fed during the years of rationing. What to do with an old man—an artist, in a way, with his creations expressed so tangibly in this garden, in years of humdrum work, in dedication to duty, and in oil paintings of a dark, violent sea?

"Do you eat rabbit down there in Mexico?"

"No, but once I ate baby goat. It wasn't bad. As good as rabbit, anyway."

An ash from his cigarette fell on his sleeve. He groped for a spade and leaned on it. Dust in the suspended air marked the place where he pushed the earth into little mounds.

"A few years ago, this was a garden of paradise."

"Still looks good to me," I said. It felt like a timeless moment.

The back door opened slightly and we were called for dinner. In the background, I heard the telephone ring.

"We'd better go." Prompt submission to my grandmother tore us away from the garden. "Don't tell Nonny about the goat. She wouldn't like it."

He was referring to my grandmother's sensibilities. She had instilled in the family a pride about food and a fixation on neatness. There was an order to life that one came to understand only by living through it. I would tell her later about Mexico, the good things.

I touched the pepper tree and looked at the wheelbarrow, enjoying the smell of home cooking and my grandfather's presence. Whatever the present moment was, I wanted to hold onto its healing renewal.

What would happen if I stayed, if I didn't go back with Len?

I took a deep breath and walked inside.

Staying wasn't really an option. I had to go back. I couldn't abandon Len now that I knew of his life-threatening diagnosis. Grandpa never abandoned us. I had to try.

🜖

After dinner, we talked about what had happened in the scant few months since I had left. I decided not to mention the discovery of Len's heart condition. My grandparents inquired about life in Mexico and why it was so important for us to remain there. I braced myself as my grandmother gave me a piece of her mind.

"You're so far away and living with strangers. Why? Just tell me why!"

They might have guessed the answer. "It's important to Len."

"Humph." My grandmother was not impressed. "Call your mother. She's working late and wants to see you."

🜖

My mother, employed at Jessop's Jewelry Store, had worked in the business sporadically since the end of the war. A lovely woman, she offered an attractive image, superb sales skills, and a well-earned reputation as a diamond specialist.

I had lost a part of my mother when I was five. At that time, she had what was called a nervous breakdown and had to be hospitalized. Psychiatry was still a new science, and we never quite understood the "what" or "why" of what happened to her. She was subjected to electric shock treatment, and when she returned to us, she seemed a little different, more distant. Unspoken fears haunted her.

During my childhood in Chicago, she and I would return home to our apartment late at night after a movie out. She would open the door and shove me in.

"I'm afraid," she'd say, "but you're going to be brave." She'd give me a little push. I'd rush into the darkened room unafraid, not understanding her hesitancy. I trusted her completely, knowing she would never put me in harm's way.

Over the years, we all learned to handle her with kid gloves. Things had not changed.

I saw her curly brown head through the window. Dressed in a deeply colored blue-green suit, tailored and well-fitting, she wore a thick strand of pearls, as well as a lapel pin made of clusters of tiny seed pearls in the shape of a fan that looked like an exotic sea plant. She didn't see me as I halted in the doorway under the sign, "Jessop's Jewelry." Red fluted goblets, probably Venetian glass, were arranged in the display case behind where she stood. Christmas carols played softly. A square clock with an ebony façade sat next to a tray of amber jewelry.

Mother looked up and noticed me standing there in front of her. Her eyebrows rose in recognition. "Come, come," she motioned me forward. "Hi, Kiddo. Where's Jeanne?" A faint infusion of light from above shone down on a tray of twinkling diamonds. She carefully arranged them, one by one, in neat rows.

"She's with Len this evening. I thought it would be easier to visit everybody this way, first." I unbuttoned my coat and looked about the store. "I'll bring Jeanne over as soon as you let me know your schedule."

"Well, you better. I'm dying to see her. I get my break soon."
She put the tray back inside the case and locked it. "Diamonds
are a big item this year. My sales have been good."

The surreal gentility of the jewelry store was not conducive to
intimate talk, so I walked around, surveying all the gorgeous
things, and waited for her. There were clusters of pearls on a table
beside the front door, a beautiful collection of iridescent neck-
laces and bracelets.

On her break, we walked to a small coffee shop where she
ordered a sandwich for herself and a pot of tea for me. Her left
knee bounced nervously.

"These last few years have not been easy." She tugged at her
jacket sleeve to straighten it out, poofed up her hair, and wriggled her shoulders.

"Are you okay?" I asked. A jukebox played an Elvis tune in the
background. From the player, a steady thump.

She didn't answer my question. Instead, she said, "It's amazing how your father, a man who has raised millions of dollars for
others, couldn't do something for his own family." The words
poured out in a tense, angry tumble. She looked out the window
and picked at the cuticle of her thumb. "I'm lucky to have a nice
place to work."

I moistened my lips with tea and said, "So, I hear that Daddy's
selling appliances. I know it must be hard for him. I'll go by and
see him tomorrow. Isn't he working right around the corner from
Sunshine Carpet?"

"Sunshine Carpet," she said. "That's where Alice is hanging
out these days."

"Well, yes, in a way. She's trying to get a business started with
Mr. Johnson."

"Don't get me started on that one," my mother said. "She
thinks she can twist every man she meets around her little
finger."

I was shocked. My mother had her faults, but I had never heard her utter one unkind word about another human being.

"Your dad stopped in the other day, and there she was, snuggled up to Mr. Johnson. Some way to run a business."

"I don't think she means anything by it." I swallowed.

"Probably not, but she's one to watch out for. She's really quite notorious. For unbridled extravagance and, I must add, for shady deals."

"Like what?"

"Last year, she was racing horses at Del Mar. She told me some doctor gave her two horses, but she couldn't afford the upkeep and had to let them go. His wife found out and there was a big row."

I wanted to change the subject, and when I mentioned Jeanne, she brightened and asked a million questions. In the intensity of our conversation, I had not paid attention to the hour. At length, she glanced at her watch, put it to her ear, and listened to it. "Not much time. Have to go in a minute. Too bad we can't go for a drink."

"What do you mean?"

"There's a new bar just around the corner. They make great martinis. Beefeaters Gin. Yummm."

"I don't drink," I said. *She knew that.*

"Too bad, Kiddo." She tapped her red oval-shaped fingernails on the table.

I didn't know how to interpret the "Kiddo." She'd never called me that me before. "Well, maybe next time," I said, trying to humor her.

"Oops," she said. "I have to take a pill."

"Are you sick?" I was beginning to feel scared and uncomfortable.

"No, it's some new thing. They call it a tranquilizer." She popped a pill in her mouth. "The doctor said it would calm me down. I don't see much difference, except it makes my mouth real dry."

I didn't know what to say. I waited a moment, not looking directly at her. And then, plunging in, I summoned up my courage and told her briefly about Len and his heart condition. I emphasized the chaos and turmoil of our life in Mexico.

"It's just that we're always short on money," I said. "I'm working, but can't much longer."

"Well, he's just got to leave you alone. You can't keep having a kid every year."

"It's funny," I said. "You see, he does leave me alone. I hardly ever see him. He's out with the gang all the time. It's frightening to be alone so much at night, you know?" In that moment of sudden intimacy, I wanted consolation. I wanted to tell her what I hadn't admitted even to myself, that I often submitted to drunken caresses that left me feeling empty. Could I possibly tell her?

Her eyes met mine. "Oh, he's still young." Her manner was abrupt and she shrugged it off.

Maybe she thought I was asking her for money. I wasn't. I just wanted to get the weight off my shoulders. In the café, with the misty light coming in from the windows, I was like a kid again, wanting reassurance.

"He likes to go out, you know, to the *cantinas*," I went on. "He likes to play host. Pay for rounds and rounds of drinks. He can use up my week's pay in a night."

She looked at me and said almost automatically, without feeling, "Well, you made your bed. Now you have to lie in it."

Outside, Christmas shoppers strolled in the mall. A gleam settled over the store fronts, shimmering in the glare of the decorated windows. I sat with my head bent, thinking. *All right, I'll handle it myself.* I felt no easier in my mind and every bit as anxious.

I loved my mother uncritically and obediently. All through high school, I couldn't go to the beach with boys or stay out late. She chose my clothes and I didn't rebel, not over things like that. I found freedom in the books that I read where I could live in a deep, hidden world. She could be explosive and I didn't like to stir her up.

That night, however, I couldn't sleep. My pillow was hard. I'd seen something in my mother that I'd never seen before; something I couldn't put my finger on. There'd been a strange frenzied quality about her, something different. I dismissed it, thinking at the time that she was concerned about my grandfather as we all were. But her manner that night haunted me. I made up my mind to light a candle for her and for Len the next time I went to church.

ॐ

That Jeanne should be in the hospital only the day after Christmas was a shock to all of us.

Bolstering my courage, I asked, "What exactly happened, Doctor?" I was wearing my blue, dingy raincoat and my heart raced underneath it. I was still traumatized by the wild ride to the emergency room.

"Apparently, your daughter aspirated some of the hair from her stuffed animal. Not uncommon."

I looked at the baby who, by now, was sleeping peacefully as if at home in her own bed. "But it happened so quickly. She just turned blue. Started choking. Couldn't breathe."

"Lucky you got her here so quickly. Let's keep her a day or two just to be sure."

A while later, hospital ritual set in and Jeanne, with me beside her, was ensconced in a room in Pediatrics. It was almost dark. There was no sound to be heard, except the soft rustle of nurses in the hall. Jeanne slept deeply. Outside of an occasional flutter of eyelashes, her face was at rest. I could hardly bear to look at her. I was overcome with guilt. *I should never have let her have that stuffed toy.*

The door opened and someone turned on the light. I glanced around. I couldn't believe who came in. It was Janille Enright, my high school buddy. She wore the crisp uniform of a student nurse at Mercy Hospital. Straightening up, I walked to her, hands outstretched.

She hugged me. "I heard what happened. She's getting great care."

Keeping my voice as calm as I could, I said, "She could have died."

Raising clear brown eyes to me, Janille went on, "But she didn't. She'll be fine."

I desperately hoped she was right. The room was fragrant of the pine used for disinfectant. After taking two deep breaths, I said, "God, it's good to see you." In her eyes, I read acceptance. For the first time in weeks, here was someone without a hidden agenda.

A prim cap that framed her pretty face shimmered under the fluorescent light. She moved a little closer. The starched folds of her blue and white uniform made a crunching noise as she sat down on the edge of the bed and we talked. She inquired politely about my family, life in Mexico, and Len.

"You know," she leaned forward, "when you married him, we all thought you hit the jackpot. He's a great guy."

"It's strange," I said. "Len's like a magnet. Wherever we go, he attracts people."

"He's a charmer, for sure," she laughed, "and so good-looking. When he was an X-ray tech here, we students would go up there to the dark room. He'd let us go in and smoke. Always had a funny story."

I shifted in my chair in slight irritation. Just then, the door opened. It was Len.

"How's my girl?"

From the minute he came into the room, we all felt his presence. Jeanne's eyes fluttered open and she smiled. She glowed at the sight of him, as if a light passed between them. I too felt an instant reaction.

What terrified me was that there had seemed to be no end to crisis. Trouble stalked us. First Len's heart condition and his enigmatic silence about it, then my mother's peculiar behavior—an outward show of togetherness covering signs of inner tension, which had filled me with dread, and now Jeanne's accident, all in two weeks time. Our lives were so precarious.

Yet, when I saw Len that evening, I felt a welcome relief. I focused on the positive side. Len was ambitious and energetic, possessing an instinctive ability to make people like him. He'd just persuaded a doctor friend to agree to send him twenty-five dollars a month to get him through school.

Maybe I would get through this if Len would just explain things to me. I asked for more information about his heart.

"There's a lot of talk in Houston about artificial valves. It's just talk now, but someday. I'll just have to live long enough to get one," he joked.

As we set out for our return to Mexico, my fears returned. We had less money in our pocket than we had come with. All the cash that Len earned that Christmas at Sunshine Carpet had to go to pay for the hospital bill. As might be expected, he brushed it off.

"I'm doing this all for you," he insisted, "and for Jeanne. Someday, you'll be glad." A marble-hard look in his blue eyes warned me not go any further.

For just a flash, I again thought about not going back to Mexico with him. But when I saw the light in Jeanne's fairy eyes, I knew I had to go. I felt myself being sucked in yet again. Desperate and stubborn, I told myself that Len would survive.

Part Two

Sixteen

Once More Into the Breach

The dark mountain peaks were deeply etched against a cold starry sky. When we finally reached Monterrey and our home, I slid out of the car and slowly walked toward the entrance. As I bent over the lock, Len stood behind me, holding Jeanne. My senses, often telepathic, told me that something was wrong.

I pushed the door open. An instinct guided me to leave it ajar. There was no lamp. It had vanished. *Perhaps I had placed it somewhere else.* But that was impossible.

Reaching behind the door, I switched on the overhead light. A single small bulb flared out of the darkness, creating a nightmarish atmosphere, the sense of unreality heightened by the thick layer of dust that covered the table, sofa, an overturned armchair. Cupboards yawned. Drawers sat pulled open with their spilled contents on the floor. A gritty stillness pervaded the place.

A thin, icy breeze sent swirls of dust dancing across the gritty floor.

We had been robbed.

Curses and questions broke the quiet as Len stumbled through the rooms.

"Damn it! Look at the mess in the kitchen!" he yelled in a fury.

Many articles, mostly wedding presents, had been taken: the lamp with an absurd copper teapot base, the electric toaster, and some of Len's instruments. I rushed to the bedroom and checked the closet. Fortunately, the lock had held and the closet crammed with critical items was intact. I unlocked the door and made a quick survey. Gentle puffs of dust escaped from blankets, clothes, and linens as I poked and peered to check the contents. We could at least make the bed. Thank God, the radio was there.

I heard Cha Cha talking to Len in the living room in a soft voice. She must have heard us arrive and had entered through the open door. I left the bedroom and followed the sound of the voices.

"It was the *policia*; they did it. We couldn't do anything," Cha Cha cried.

"The police?" Could I possibly have heard right? "The police of the *colonia*?"

"They were *como se dice, borracho*. Drunk!"

The authorities could not be trusted. I was foolish to have told them about our departure.

And yet, I knew that what had happened was more than that. This was one of the many things that happened in Mexico, the general turmoil of everyday life. There was no travel guide or map or any sense of direction. Life reshaped itself on a moment-to-moment basis. I had to be ready for anything. Little by little, I was experiencing the way of dispossession as things I had once known or cherished were stripped away from me.

"I'm glad you're back," said Cha Cha. "Tomorrow, you can fix things."

"Thank you, Cha Cha. It is good to see you. Very good."

Actually, when she took Jeanne's hand there in the dusty room, I remembered Cha Cha as she had been at the cathedral—a little guide, and quite a good one. I appreciated her now more than ever.

"Señor Sanchez—he has been asking about you."

"Oh?" About Señor Sanchez I didn't know what to say. Bewilderment, culture shock, and endless surprises often left me without a voice. It had nothing to do with speaking a different language.

Together, the three of us restored some order until the next day. Then, the cleaning-up process began in earnest.

"Into the breach," I said with as much energy as I could summon.

"What did you say?" Len asked.

"You know, 'Into the breach.' Shakespeare. Henry the Fifth rallies the troops."

"Very funny."

⚜

For many weeks, I harbored the hope that Paula might return. The fact that I needed to find a new maid served as merely a counter irritation to the break-in. I had to think of Jeanne and the baby to come. Preparations for the birth had to be made, and that included making a reservation at *La Murguerza*, the maternity hospital. I also needed to do something about my students. Recapitulating my worries to myself, I knew that I had to find help.

Several days later, María Elena took me to an Indian village tucked away in a hidden mesa in the surrounding mountains. Yellow, tidy, adobe homes squatted at the foot of a high cliff. We stopped before a low adobe hut, got out, and approached the entrance. A low voice, almost inaudible, bade us enter. There, we met a fifteen-year-old girl who was sitting quietly in the semidarkness of her family home, close to a small, withered old woman. *La Vieja* sat on the floor, a small folded figure facing the open door into the street, which was now filled with pale light from the morning sun. The old woman had a distant, foreign look, and I got the impression that she had lived through many years of change. She spoke to the girl in a language I did not recognize—a native tongue that bore no resemblance to Spanish at all.

The girl was neatly dressed in a striped skirt of many colors and a hand-woven red sweater. When she stood to greet us, she had that same elegant poise that had so captivated me when I saw the young Indian in the *mercado* months before. Her thick hair, pulled back into two dark braids, nearly fell to her waist. Before her sat a basket of *masa* and a set of ancient stone tools for mashing it. She was quiet, yet assured. María Elena spoke to the younger woman in Spanish and explained the situation. Almost simultaneously, the young woman translated into her own dialect as the older woman listened impassively. Nearly twenty minutes of discussion passed. There were questions about wages, time off, and transportation.

We struck a deal. Luisa, our new girl, would accompany us home, and what had been mutually understood was accepted with smiles. If Paula should return—and I still hoped she would—we would keep both of them, as was the custom. The younger girl would be responsible, primarily, for caring for the children. When at last we rose to make our farewells, Luisa lifted her chin to the thin old face of the woman, closed her eyes, and received a kiss.

As Luisa gathered her things, I returned to the car with María Elena.

"*Mira,*" she said, indicating the forbidding beauty of the mountains rising out of the mist.

Way up on the slopes above, a herd of goats grazed the jagged cliffs, clearly visible in the transparent air. Behind the row of houses lay the cemetery—a hillock strewn with stony markers and crosses.

We had caught the attention of the village, and several of the inhabitants gathered around the house and in front of the car to say "goodbye" to the girl. I noticed faces, many of which were severely scarred. Probably small pox. And yet, the village, although remote, was charming, clean, and orderly. The people lived simply. Here were people carrying root vegetables in baskets; there, they pastured cattle.

Purple rocks and crystal blue peaks bestowed a sense of nature's power all around. Down from the mountains, the unpaved road turned back to Monterrey. As we continued our descent, I watched the winding road, grateful that María Elena had taken the time to bring me here. She was open, available and encouraging in a way that my own mother had not been able to be.

"Thank you, María Elena." I was glad that she was driving because the road toward Monterrey was difficult and steep. Her green and white Cadillac raced down the unpaved road, leaving little clouds of dust trailing behind.

"*México es precioso,*" she said. As we approached a crumbling one-lane bridge, she honked the horn, for that was the protocol. We raced forward before anyone else got there.

Each passer-by with sombrero and serape attracted my attention. *Are they also headed for Monterrey?*

Luisa, with her few belongings gathered around her, tall and erect in the back seat. She had a lean, energetic, and intense presence. Although she was only fifteen, from a distance she looked more like thirty. A mature calm enveloped her.

We passed farmhouses decorated with dried *chilis*, where old women sat on the steps, and a few spotted dogs licked their paws or chased playfully in the field. It was a bright, cold day, and the ruts in the road had cracked with dryness. To one side of the road, a man in a striped serape stood amid a cluster of baggy-kneed cattle. Almost every mountain pass and every curve in the road offered a hint of village life. I felt hopeful. Luisa would make it possible for me to complete my work with my students.

At last, we got to the highway and the fast-paced, crazy way of driving where there was always a sense of frenzy and gamesmanship. A strong wind had come up, and with it whirls of red dust, which blotted out the airport. It was as if Monterrey had momentarily withdrawn from the rest of the world. I told myself to relax. Maybe our troublesome times were behind us.

Seventeen

Laughter in the Garden

*J*anuary and February passed swiftly. We settled down to a routine with me teaching and Len in school. While out and about with my students or at the *mercado,* when six o'clock came, I was aware of a rising excitement within me—a lifting of the spirits. I could hardly wait to get home and be with Len for dinner. Those moments together passed all too quickly, and I would hope that he would forget the Green Cross for just one night.

But he seldom did. And after he'd gone, I struggled with my need to see him, to be with him. When he returned with cheeks flushed, eyes bright, and smelling of rum, he would take my face between his hands, kiss me, and say, "Good night," sometimes patting me like a puppy.

I had been set aside. My loneliness mounted as the nights wore on, and I turned more and more to books and reading to fill the void.

By the end of February, it was time for me to go on maternity leave. When I finally said "goodbye" to my students, my misgivings returned, and I felt a deep regret at leaving my post. My work had brought more than money; it brought me a sense of freedom and purpose all my own.

"But I promise to return as soon as possible." To my embarrassment, I failed to say, "After the baby is born." Instead, I said, "As soon as I am able."

This moment marked the beginning of a tormenting distrust of Len, either as a husband or that his plan would work out. Since our return, his schedule had been even more rigorous with late nights out, the Green Cross, and study sessions with the gang. Thus far, this strategy had only worked well for him.

"I take it you have no objection to my putting so much time in on the books," Len said when I expressed my concern, "and I can't believe you would want me stop treating the poor at the Green Cross."

"Of course not," I replied, "the situation is quite understandable." This statement, of course, was untruthful. However, at nineteen, to question my worldly and charming husband was quite out of character. I said, "Good night" and went to my room, opened up the shutters, and stared out into the hushed night. When he told it, the story sounded so authentic, and yet, he always kept me off balance.

Later that night, after he was gone, I took out our bankbook and reviewed the situation. The commitment for twenty-five dollars a month from the doctor in San Diego would be helpful. Still, it would take careful management to get us through the spring until I could go back to work after the baby was born.

I noticed a change in me. I sensed a movement forward, something like fate or destiny pulling me, and made up my mind that I would have to make peace with the situation.

It was on one of those nights I had come to appreciate—those quiet nights—with Jeanne sleeping peacefully, that I read late into the night, uninterrupted. Only a few hours before, Len and I had sat talking steadily, our faces turned toward each other, or turned now and then to the window, with the howling winter wind and the red dust outside. We talked about the semester, about us, about medicine. I sensed that something was wrong.

"Tell me," I said, "what's bothering you. I have an instinct for sensing trouble and I sense it tonight—in fact, since we've come back to Mexico. Have I said or done anything to hurt you?"

There it was. I put my cards on the table.

"You've done nothing to hurt me. It's just that you've got to talk to the doctor about birth control after you have this baby."

I was taken aback momentarily. This was the first time he had mentioned such an outrageous idea.

"You know that it's forbidden by the Church." I felt myself grow hot. "It's a mortal sin."

He sat there, so calm, smoking a cigarette. "Nobody pays any attention to that down here. You have to be practical." There was a coaxing sound to his voice.

"Women here *do* pay attention. Every Sunday, the church is filled with young families," I insisted.

"Yes, and with their stair-step kids in tow and babes in arms. Sooner or later, they come to their senses."

I reached over and took his hand in both of mine. I tried to tell him why birth control was a mortal sin, and why I was hesitant to risk my immortal soul for expediency.

Len interrupted, "Why don't you grow up? I tell you no one down here pays any attention to the Church." His features had frozen into a mask of contempt.

"I do!" I said, desperately thinking ahead, wondering if there was any method that the Church might approve of besides the ill-conceived rhythm method. Life could not be destroyed. Glancing at Len, I thought how pink his face became when he is irritated. I was angry with him, but I realized that there might be some truth in what he said.

"Well, just ask your doctor. I've heard there are some very effective things you can do."

"Like what?"

"Like foam."

I felt like I was facing a new adversary. "How do you know so much about these things? Anatomy class?" I said it sarcastically, wanting to hurt him.

"Let me share a secret with you. I've talked to a friend. May Hinajosa, to be exact. She wants to meet you."

"You mean the American lady who's married to that wealthy banker? The ones who live in the big house over the hill?"

"Yes, I met them before you came down. Went to a few parties there. I'll arrange everything. After all, she's Catholic, too."

I said, "So are you." *And so is your family.*

Wild memories spun around in my head as I recalled my conversation with Alice. *These were people who clearly made up their own rules as they went along.* Len turned slightly, his eyes roamed toward the door. He seemed restless.

"What about the baby?" I asked.

"Do you mean Jeanne?"

"No, I mean the baby that could be born any minute."

"So? What about it? What's done is done!" He said it with a deep look of regret on his face.

I began to feel alternately guilty and determined. A Mexican polka came from the kitchen. The sound interrupted our conversation and I forced my attention to Luisa. She entered and set supper on the table: coffee, flour *tortillas*, scrambled eggs, and cheese. We took our respective places at the table.

"Well, just talk to some people," Len said over dinner. After dinner, he made a feeble attempt at reconciliation and squeezed my hand.

In an ideal world, Len and I would have discussed these issues before marriage, but we had not. We lived in a world of silence where sex and money were taboo subjects. There was no common ground to make a family out of us, no consensus about anything except the "I've got to be a doctor" theme, which I had come to resent.

He slammed the door with finality and left. For once, I was glad to see him go. *The Church forbids it,* I told myself. *Go and see May Hinajosa? Who was she and why was she talking about my private affairs? One mortal sin is enough to go to hell.*

I turned to my book, *A Portrait of A Lady,* focusing intently on the words. Some of the really unpleasant characters were Americans. But the important thing was that it was the Americans who were transformed, matured, and became something wonderful. I wanted to become one of the latter. Reading was my gift, my salvation.

Henry James had an amazing ability to tell a story. Shrewd as to the subject of Americans abroad and astray, he spun a tale of fortune, sex, and foreign lands that overtook me and absorbed my huge, elemental fears. His novels had become my constant companions, a reality within a reality. No talk of birth control. No mention of mortal sin.

A soft tap on the front door broke the spell. "Hello, may I come in?"

It was Ralph. I was not surprised for he frequently stopped by to play the piano and keep in practice.

I opened the door. "Yes, Ralph, what is it?"

"I've got a few free hours. Do you mind if I practice for a while?"

"It's all right with me. Come in."

Although I did not particularly like Ralph, I warmed to the idea of having a man in the house, just in case the police should get any more ideas. Since the break-in, I had been sleeping with a large butcher knife under my pillow. "Please, make yourself at home. I'm reading in bed, so if you don't mind—"

"No, go ahead. I just want to practice and won't be long."

"Stay as long as you like. Just lock the door behind you."

As usual, he played Bach—splendid, strong, formally perfect. It was to this pleasant accompaniment that I read Henry James late into the night. The music finally stopped.

I slept uneasily that night, passing from one restless dream to another. Pictures of stories, infinitely beautiful and infinitely disturbing, floated in my brain, yet I felt joyously lucid.

Startled, I awoke and there at the foot of the bed stood a man. It was my grandfather.

I was soberly, painfully awake. I looked at him.

"How are ya, kid?" He didn't move his lips to speak, yet I understood the message. His smile overflowed with love.

I felt myself falling from sensation to befuddlement and then my initial shock gave way to wonder.

"Oh, I feel like a cornered animal, Grandpa. I don't know what to do." I just thought it. No words were necessary, for we were linked in some strange telepathic way.

"I just came to check up on you. I love you. You're gonna be fine." I heard him laugh. It was the laughter that came from his garden when things went especially well. Soft, melodious, happy laughter.

As I understood his message, a great rush of energy came over me. It was as if all the love and wisdom of the world washed over me in a warm wave of golden light. I could not take my eyes off of his incredible brightness.

"This time in Mexico will be good for you." I noticed that he was wearing his Masonic pin and ring, and from them emanated streams of light. Just as I began to tell him how much I had missed him, his image faded away. Right there in the center of the room, the center of everything where his radiant presence had been, only an empty space and silence remained.

The delicate aura of the vision pervaded the room. Startled, I found myself staring into nothing. I felt deeply and deliriously comforted by the appearance. For a couple of minutes, I sat there not quite believing what I had seen, but at the same time knowing that this experience had touched the core of my being. I felt powerful and more alive than I had ever been.

Labor started a few hours later. It must have been close to dawn when the pains began. Len had still not returned home. I told myself, *be still and let the vision and the light and the laughter come over you.* I waited, tense, expectant, while the pains grew stronger. Hours, it seemed, I waited. Sometimes, I could hear the faintest whisper of laughter.

Eighteen

La Primavera

At first, I slept between the pains, languishing in the dream-like atmosphere of the vision. There, in that other world, I felt safe and nurtured until another pain washed over me, and I reeled back into the reality of the room. Could this be the same room where Grandpa had come to see me? He'd made it so magical.

The length of the pains and the frequency steadily increased. The contractions intensified and I doubled over drowning in the force of it, and then came up again as if for air and the warmth and security of the images from the mind place. Pain, vision, pain.

My grandfather's appearance haunted those first hours of labor. After several such cycles, I realized that this was not like the first time, not like the prolonged labor with Jeanne. Things were happening so quickly. There was no purpose in risking having the baby here. I needed to get to the hospital.

"Luisa, Luisa," I called from my room, until at last the drowsy girl appeared in the doorway and rubbed her eyes. I motioned to the closet.

"*Mi bolsa. El bebe viene.*" I gasped. Another pain came over me just as a screech of tires and a braking car pulled my attention to the window.

"*El Señor.*" Luisa pointed to the doorway and, taking my arm, she helped me up and grabbed the bag with her free hand. We met a grinning Len at the door.

"Get me to the hospital now. Right now!" I leaned on Luisa as she walked me to the car.

"Huh? Waz' goin' on?" Len leaned on the doorframe; his eyes roamed the room. He looked first at me, then at Luisa, then back at me and smiled all the while.

"Get me to the hospital, now!" We pushed passed him through the patio toward the street and the car. Luisa slammed the door and went back to the house. Jeanne had begun to cry. Len stumbled to the driver's side. I felt another pain coming and I thought my back was going to break in two. "Hurry," I gasped again.

Len gunned the engine and the car jerked forward, narrowly missing María Elena's green and white Cadillac stationed at the corner. "Wow, what a night. Whoopee!" He steered around the corner and ended up on the wrong side of the street.

"Please slow down. Slow down!" His crazy driving frightened me.

"You said to hurry. Thaz' what I'm doin'." We raced along on the wrong side of the river road. *Thank God it was early morning or we would kill someone.*

"Please, Len." Now I was really frightened. "Take it easy."

The car teetered back and forth from one side of the road to the other, but he only increased the speed. Before I could say more, another pain rushed in on me. It was so crushing that I finally let go and slipped into total blackness and temporary relief.

At the first peek of morning, we careened round the *glorieta*, the plaza; the hospital was just on the far side.

I thought I saw a tiny flash of form, a figure. Yes, a man dashed across the road from the *Colonia Independencia*. Our headlights showed him to be young and agile. His serape flapped nervously in the breeze as he dodged the path of our speeding car. Len hit the brakes.

"Damn it." He swerved, narrowly missing the man. We veered close to the river's edge, but somehow made the turn. A circular drive opened; it was the entrance to *La Muguerza* hospital.

The gray stone building loomed directly in front of the car. We came to a sudden stop just as another pain took over. The sound of the squealing brakes or the smell of burning rubber alerted someone, and two shadowy figures rushed out of the hospital to the car. Silent hands wrenched me from the car into a wheelchair and then on to a gurney. A bulky figure made a gesture of impatience toward Len.

"Get him out of here." I recognized the voice. Looking up, I saw the long, thick mustache. It was my doctor, Salas Garza.

"Get him out of here," he shouted again, and I knew he meant Len. Another pain hit as two nurses wheeled me away and into a small alcove. There, they stripped me of my clothes and briskly wrapped a blue hospital gown around my shivering body.

The double doors swung open into the delivery room, and silent automatic hands placed a mask over my nose and mouth.

"Breathe, *Respire, sí, sí.*"

I breathed a deep breath, and still another, until I was floating in empty space, oblivious of everything except voices far away. Breathing again, I could feel the freedom of weightlessness and the delightful spin within a twilight world. Floating. Just floating. There was no pain here, no memory of pain. Only time, just endless time. Somewhere far away, I heard voices again, but they were not important in this wondrous place of rest and timelessness. From far, far away I heard a cry and someone shouted.

"*Es un niño. Mira el niño.*" I could barely hear the voice, although I knew from the force behind it, he must have been shouting.

Then came another cry, a loud lusty cry.

Someone much closer said in my ear, "*Tiene un hijo, Señora,* a son."

Coming forward, out from the darkness, I saw the crying baby. Dr. Salas Garza held my boy for me to see. And then I retreated back again into the emptiness, unresisting deep sleep.

৳

Twittering birds woke me the next morning. Soft, lively bird song teased me into opening my eyes. I found myself in a great airy room. Cheerful chintz drapes framed picture windows, which nearly covered one whole side of the room. Sunshine streamed in. Tinkling glasses and rattling trays caught my attention from somewhere outside the room, and then came the marvelous, un-mistakable smell of coffee. Carts and trays clamored in the hall beyond the closed door. I realized that I was famished.

The door burst open and I was greeted by *"Muy buenos dias, Señora. Congratulationes. Ójala que todo está bien . . . "* A small woman with dark eyes that sparkled pushed a cart in my direc-tion. Her stream of Spanish flowed continuously and, although I couldn't get the meaning of each word, I savored the pleasant, melodious flow from the lovely nurse with shining dark hair, round face, and delicate figure. The nurse, clad in starched white linen, hovered behind me chatting all the while. She raised the head of the bed and fluffed my pillows. The Spanish continued staccato-like—a good sound to wake up to.

"¿Qué dia es, Señorita? ¿Cual es la fecha?" I'd lost track of time.

"Hoy es la 21 de Marzo. Es La Primavera." She handed me the newspaper.

Even so, I calculated that the baby must have been born on the twentieth, the last day of winter. It was appropriate. Jeanne had been born on the twenty-third, just a year ago, and the first day of spring. My companion continued her rapid-fire discourse.

I was not to get up; I was to rest and, most of all, to enjoy my breakfast. That much I could understand. She placed the tray on the table, which she swiveled in front of me.

"*Quizás mañana, puede comer allá.*" She pointed to a charming low table near the window. "*Pero, hoy, tiene que quedarse in la cama.*" Huge dimples accentuated the words, stay in the bed. "*Sí, en la cama.*" She continued to chatter as she poured coffee into a china cup. Then, she uncovered delicious surprises which hid under covered trays in front of me: fresh orange juice, tiny crescent rolls, cream of wheat, real cream and butter. I learned that the doctor would arrive shortly after breakfast.

The nurse fussed about the room and me as if getting ready for a visiting dignitary. At last, Dr. Garza made his appearance, checked the chart, checked me, and grinned.

"It's customary to stay at least a week," the doctor said sternly. Then, he smiled, "That way, you'll get a good rest and feel very good when you go home."

"But I feel wonderful, just as you said I would. It was all so easy." I couldn't keep from comparing this experience to the one in the States. Jeanne's birth had not been easy. I recalled the post delivery hemorrhaging and the emergency "D and C" a few days later.

Dr. Salas Garza seemed to read my mind. "You *will* stay a week! Here, the practice of medicine is an art. In your country, it is viewed as a science."

"Yes, I remember you told me that at our very first meeting." After all, he had trained in the States, at Bellevue in New York City. He knew both systems, if anyone did. "Do you think I will be able to nurse this baby?"

"Why not? Your body was made to have babies, just as I told you."

Looking at him, I thought, *and yours was made to play football*. He had a large, muscular frame, huge hands, and the presence of a man who commanded respect. Dr. Salas Garza cut an imposing figure in his blue worsted suit, meticulous white shirt, and stylish gray and blue tie. He was one of the most sought-after obstetricians in the state of *Nuevo Leon* and, of course, a professor at the medical school. His light brown hair was cut short, emphasizing his athletic build and lending an almost martial air.

"Everything went very well. The baby weighs three kilos ten." He surveyed me much as a general would survey a battlefield in which he had recently won a tidy victory. "Later this morning, the nurse will take you to see the baby. Very healthy baby, *mucho hombre.*" He turned to go, then hesitated. Looking back at me, he said in a gruff voice, "*¡El es Mexicano, un Regiomontano! ¡Hasta mañana!*"

And he was gone before I had a chance to say a word.

Made to have babies. That was good news, yet also disconcerting considering the last conversation that I had with my husband. *No wonder Mexican women have so many babies. With that twilight sleep, it was all too wonderful.*

I was glad to be here. I had a private room and it was spacious, pretty. Two high-backed chairs to one side overlooked a lovely garden below. There was a mahogany chest of drawers and floral pictures on the wall. These accommodations were absolutely elegant, all so very different from the way it had been in the States.

At Mercy Hospital, I had been in a ward with five other women. Here, I had a room all to myself with nurses who came in to check on me and to bring snacks and meals. During the morning, they brought flowers, and sometimes they brought gifts that had been left at the front desk. It was all too good to be true. I felt that I had been transported to a lovely resort and was enjoying a secret vacation. This was no ordinary hospital. It was only for mothers and babies.

Nurse Francesca was a cheerful young woman, quick to laugh and prone to long spells of chatting in Spanish whether I responded or not. She walked with a quick gait and had merry eyes. Everything in her presence broadcast optimism.

Soon, we were off to the nursery. All the expected sounds hustled and clattered about us as she rolled the wheelchair over shining tile floors. She sang to me, "*Sí, nos vamos a ver el bebe, el güero.*" We were going to see the baby—*that* I understood.

The fragments of rapid-fire Spanish became more and more meaningful. I'd learned the words for bedpan, bell, tray, and *el güero*—the blondie.

Down the hall we sped. Nurse Francesca chuckled all the while until, with a smooth stop, she parked me in front of a large glass window. There, a curtain pulled back and the scene revealed four rows of bassinets with tiny sleeping infants covered with blue or pink blankets. In a single sweeping glance, I saw their bare heads and thick mops of dark black or brown that crowned the babies, except for one. There in the second row on the end, *el güero,* my son, attracted attention.

Francesca motioned to the attendant inside the window. She lifted the baby, brought him close to the window, and pulled the blanket back so that we could take a better peek. Gazing at him, I noticed big dimples in each cheek—the mark of a Burns.

The surrounding entourage—fathers, mothers, grandparents, friends—clustered around this custom-made universe for babies. Some of us pointed with enthusiasm, others waved at newborns.

"*Mira el güero, el güero,*" an expression of appreciation to the tiny blond, almost white-haired, light-skinned baby, the only one of this fair shade in the hospital. I felt my cheeks go hot with self-consciousness and retreated into my habitual silence. Compliments showered upon me from the group and I was forced to engage them.

"*Sí, es el mio,*" I said, urged on by the attention.

"*¿Nombre?*"

Staring back, I composed my features and replied. "*Leonardo. Leonardo Daniel Burns de Henderson.*"

And they replied in varying rhythms, "*Que precioso, que precioso.*" I heard it over and over. I agreed; he was precious.

Salas Garza was right. Under the benign supervision of nurse Francesca, I healed quickly and, except for a slight hernia—not an uncommon occurrence—the newborn was perfect in every way. And wonder of wonders, I was able to nurse my baby. By the third day of my convalescence, I began to visualize my return home. The plump healthy baby and his delightful smile played on my heartstrings, and I was grateful for such good fortune.

Abandoning the wheelchair, nurse Francesca and I made the ritual morning stroll to the nursery where the thin chorus of wailing babes always stimulated the fullness in my breasts and made the milk run free. There were no decisions to make, and for the first time in months, I contented myself that things might work out after all.

All that was missing was Len.

I kept wishing that he'd show up. Now that he had a son, I thought he'd become more involved. Maybe Salas Garza scared him off? With all the other families gathered around the babies, it was so glaring that I was alone.

Nineteen

An Intimate Encounter

Outside, a large dark bird swooped by the window and I tried to make up my mind about getting up unaided. I was waiting patiently for Francesca to help with a bath when a knock on the door broke my reverie.

"*Venga.*"

"Gail?" The voice of a woman preceded her entrance through the door. She was American—slight, with wisps of gray framing her delicate face. She wore no make-up, no jewelry, and not even a wedding ring. A clean cotton dress whispered as the starched skirt swished across the room.

"Yes?"

"Hello, I'm Kitty. My husband is a medical student here. We're from Loma Linda in California." She smiled sweetly and, as her kindness closed in, I felt myself connected to a woman whose life had to be so different from my own.

"The Seventh Day Adventist Community?"

"Yes, there's quite a group of us here." She pulled up a chair and immediately animated a shadowy patch of gray near the window.

The sun was low over the horizon outside, and I saw beyond her a mist over the mountains.

Kitty drew her chair closer to me. "Congratulations. I've told the others. How are you feeling?"

"Incredibly well—nothing like my first delivery. It was long and hard and there were many complications. This time everything went well."

"Enjoy your rest here." Kitty patted my hand.

How pleasant she is, her manner, her soft, soothing voice.

"I've taken a casserole by the house, and everything was just fine," she said. "Your little daughter is adorable and, oh yes—they asked me to tell you that Paula is back."

"Paula is back? Hallelujah."

We chatted for several minutes and she left, promising to come and check in on me when I returned home. I watched her leave. Afternoon closed in, and I felt myself alone in a life too much my own.

Leonard, for his part, had taken a dodgy wait-and-see position claiming that he was incredibly busy. He told me that the task of holding down the fort at home created a frantic schedule for him and he came by just once during the week.

"And the baby—have you seen the baby?" To my utter surprise, he seemed to show no interest in his son.

He smiled at me with a faint smile, "Yes, cute, very cute." This platitude was followed by a long silence surprising in its duration. When he looked at the baby, there was no sign of emotion.

I was elated to see him, yet heartbroken at his attitude toward his son. His visit brought about an abrupt change in my peaceful state of mind. I couldn't fathom why he was so distant with his new namesake.

Nevertheless, thanks to rest, proper care, and the attentions of Salas Garza, I managed to avoid any complications and remained in the hospital for a full week as ordered. Cards, prompted by Kitty's chain of communication, came in with good wishes and offers of help.

On the day before my release, as I made ready to go home, I had another surprise visitor—one who would tip my already unstable world.

Twenty

Headline News

It was the last afternoon. I was to go home the next day. A lovely sense of anticipation came over me as the hours progressed. Bustling sounds in the corridor told me that it was the visiting hour. Gingerly, I swung myself over the edge of the bed and inched slowly to the chair overlooking the garden below. Then, just as I was complimenting myself for completing the task on my own, a woman entered the room. Deep shadows under her eyes led me to believe that she was not well. For my part, initial annoyance marked her entry. I wanted, instead of visiting, to think of my next move and to plan my strategy.

Perhaps she's here by mistake. Perhaps this woman has come to the wrong room. She's clearly not a Sabbie with all that jewelry and make-up.

"You must be Len's wife," said the woman. She was attractive, trim, and athletic with a pretty, oval face marred only by the deep worry lines.

She received a nod in reply as I thought with sympathy how desolate she appeared. Her whole body seemed to expand and dilate with sadness. The woman's face was white; her mouth, tense.

"I'm May Hinajosa, Pepe's wife."

Just then, Francesca, punctual to the minute, whooshed through the door and past the visitor. "*Aqúi está su medicina.*" A rapid rush of phrases followed.

May must have noticed that I did not catch all the words and instantly translated for me. "She wants to know if you'll get up for dinner tonight. If you would like a tray by the window."

"Oh yes, *sí*," I replied to one and then the other.

As Francesca glanced at the visitor, a peculiar interest blossomed in her face. It was as if my nurse could not pull her eyes away. At last, she turned back to me and said, "*Muy bien Señora,*" and hurried out of the door after casting one last curious look toward May.

I wondered why my nurse was so interested in the Hinajosa woman. I didn't even know who she was. Then, it dawned on me; this was the woman that Len wanted me to meet—the foam lady.

"Oh, yes, May Hinajosa. Len has mentioned you." She was certainly handsome, about my mother's age. Immaculate, precise, she was wearing a powder-blue wool suit.

"You are just as Len said." May studied my face.

"Oh, and how is that?" I tried to sound composed as this strange woman scrutinized my face.

"Very pretty and such a quality of refinement!" And then, more circumspect as she looked down at me, she sighed. "I didn't realize how very young you are."

I could hardly repress a grin. "I don't feel young." I became aware of my ridiculous desire to laugh. "Please, sit down." So, this was May Hinajosa. For some reason, she was not what I expected. "Len said you live over there in *Del Valle.*"

"Yes, it's a lovely area. As soon as you're able, I hope you will come by. I look forward to entertaining you and Len later this spring. Perhaps you'll join our canasta club. We're a small group of American women—mostly from Texas, like me—and all wives of local businessmen."

I looked at her closely and noticed tiny lines radiating from the corners of her eyes.

"I don't play canasta, but a visit sounds, uh, sounds nice." I stumbled over the words. I felt discontent with my appearance and ashamed of the fact that I was not bathed. The linen shift I was wearing was patched and mended.

She went on, "I'm so grateful for the time that Len has been able to spend with me. The last few days and especially the nights have been so—" she choked on the words, "so difficult."

I felt angry with myself for not knowing what she meant. Then I realized from the tone of her voice and the way she looked at me that she was clearly upset by some recent event. She was not ill. There was more to it.

"Len—your husband—has been so kind, so helpful."

I didn't know Len knew how to be helpful. *Why is he helping this woman? What's going on?* I waited for her to explain further. I hypothesized that her husband or one of her children had been injured, or worse, was dead. She gave no details. My patience was both polite and implacable. I didn't know the woman or why she had come to see me. I sat there scarcely believing my ears at the immediate intimacy of her voice.

"When Len told me you had a baby boy, I had this made for you." She handed me a large flat box. It was meticulously wrapped with silver and white paper. A huge, blue satin bow perched on top. The box was bulky, but lightweight, and I angled it so that it balanced on my knees. "Please, open it," she insisted.

Off came the paper and the large fluffy bow fell to the floor. Opening the lid, I peered inside the box. There, enfolded neatly in tissue paper, lay an exquisite baptismal outfit. Lifting it up and in front of me, the long dress flowed gently to the floor as the light from across the room shone through yards and yards of sheer batiste. Instead of replacing it in the box, I lay the christening gown across my lap to better explore the delicate hand-made tucks and tiny blue bows, so pale they were almost white.

"Ice-blue" best described the ribbon color. A tiny bonnet trimmed with lace and satin rosettes completed the set. I looked at May and struggled to make conversation.

"Lovely. It's really lovely," I repeated. I was enchanted with the gift and yet concerned about the cost of such an expensive item. "Thank you so much," I looked up from the box. "It was very kind of you."

She looked into my eyes and must have seen something—some slight loss of spirit, a moment's expression that flashed mistrust and she quickly said, "I just wanted to do something special for you. I commend your struggle. Yours and Len's." She took a breath and went on. "Besides, I just wanted us to meet and say 'hello.' Your husband is such a wonderful man, so—" she choked up again, "so compassionate."

I still felt sorry for her, but without knowing why. *Striking, she's really quite striking in that smart outfit so neatly tailored, leather bag, and matching pumps. And that curly dark hair. Long red manicured nails—those, too.*

"Everyone admires Leonard so much." When she spoke of Len, her words were so animated that she sounded like a woman in love. "He's just charming. But then, dear, you must know all that."

Her words were exasperating.

She tilted her head forward and stared at me. "Oh! By the way," she added, "Len said you wanted me to do some shopping for you, next time I go to Texas."

"Shopping?" The change of subject threw me into puzzlement.

"Yes, Len said I should bring back some," and she whispered confidentially, "foam for you. It's easy to use and they say ninety percent effective." Then she winked and with a knowing look said, "It's difficult to get these things here. Don't worry, I'll take care of it."

"I don't know what to say."

"Your assurance to me that you'll take the time to be completely recovered is all I want. This visit has brought me great joy."

May turned and was gone in a wake of French perfume, leaving me with dozens of questions. She had invaded my sanctuary. Her talk about Len upset me. Shaken by a flood of emotion, I considered whether I could begin to decipher the truth.

I sat there dumb as I realized that many of those evenings when I was alone, afraid, and sleeping with a butcher knife under my pillow for fear of the police, Len was probably with May, in *Colonia Del Valle* comforting her over some mysterious problem. *Her problem was more important than I was.* I sat by the window and watched the rain. I took no notice of Len when he made his appearance.

He waved the paper in front of me. "Did you see this?" he gasped, effusive as he pointed, "The headlines?"

"What are you talking about?"

"Look at this." There in bold letters, the gruesome array of pictures and facts told the story.

Local Banker Crashes Airplane
While Serenading Sweetheart

"Who are they talking about? Someone we know?" I queried, not believing what I was actually seeing in front of me.

Len said, "Pepe Hinajosa! Wow, what a scandal."

Some seconds later, I added, "She was just here. May. She came to thank me, and you, too, I suppose. And to give me this." I held up the dress.

"Nice lady," he said, "real nice." There was not a hint of embarrassment. "Been over there a couple of times lately, just to cheer her up. But this! Poor thing, she must feel terribly humiliated."

"So, that's why Francesca kept staring at her," I said.

Len read the story: *Well-known businessman Pepe Hinajosa was injured yesterday when he crashed his plane into telephone wires while scattering rose petals and singing love songs over a loud speaker to his teenage sweetheart. The injury is not serious and Pepe should be back on his feet in a few days. His family offers no comment.*

I was shocked to see a picture of the crashed plane below the headline. Worse yet, further down the page, another picture: Pepe's astounded face stared out at the reader. Latin good looks, dark eyes, and sleek black hair, graying perfectly just at the temples. There was also a picture of May.

No wonder she had dark circles under her eyes. How did this involve Len?

I refrained from any response and kept quiet. This was Len's story and I wanted to see what he would do with it.

"Some scandal," he said. "Well, we all have our foibles, and Pepe's is just part of this culture. That's just the way it is here. Too bad. He's really a nice guy. They were both really nice to me when I first arrived."

"Where did you meet them?" I pressed for more details.

"Oh, at a party in *Del Valle*. Pepe introduced me to Señor Sanchez. That's how I found the house."

I waited in rather pathetic hope that there would be more. Instead, Len said that he couldn't stay long. Of course, this was just his well-intentioned way of steadying the situation. If I longed for more of an explanation, I knew it would not be forthcoming, and I was too afraid to ask, too afraid to know if something had been going on between him and May.

There was more. "Look what she gave me." He held up a 35 mm Zeiss Ikon camera, one that he had been eyeing at the camera store downtown ever since he arrived in Monterrey. "She said it's a belated Christmas present. Now, I can take really good pictures of the kids."

"Pretty expensive, don't you think?" I asked. I was delighted to hear him utter the word "kids," but at the same time, thoroughly confused about him and May.

"Look, she wanted to. She's grateful in a way, I think."

I didn't want to talk about May. I wanted to focus on us, our baby, and our life.

"Won't you see your son? Visiting hours at the universe for babies is nearly over," I joked. "Everyone who sees the baby says he's such a delight."

"Sure, I'll stop by on the way out." Len sounded like a child who had been scolded about doing his homework, as if he had to convince himself that it was worth the effort to stop and see his son. As he came close to me, there was a wary warmth to his embrace.

"Bye," he said, and the twinkle in his eye made his touch seem unguarded and more flattering. "I love you," he whispered, capturing my attention with a breathtaking—albeit furtive—smile. "I'm really proud of you."

His words only added to my confused anger and frustration. I listened as his footsteps clicked in retreat down the hall. It sounded like the direction of the exit.

Outside, a spring rain had hushed everything. Tears trickled down my face like the rain on the window. In the silence, I got a sense of my grandfather, a sense of something soft and gentle embracing me. The contact was undeniable.

Twenty-one

A Tumble of Questions

As the night wore on, I played the conversations between May and Len and me over in my mind, time and again. Len must have had to re-work his story for my benefit. Perhaps they both did, he and May. The smell of dampness mingled with the smell of the flowers in the room. Outside, the sound of the wailing wind and shrill rain played on my nerves.

I came by degrees to realize that I was angry because of my sense of submission. One fantastic scene from the afternoon merged into the next; one question tumbled unanswered after the next. I cursed my own weakness for believing Len. I cursed my slavish obedience to the Church. *Why had I submitted so meekly to coming to Mexico?* Overtired brain teeming with these thoughts, I found myself stranded in a sleepless, restless night.

Len can't be trusted, and yet, so much depends on his finishing school. If I don't falter, we may yet come to the end of the trail, and Len will practice medicine, and the children will have a future.

It looked like this would mean submission for me, again.

I tried to put the pieces together.

Is he having an affair with May? . . . She's not his type. She's attractive, has money, but too old. Besides, he doesn't have to have sex with a woman to seduce her. It's the power he loves. Then again,

171

how did the two of them get to the topic of contraceptive foam? How dare they violate my privacy? Then there's Pepe. He's everything that Len wants to be—rich, successful, and a respected professional, at least until he made the headlines. Maybe it's Pepe. Maybe he's the real attraction. And the gifts? Expensive ones. Alice Denny had a way of wheedling presents out of rich people, like those two racehorses. Maybe Len was more like her than I ever imagined.

In the small hours of the morning, I tried to imagine a future in which everything came out with a happy ending. Like a calculating machine, I added pros and cons. I thought through what needed to happen until the fatigue and ache inside my skull took me into sleep. What awoke me was the sun shining straight into my eyes.

Twenty-two

Dust and Roses

Three days at home. My arrival had been heralded with flowers, cards, and gifts for the baby. Exotic casseroles from the Sabbie community filled the refrigerator.

You really have to like those people.

There were notes with offers of help. A floral arrangement from Rosemary and Mario sat on the dining room table, and a bouquet of roses had been placed at my bed stand. The card read: *from May and Pepe.*

Then, I saw Paula. The sight of her warmed my heart. "*Entonces, estás aqúi,*" I said and squeezed her hand.

"*Sí, Señora, tengo un novio.*"

So, it was a boyfriend that brought her back.

"*Que bueno,*" I answered her and smiled.

I never said anything to her about her disappearance. She never said anything about the skull, which by now lived indoors. It held a place of honor on the bookshelf next to *Gray's Anatomy*. Len had kept his word. He printed the name of every articulation of the human skull. His tiny, precise writing covered the cranium in a red, black, and green code that had important meaning for him.

Silence fell. Until that moment, everything was so normal—deceptively normal. Paula was in the kitchen separating a kilo of beans from the small pebbles that came with the lot. Little beans were spread out all over the table. She carefully pushed them one by one into a bowl, leaving behind the gritty remains. Tomorrow, they would bubble on the stove with garlic and onions, but today the task required infinite patience.

The babies were asleep. Normally Len would be gone by now, but tonight he lingered. It was early spring and the air already felt warm. Night filled the sky with stars.

We sat together after dinner. He told me about his classes, of Pepe Hinajosa, of pictures he had taken with his new camera. Our table talk was not what was in his heart. His grim determination and stony calmness offered hints that something was wrong. Finally, he motioned for me to come and sit next to him.

Len settled into a comfortable chair and rummaged through a folder of mail until, at last, he found a crumpled letter and took it out. Smudged ink and ragged edges suggested that it had been stored there after hiding away in his pocket or a book. He took a long pull at his cigarette—head thrown back as if he wanted to prolong the moment. Then he shot a searching glance in my direction.

I pulled a footstool next to Len and sat, knees touching. "Yes?"

A moth caught my attention as it frantically fluttered at the closed windowpane seeking the light inside.

"I've something to tell you." He held my hands and stared at me with a steady unblinking gaze, one eye slightly hooded, smoke curling from his mouth.

"What? What's happened? Something at school?" A sudden flood of suspicion crept into my heart. *Was this something more about May Hinajosa?*

He held a wrinkled letter in his hand, drew in long on his cigarette, and handed the paper to me.

Your grandfather, Fred, died on March 19. He suffered greatly, but in the end, went peacefully. The Masons buried him at Greenwood Cemetery.
Nonny

The letter was short and to the point.

I felt numb. "I think I knew," I said. "You see, he came to me."

"He what?"

"I saw him. Here. The night Lenny was born. The letter says Grandpa died only a day or so before. He came to say, 'Farewell.'"

"What can you possibly mean?"

"Sometimes, when I play that night over in my head, I see that we're connected . . . .And the night he died, he had a strong desire to see me and to tell me something. We were connected."

"Did he tell you something?"

"Not exactly. He conveyed a message with his eyes. No words were needed."

"Well, what was it?"

"I needed warmth, encouragement . . . .Grandpa filled me with his eyes. I don't know how else to say it."

Len's eyes were big. "So, you found a way to communicate with him after he died?"

"I didn't even know he was dead. He seemed so alive."

"What did he want you to know? Any idea?"

"Yes, he wants me to be free."

"Free?" He creased his eyebrows.

"Yes, free to choose my own way, free of the Church, free of your desires. I still feel the connection with him. I always will."

"Are you giving up on me?"

"No. I agreed to go through this with you. The choice is mine. But when you're done, it's my turn. Just so you know."

"It's a deal," he said. He tilted his head down toward me with gentle eyes and a sincere smile.

"These last weeks when I was alone at night, when Jeanne was asleep, all I could think about was literature—Henry James, T. S. Eliot, Shakespeare. It's kept me going. I want to finish my degree in English."

"You mean to teach?"

"Don't know. Maybe I'll write."

"So, you're not shocked that he's dead."

"No," I said. "Your telling me makes it final. I mean the words of it . . . so sobering. I feel a strange emptiness. Somehow, I knew in December that I'd never see him again. Still, his visit surprised me. Once you've seen a vision, you never forget it. He journeyed across time and space just to say he loved me."

"I love you, too." I think he meant it at the time.

"Love is a beautiful activity," I said and smiled warily. "Now that I know for sure that he's gone, I feel stronger—as if some part of his energy passed through to me."

"Well, maybe it did, Dear." He never called me "Dear" and I wasn't sure he was really talking to me. "Your grandfather was quite a man." Len took my face in his hands and gently kissed me. I took refuge in this sweet act of compassion.

Maybe things would be different, now.

Like a devotee sitting at his feet, I was primed to soak up every gesture of love and fidelity, utterly beguiled. Len's presence made the loss easier to bear. His tender words undeniably softened the blow. I looked up at him, and the space where he sat became timeless and motionless filled with love and hope and forgiveness.

Why did Grandpa dislike him so? In my grandfather's house, no adventures really took place, those of any grand scale. Family came first and an orderly routine came next, even at the cost of dreams. Sunday dinner at one P.M. with grandpa at the head of the table—good china and crystal goblets. Up at six every day. Early to bed. If you would like to go off to far lands, that was done in painting or vicariously by listening to the radio on Saturday night. Maybe Grandpa resented Len's unwillingness to make the same kind of sacrifices.

After some moments, I pleaded tiredness and longed in my heart for privacy. Perhaps in sleep I could forget that I'd never see my grandfather again. I got to my feet. As I turned to the patio, there—where our street merged into bleached brush and thorny cactus—I stared into the dust and the moonlight, and then quite automatically stumbled back toward the nursery. The new baby snuggled in his crib and looked like an adorable plump little imp. His skin was pink, soft, unflawed.

And closer to the window, sound asleep in the glow of the moon, lay Jeanne. I looked down on her doll-like face, her nose delicate and pointed upward, well formed. She held tightly to her blanket, which partly covered her pert, oval face. Only a few hours before, she had pleaded like a little coquette. "*Dulces, dulces.*" Clever eyes, cornflower blue, had twinkled at Paula, who could not resist Jeanne's charm, and popped a piece of candy into her mouth.

I lay awake listening to the night sounds. There were clues that last Christmas with Grandpa, clues that one could not miss. Now it was final. No more strolls with my grandfather.

Adventures into the backcountry of California were gone forever. Pleasant memories—the Borrego desert, Mount Palomar, small ranches in Ramona where you could find exotic birds—gone forever. I wondered what Grandpa would have done in Mexico. It was a magnificent country, but wild, hellishly hot, and then icy cold. Monterrey was the land of vultures and cattle. In the mountains, there was iron ore and silver. I thought he'd like the landscape—wide and full, elevations and declivities—a tangible wild beauty.

Recurrent thoughts of Grandpa filled the night. Then, all I could do was sob for hours into my pillow. And in that sadness, I discovered a curious inner presence, an inner self, watching from afar.

The night that Len gave me the news, he didn't leave. He stayed, read, and worked at home. I confess that I looked forward to future evenings like this with much pleasure. In my heart, I knew it would not last.

I never saw my grandfather's spirit again. Now that I had the actual paper, the words in front of me, the physical shock gave way to psychic shock. I didn't want to feel. I wanted to protect myself, but my grandfather would have none of it.

The circuit was alive. At night, I dreamed my way back to my childhood garden, down the path to the Victory garden. There was the aroma of sweet peas, very strong, and sometimes a whiff of Green Mountain. I heard a whisper.

"There is no situation which you can't find your way out of."

Twenty-three

Diamonds Sparkle

*I*t was spring. I had a new baby and I felt great. I made plans for my life during the coming year, for it seemed to me the year had just begun. It would differ widely from the year that had just passed. The dinner to which we were invited gave a hint of what was to come.

The weather had softened into one of those April days when the sun, low in the sky, cast a soft glow over the Hinajosa property as we drove up. Their home was large, airy yet comfortable, with a white tiled floor so slick it gave the impression of water on a lake.

May was gentler than I remembered, yet very controlled. "We've all been going through a distressing time, my dear," she said.

Her embroidered gown of red and black rustled as she led us through the garden. She treated me like a long lost friend. Perhaps there were reasons why May would want to go to considerable lengths to ingratiate herself with me, but I think I can say that the interest we took in one another at that point was genuine. Each was an object of curiosity to the other. Our lifestyles reflected extremes, but her goodwill touched me. I could not ignore her warmth and friendliness and glimpsed the lifestyle of many Americans who lived in Monterrey, those who were not students struggling to get along.

"You will forgive me if I don't go into it at length," she went on. "This mortifying event with Pepe—we leave the house as seldom as we can. We look into each other's faces like strangers." She paused and breathed deeply. "The latest news fills me with no less alarm than that of the scandal itself. Pepe may have to pay some enormous bribe to keep the law off of him. Thank God no one was seriously hurt. Pepe is depressed. He promises not to see the girl again—just a sentimental history, he tells me. But can I believe him?" She fingered a diamond choker around her splendid neck. "He gave me this." The diamonds sparkled in the evening light.

"It seems that the law here is greatly influenced by money," I said. I could find no answers. Her manner was simple, direct, and I was taken aback by her frankness.

"Here I am going on about myself," she said. "Len tells me you've had a death in the family. I'm so sorry." She sighed and from a cabinet withdrew some beautiful paintings of her two children and showed them to me. Two boys, early teens.

"What in the world is equal to these darlings?" She looked at me with tears in her eyes. "I'm going to protect my nest." Tears welled up in my eyes also. I could see that she was in much pain. I, too, was in a vulnerable position.

Len and Pepe interrupted us. They were surprised to see us sitting in tears.

"We were talking of life and death," she said.

"I'll see about our drinks," Pepe said and moved toward the kitchen.

At the thought of drinking anything, my breast began to swell. I felt pressure. "We can't stay too long; I'm nursing the baby."

"That's great," May said. "And there's a side benefit, you know. They say it prevents you from getting pregnant."

Len approached us, but May made a gesture with her eyes and he followed Pepe to the kitchen. She saw an opening and went for it.

"Now, Gail. This thing about birth control—God knows they don't have it down perfect. But there are things you can do."

"But May, I'm Catholic."

"So am I, my dear. You were probably raised like me. I'm Italian American, Catholic all the way. We went to Catholic school from day one."

I nodded my head. "So did I."

"I'll bet you had those priests from Ireland, too."

"Well, as a matter of fact, the Monsignor at our parish—the one that married us—was from Dublin. He was very strict."

"I know what you mean. We had the Irish, also. Hard-liners. Here, it's different. Go and talk to the priest in your parish. He's all Mexican, Padre Morales, a kind of mystic some say. Speaks perfect English, young and handsome. He's extremely devoted. You'll like him."

"I'll do it," I said.

"You're delicate. You can't take chances with your health. Besides, you have two children to raise. And Len needs you. He speaks about you all the time; but I won't intrude into your private affairs. I'm going to Texas next week. Is there anything I can bring back for you?"

"You could bring me some baby food; it's so expensive here. And," I added, "anything by Walt Whitman."

"Who?"

"Walt Whitman, the American poet. Anything you can find."

"I'll do it, gladly," she said.

In the end, Pepe was acquitted of all wrongdoing. Rumor had it that he paid off many people. From the outsider's point of view, the marriage healed. May brought me a book of Whitman's poems, as well as the infamous foam from Texas, but I didn't have the courage to use it. That would require much more thought. I decided to go see the priest.

ॐ

The confessional was dark and I was certain he couldn't see me through the slats. Surely, he had to recognize my voice. I had just been there two days before to make arrangements for the baptism.

"I believe in marriage, but it all seems so rigid, Father. I have so much fear that I'll do the wrong thing. I feel trapped, and either way I go, I suffocate. I've given up my freedom and there's no security." I explained the situation. "I feel like someone is reading over my shoulder. It's the Church passing judgment on me, on my secret self."

His response surprised me. "Christ is the alpha and the omega. Nothing is alien to him. There is no activity, however humble or simple—so long as it is done in the love of God—that can, or will, shock Him. There is no need for a young mother to fear that in living in the world with faith and with grace, you will lose your soul."

Spurred on by the impulse of his words, I asked, "But father, isn't it—I mean birth control—a mortal sin?"

"To act worthily and usefully is to achieve unity with God. To be so united is to leave behind the self-centered, and so, you will advance. That is what needs to be born."

He didn't really answer my question. He's a Jesuit, a mystic, and an intellectual. I can trust him.

The priest went on. "To love is to be drawn together. In being close, we can get even closer to the center of our center. Unless we really love, our inner life is shallow, fragmented. I think you love. Go in peace, my child."

That night I had another dream. There was the fragrance and there was the sparkle of his diamond ring, the Masonic one.

Grandpa said, "All the answers are inside of your head and your heart. You gotta' do what you gotta' do."

That was the last time he came to me in a dream. I knew I was on my own.

Twenty-four

Simple Innocence

I asked Rosemary and Mario to be godparents. I only knew the sketchy details of her life, but these few facts alone were a tribute to human resilience. Endless bombings, hunger, and a myriad of deprivations marked her childhood in Germany during the war. We were the same age, but her growing-up years had been so different from my experience of the war years in Chicago and San Diego. Now, we were both here in Mexico married to men who wanted so desperately to become doctors. I knew that in Mario and Rosemary we had made the right choice of godparents. Together, they seemed solid and very much in love.

After a Sunday mass in April, we assembled together around the baptismal font in the back of the church—Rosemary and Mario, the godparents; Len with Jeanne in his arms, and me.

"In nomine patri et filii et spiritu . . ."

The priest droned on. It was Padre Morales—Jesuit-trained and elegant. I still felt self-conscious in his company after our talk in the confessional.

At the words of the prayer, my sense of security deepened and expanded. Those thoughts that troubled me smoothed out, and a calm tenderness flooded over me when I looked at the baby, so neatly snuggled into the crook of Rosemary's arm.

The Latin droned on and I found myself drawn in by ancient ritual. The church, Our Lady of Lourdes, was beautiful and only recently completed. Modern, serene, and cool—today, it was suffused with the faintest smell of incense. The lovely statue of the apparition at Lourdes created a sense of refuge.

My silk dress was rose in color, almost the same shade as the expanse of marble beneath my feet. For a moment, the alcove slipped from my focus as I remembered that this was the dress I had worn when I received my scholarship at the University of San Diego. Bishop Buddy had personally handed me an envelope with the award inside. In a rush of memory, I recalled the details until the flash and glitter of sacred vessels brought me back to my place at the baptismal font.

Early afternoon sun painted the baptismal font and surrounding alcove a mellow gold. The baby's head tilted slightly backward, lips parted. Widely spaced eyes like navy-blue jewels betrayed no hint of fear. *Surely, Len would now be drawn to this beautiful boy, his first son.*

The priest took a pinch of salt, the salt of life, from a silver container and placed it on the baby's tongue. A grimace of surprise was offset by a flutter of dimples as his tiny tongue explored the new taste. Under the circumstances, who could blame the little one? A tiny bubble of saliva showed as he opened his mouth. The white baptismal gown with ice-blue ribbons, the strange gift from May Hinajosa, flowed halfway down to the floor, and the little bonnet with rosettes was now slightly askew as the baby wriggled from the salty new experience.

"*¿El nombre?*" The priest glanced at Mario and Rosemary.

In unison, Rosemary and Mario replied, "Leonardo Daniel."

Padre Morales poured the water of life, the water of salvation, proclaiming the name, "Leonardo Daniel."

Our baby is safe. Now he has his father's name.

That was not all he had. Our son was now a part of the official community, a member of the Roman Catholic Church with all its vitality and promise.

"*Mira la luz*," Jeanne interrupted. As usual, she was animated and I could already see the sharp contrast to her placid, easy-going sibling.

An April breeze sighed strangely, the bank of candles flickered, and the ceremony ended. I moved forward, alone, to retrieve my baby and give thanks to the priest and the godparents.

⚕

There was the usual Sunday parade on the road. Families wearing their finest strolled on the sidewalks, teenagers sped in cars they hardly knew how to drive, and slow-moving servants returned to work for the evening meal. In the background surrounding the *colonia*, jagged mother-of-pearl peaks split billowing banks of clouds.

We had planned a small reception, and upon returning home, it was not long before students and friends packed the living room and began talking loudly, sipping tequila, and filling ashtrays. I held the baby, who soon lost his amazing composure and fidgeted to eat. Carefully, I unbuttoned my dress, shielded my breast as I had seen Mexican mothers do, and gently gave him the nipple to feed. He eagerly clung on.

Stiff and a little self-conscious, I made sure to cover myself with a lacy white blanket, a gift from Rosemary. The baby in his simple innocence made sucking sounds. Rosemary waved at me from across the room and disappeared into the kitchen, emerging in seconds with a tray of tiny sandwiches.

"I understand that you're a teacher," a young man sat down opposite me. His lips barely touched the cup of coffee Rosemary had handed him.

"Yes, I enjoy the work and I meet many people that way." Discreetly, I pulled the blanket even closer.

"And you're already working?" His eyes strayed to the baby at my breast. His words did not convey disapproval, only surprise.

"Not yet, but I will. It's necessary. I do what I can to support my husband."

Out of the corner of my eye, I could see Len. He sat smoking at the table now laden with bottles of wine, tequila, and sandwiches. His eyes glared at me and I could only catch snips of conversation. He poured himself a drink.

"I'll be going to Houston in June," I overheard Len say to Mario.

What? I could hardly believe my ears. *What could this mean? Going to Houston?*

Mario said something to Len and a storm of chuckles rose from the table behind me. *Would he leave Monterrey? Would he leave me here alone with two babies?*

A coldness trickled through me. Once again, I noticed that the man opposite me was staring at my face. Rosemary passed a tray to him. He politely accepted a finger sandwich and leaned a little forward.

"You're very beautiful. You remind me of someone." He smiled approvingly. "Yes, that's it: Grace Kelley."

Uncomfortable with the tack the conversation was taking, I decided to redirect the theme. "And what of Costa Rica? Is it like Mexico?" I had never met anyone from Central America and was curious. More than that, more personally, I was nervous with the baby suckling at my breast and felt flustered by conversation that remotely related to my physical body.

The young man began to speak of his country. With all the animation of a Latino, he described volcanoes and rainforests, beautiful beaches, orchids on mountain slopes, and wonderful Continental food. More laughter came from the table behind me and soon the gang had surrounded Len. Once again, he was the center of attraction. I tried to create a sense of ease, but it eluded me. The man next to me went on with the story about his country, and I became pleasantly distracted with his description—green tropical forests, brightly colored parrots, wide lonely beaches, howler monkeys.

"It is much more European than México," he said, "and quite a wealthy country. By the way, my name is Roberto Mendoza. I'm a fourth-year student here. You have a fine boy there."

Len yelled, "C'mon, Ralph! Play a tune!"

Everyone was talking at once. Ralph took a seat at the piano and played a polka.

"I live with him," Roberto said and pointed to Ralph. "We both rent rooms from a woman up the street. Not much space, though. Guess that's why Ralph keeps his piano here. He's told me about visits here."

"Oh, yes, he drops in at all hours."

"Ralph says when he comes to visit he has to keep on his toes to converse with you."

"I'm sure Ralph is exaggerating. Besides, we don't talk. He plays and I rather enjoy it."

The afternoon wore on. We said, "Goodbye" to our guests amidst the many expressions of "*Congratulationes.*"

"I hope to see you again," Roberto said as he left.

It occurred to me that what I had overheard, this latest development about Len going to Houston, might be some kind of mistake. *Surely he couldn't leave me here in Mexico. Not alone with two tiny babies. He couldn't. He wouldn't.* I wanted to know more and I anxiously waited for the last of the guests to depart.

Before I had a chance to say a word, Len turned on me. "How could you? And in front of my friends!"

"How could I? What are you talking about?" He seemed out of control. *Was it the tequila or had I insulted one of his friends?*

He threw the little wrapping blanket in my face. "Exposing yourself in public that way, like some chippie!" His puffed-up red face was just inches away from my nose. He was breathing hard.

Dumbstruck, my features froze, and then I recovered enough to say, "I was just nursing the baby." A hurt feeling akin to pain rushed over me. My throat went dry. "Señora Montemayor—"

Len cut me off. "You just whipped it out in front of all my friends."

"Yes," I said with my head bowed as hot tears rushed to my eyes. Ashamed of myself, ashamed of Len's reaction, I knew this would be just another good excuse for Len to distance himself from the baby in my arms. I stroked his little face as he nestled close. But I felt numb in my humiliation.

I took the baby with me and moved outdoors to one corner of the patio where I could just barely see the tall, obelisk bell tower of our church on the far hill. Never had I been so rebuffed, so openly mortified. I could still feel the sting of Len's words. I needed a moment all to myself; away from him, I could pull myself together. There, in that solitude, I recalled Señora Montemayor and the natural way she nursed her baby. That was how it had been in the days of my mother and my grandmother. There was nothing wrong with me or with what I had done. It was Len who had a problem.

The baby turned slightly in my arms and stared into my eyes. The evocative aura of the baptism and the look in my baby's eyes left no doubt that birth is sacred. Anything to do with new life was holy. All trace of chagrin dissolved as I recalled Our Lady of Lourdes, the tilt of her head in a gesture that offered the elixir of life. I had done nothing wrong and I refused to be ashamed. For a second, I felt animosity toward my husband, but then I realized how absurd this was; he had been drinking.

Still, I was irritated about many things. I didn't want to waste my time having a tantrum, but I had to admit that I was angry about being so passive in the marriage. I didn't want to give way to subservience again and again. I wanted to earn a living. I wanted to create my own kind of freedom, one that I didn't need to tiptoe around.

The next morning, Len told me that he had arranged an externship at Houston General Hospital. Humming softly like the April breeze through the bedroom window, I watched him dress. His distant attitude lingered, but did not concern me.

"When do you leave?" I asked.

"Not until June. There's lots of time before finals."

"Yes," I said, "enough time for me to get my job back." An unconscious process of sabotage stewed inside of me. I didn't know it then, but I wanted revenge.

Twenty-five

Money Talks

A warm voice with a Midwestern accent caught my attention. The woman's back was turned to me and she had her hands on the grocery cart as she bent over to a little girl by her side. "See, Ginny, we can have cookies tonight." The child, a girl of about four, reached up and grabbed the package.

I approached them. "Are you American?"

The most remarkable thing about the woman was her large lucid eyes that first appeared startled at the intrusion and then warmed. "I'm Julie Monsour," she said. She was dressed in a deep-brown maternity smock. Her hair, parted in the center with a luxurious knot behind, accentuated full and sensual features.

"You're the new one," she added and chuckled. "You're not a Sabbie, I hear." She wore make-up, rings, and smelled of nice perfume—definitely not a Seventh Day Adventist.

"No, I'm not. And you're the first American woman I've met in the *colonia* who isn't."

"Well then, we should be friends. I owe you an apology for not coming to meet you. As you can see, I'm going to have a baby next month and I've been chasing around getting things ready." Her friendly manner made me say more.

"I've been busy, too, getting settled, trying to figure things out," I replied.

"Come for coffee this afternoon. Please do."

And so it happened. That afternoon, coffee became the routine. Julie had a handle on life in Monterrey. She was a few years older than I and, like her husband, had completely mastered Spanish.

I'd bring my two children with me and Jeanne and Ginny would play. Julie and I laughed together like children over the antics of the medical students, my cooking disasters, and my broken Spanish.

The rooms of the Monsour house led into each other. Their house was large and nicely furnished with a shiny tile floor. The smell of food cooking in the kitchen permeated the atmosphere, and I felt immediately at home. In one of the larger rooms, there was a long table with heavy, monastic-style chairs.

"So, Len's going to Houston this summer," she said. "Aren't you afraid to be here alone?"

"I'm uneasy—not afraid."

"You've got guts," she said.

"I don't have much choice."

With her dark good looks, Julie could have passed for Mexican. Both she and her husband were Arab Americans from Detroit. He had already completed his third year. Upon completion of medical school, he could look forward to joining his two brothers who had a clinic in Detroit. Zack was a vigorous man, very earthy, with enormous zeal for life and his goal: to complete his training. With his strong, stocky build, he resembled a wrestler more than a physician.

"Come over for dinner on Saturday, and afterwards we'll go to the movies. Grace Kelley's playing in *The Swan*. Everybody's talking about it since she's getting married soon."

❦

I accepted the invitation and Saturday could not come soon enough to suit me. It was a moody, fitful day, low clouds scudding across the West, a hint of rain in the gusts of wind. When we arrived at the Monsour house, I discovered that the maid had set out a traditional Mexican dinner—*arroz, frijoles* and *enchiladas verdes*. I had no sense of foreboding when we gathered around the table. Zack sat at the head of the table; Len next to him flushed with excitement of school talk, his eyes aglow. Dinner proceeded in an uproarious and lighthearted fashion. Beer glasses were filled and refilled.

We left for *el cine* around seven, and when the film was over, we left the theater and went out into the dark night. The evening had been a huge success, so far, with dinner and a fine film. Grace Kelley played the role of Alexandra, a beautiful and naïve princess about to marry the man who would be king.

"She's a real beauty," Zack said as we walked to his car.

"Have to watch out for really beautiful people," Julie said. "Sometimes they fall in love with themselves and need to be adored."

"Why do you suppose she's going to marry this Prince Rainier guy in real life?" Zack asked.

"Money talks," Julie said.

"I think she wants to be a real princess," Len said. "She's already got it all from Hollywood."

"Maybe she really loves him," I said.

We got in Zack's car. I sat in the back next to Len.

We drove along the wide river road out of town, past the *mercado* toward our *colonia*. A light mist made the *Colonia Independencia* on the far side of the river shimmer in the dark. Len checked his watch and said, "No Green Cross for me tonight."

Zack turned swiftly and called over his shoulder, "Hey, hombre, too much Green Cross isn't good for a guy."

They both laughed.

Thud.

I felt an impact.

"Oh, God, I think we hit something!" Julie screamed.

"Jesus Christ!" Zack hit the brakes. "Stay here; don't get out." He jumped out of the car and slammed the door shut.

"I didn't see anyone," Len said.

"They just dart across this road; never mind the traffic," I said.

"People say they try to kill themselves. Some of them want to die and do it this way," Julie said and held her stomach.

"Len," Zack yelled, "come here."

Len got out of the car. I turned to peek out the rear window where I saw the shape of a man on the asphalt road. Now I could hear other muted voices as a little crowd began to surround the car. Julie began to talk rapidly with a sort of nervous agitation, gesturing with her hands toward the *Colonia Independencia.* "They just run and don't look. What will Zack's family say? They keep us going down here. God help us!"

Within moments, a police officer appeared. He stood at the rear of the car and peered down at the body, which I could see out of the back window. I rolled down the window to better hear what they said.

The concern on the officer's face became greater; his thin lips grew tight. Len swallowed nervously. The policeman shook his head and looked at Zack. "*Es muerto, Señor, es muy serioso,*" he said in a muted voice.

The crowd gasped.

"They'll arrest Zack," Julie cried and began to sob.

"It was an accident; how could they?" I asked.

"Because he's an American." She wrapped her arms around herself in a gesture of self-protection.

My mind was too numb to concentrate. Then came a space of time that felt like hours, yet in reality were only minutes. An ambulance pulled up, parked behind us, and the attendants put the body into the vehicle. Len walked around the car to the driver's seat with Zack's keys in his hands. I pressed myself deeper into the seat. Len's voice was hushed. I could hardly bear to meet his eyes.

"They're taking Zack to jail."

I stared at him in silence.

He went on. "The man died almost instantly. Didn't suffer. The end was quick."

Julie rolled down the window in time to hear Zack yell out to her, "Call my family right away!" His face deathly white in the headlights, Zack looked like he was drowning.

Len pulled away from the scene of the accident.

"It's a strange feeling driving home without Zack." Her manner was a little easier now and less hysterical. I leaned over and put my arm around her.

She went on. "For a moment, I wondered if I'd be all right. I'll call the family as soon as I get home." She turned and looked at me, her mouth twitching, yet her eyes still soft and beautiful though full of tears.

I smiled at her and something happened to her eyes. A faint smile reflected back.

"Thanks," she said in a very quiet, low voice.

ॐ

Three days later, Zack's brother arrived from Detroit. I spent long hours with Julie and did what I could to comfort her; and so it was that I happened to be there that April morning four days after the accident. The cypress trees that surrounded the house closed in on us. Inside the shuttered house, once so beautiful and lively, the enclosure felt like a tomb, the air hot and heavy.

Zack's brother opened the front door, entered, slammed it behind him, and stood in front of Julie.

"I've just come from the police. They want ten-thousand dollars," he stammered.

"What?" Julie asked. "We don't have money like that!"

Zack's brother sat down in front of us. "That's what I told them. They claim the man had a wife and two kids. We have to pay."

"Oh, God, what will we do?" She started to cry.

"I got 'em down to five-thousand."

The maid came in and quietly began to open the shutters, letting sunlight into the living room.

Zack's brother jumped up and paced in front of us. "I'll get cash from the bank today. Zack won't get out until we pay. That jail's a stinking hell hole."

I watched as in a dream. None of this seemed real. Relentlessly, monotonously, Julie objected to paying the bribe, but Zack's brother won out in the end.

"All right, get him out," she said.

Outside the front door, a little courtyard opened to the sky, shaded from the blazing sun. Julie walked me to the door and out to the yard. I stood there a moment watching her, and then I put my hand out to her. We went down the little path together.

"Zack sits here every day. He likes to take Ginny out under the trees to play or read." She hugged me. "Nothing is ever certain in this country."

I nodded. "I guess you're right."

"Listen—what I said the other night in the car, about beautiful people—you know, wanting adoration. I didn't mean you."

"I never thought you did."

"But you're very beautiful. You even look like her, in a way."

"Who?"

"Grace Kelley."

"You're under a lot of strain," I said. "I'm taller than any woman in the *colonia* and most men. I don't feel beautiful at all."

"No, I mean it. You are. But I didn't mean you; it's Len. Well, he's a very handsome man; everyone says so. Just be careful. Men like that can mean trouble."

She hugged me and disappeared into the house. After a moment, the man came out.

He nodded to the chair where Zack normally sat. "Bastards," he said.

A sense of oppression grew upon me. It was cool in the garden, and yet the air was stagnant. The man nodded and squeezed my hand. "Thanks for being here. You're a good friend."

I met his eyes. "Is Zack okay?"

"He will be when I get him out." His voice had a cold, hard quality.

A man's life had been snuffed out. Ashamed of my self-centeredness, I walked home in a daze, past little gardens fragrant with the scent of roses and jasmine. A young man with a family had met a fatal point of intersection; now he was silent. I hadn't really considered him. No one had. My brain was clearer, now. I thought of Louis and Keely, my two macabre friends. They, too, had been accident victims. T. S. Eliot's words came to mind:

What we call the beginning is often the end
And to make an end is to make a beginning.
The end is where we start from.

I felt as lonely and as lost as I had that first day at the airport seven months ago, sitting in the café with my baby beside me, no one to greet me, and nothing before me, only a new country and experiences that I was not sure I really wanted.

A few days later, Julie gave birth to her daughter. Mother and baby were doing fine. I couldn't know that within six months she would leave Monterrey forever.

Twenty-six

Matadora

"*G*race Kelley, the Hollywood movie star, soon to be the Princess of Monaco . . ."

Static intervened. I fine-tuned the radio. More static, then Mexican music, blared.

"Now Grace emerges from the limousine to applause, and, taking her father's arm ascends the steps to the . . ."

More static.

"The lovely actress born in 1929 . . ." *(three years older than Len)* "is turned out exquisitely in white silk and lace . . ."

Again, I tuned the radio until I was sure I had honed in on what had to be the right call numbers, still there was no sound. I adjusted the antennae, but I had lost the signal.

The radio sat on the corner of the desk where I kept my Spanish books and papers. I arranged the notes for today's lesson. Kitty was due to come at any moment for my Spanish instruction.

"*Idiomas,*" she had said. "It's going to help a lot." Any minute, she would arrive; Kitty was never late. She was one of the few predictable happenings in my life in Mexico.

I adjusted the radio dial again. More static came through, then music, some words in French, and then a fragile, "*Oui.*"

198

That had to be Grace. She sounded timid. Glorious music and a triumph of sound followed. "The recessional continues amidst the pealing of all the bells in the little principality." News and fantasy entwined together in the ritual and pomp of the Church as the swan assumed a new identity. "Princess Grace of Monaco emerges on the arm of her husband." The carillon rang joyfully. Crowds cheered. Everything about the wedding sounded like a Hollywood script—gracious, sunlit, glinting with a romantic backdrop.

Despite what my Mexican friends said, I could see no resemblance to "The Swan" in my life or my appearance. She had it made: money, fame, and now a prince.

Kitty broke the spell with a light tap on the door. "Gail, are you there?"

My Spanish teacher wore a simple sky-blue, open-necked dress with short sleeves. Her skin was the color of eggshells, as if the hot Mexican sun had never touched her. Curly brown hair—touched here and there with gray—framed her kind, honest face. Of course, she wore no make-up or jewelry. She was a Seventh Day Adventist—a Sabbie—and her religion forbade jewelry of any kind, even a wedding ring.

I turned off the radio. "Come in, Kitty. I'm ready for you."

We sat at the dining room table opposite the gaunt, staring hulk of the skull on the shelf and spent the next forty minutes conjugating a few necessary verbs. Then, we reviewed practical day-to-day vocabulary. Next, Kitty gave me a list of words.

"Learn these for next time," she said. "You can practice at the *mercado*. We all do that." She handed me a list: a full range of nouns and verbs that related to food.

I went over the list. These lessons were very much to my liking, for each lesson was specific and practical. "This is great, Kitty. Now I can shop and maybe know what I am actually doing."

"Okay, then, for next time." She nodded toward the list and then lingered a moment. Usually, Kitty was all business: a forty-minute lesson, some talk of homework, and she'd dash off. Today, she had something on her mind; she lingered. Tilting her body toward me, she said gently as if not to hurt my feelings, "I hear Len's going away for the summer."

Her words came as a surprise. Kitty had never shown any particular interest in my personal life. The genuine concern in her voice broke my natural reserve and I wanted to confide in her.

"Yes," I replied. "At first, I panicked when I found out about his going. I was worried about being out here by myself with the babies—"

She interrupted me. "Of course, I can understand how that would be the case. You are really on the outskirts of town here." Her voice comforted me. She glanced around the house. "Something has come up that might interest you." She looked directly at me through her oval, wire-rimmed glasses. "A family from our church is going home for the summer. They have a nice house with all the modern conveniences: air conditioner, washing machine, everything." She looked around again, this time with a look that said, "I understand the way things are here." From her point of view, our bare household must have looked primitive, more like a student dormitory than a family home.

"Where do they live?" I couldn't help but be interested.

"It's just a stone's throw away. They don't want any money, just someone to house-sit during the summer months." I'd been feeling like an ugly duckling until Kitty arrived. She had a way of sprinkling magic and hope into my life, and as she presented it, the prospect of moving was, just at that moment, more pleasing than staying where I was.

"Let me think it over."

※

The Mexican spring bore down. It was already intensely hot and dry when Señor Sanchez appeared. The afternoon dragged on, and as he lingered, I felt uneasy. Endless stories about his business, his buildings, and other projects began to get on my nerves. Then, he got around to the subject that both of us knew was of real interest to him. He was still after me to smuggle in a car.

"You could be—how do you say—my window of opportunity."

That did it. I was fed up with constant pressure. I was not ready to become a smuggler. Any hesitation about moving evaporated on the spot. In that instant, I decided. I was straight with him, no weasel words. "I've decided to take a different place. A very good opportunity has come my way."

He eyed me curiously, and—at last getting the message—smiled thinly then offered his hand in return.

"*Mucha suerte.*" Lots of luck. He shrugged, turned, left the house, and drove off.

That evening I told Len what I had done. He was not so pleased with the plan. In fact, he was irritated. "Have you given any thought to what you will do in September when they get back?"

"No, I only want to move out of here."

"Why, what's wrong with this place?"

"I get nervous here at night. María Elena has lots of parties, sometimes people stumble into our yard and—" I wanted to say more, but only fragments of ideas surfaced.

"Do what you want, but I'm perfectly happy here." He pretended not to understand me.

"But you won't even be here, will you? I'm the one who has to live through the hot summer with two babies." I held back furious tears. *He has a big personality, maybe a big heart, but he never sacrifices for anybody.*

"No, I won't, but I think it's a big mistake to get mixed up with those Sabbies. Strange people."

"Better than getting mixed up with Mr. Sanchez."

And then as Señor Sanchez had done, he shrugged and sidled toward the door. The evening was calling him, and he announced without looking at me, "I've got Green Cross tonight."

"Tell Ralph to come and get his piano. I'm not taking it with me."

Len dissolved into the hot, black night. I sat on the patio, seeking some kind of solace or company. I turned off the lights to make it even darker. That night, the sky exploded with shooting stars. I felt very small in such beauty. I mused about moving and I was sure it was the right thing to do. The memory of my grandfather's ghost, the endless parties next door, Mr. Sanchez, and the pressure he was putting on me all added up: I needed a change.

When Len returned hours later, he made love to me. I took this to mean he was sorry and wanted to patch things up.

"No one loves you the way I do," he said.

Yet you will abandon me here. I shivered, but not from cold. I was beginning to think that his love came at too high a price.

For the time being, at least, my money problems were over. I devised a way to juggle our finances so that I could use money formerly set aside for the rent for other purposes. I bought Jeanne a new dress, one that I had been eyeing for weeks. And the bonus? Moving meant no further contact with Señor Sanchez. I wrote a letter to my mother.

May 15
Dear Mommy,

I will go on taking good care of myself, just as you urge me to do. I find myself thinking of home more and wish you could see the new baby. He's chubby and good-natured. By the way, I will be taking another house for the summer. It has air-conditioning. I have come to fear the intense heat the way some people fear tornadoes or earthquakes. This move will make the summer more tolerable.

Love,
Gail

She reciprocated with periodic notes of encouragement and news from home.

Dear Gail,

I think that your friend, Monica, would like to come to see you. I was talking with her mother and she thinks that Monica could use a change. You say your neighbor María Elena has asked you to be in a fashion show dressed like a matador. Send pictures. You say that the Mexicans think you look like Grace Kelley? Well, you are somewhat cool and remote.

> *Much Love,*
> *Mom*

A few weeks later I responded.

June 1
Dear Mommy,

I did the fashion show as María Elena requested. She was thrilled to have someone like myself who had some profes-sional training, and also because I was tall and thin enough to wear the red embroidered matador outfit that she had bor-rowed for the occasion. When I walked down the runway in the suit at the closing, the audience rose and applauded. I felt proud and noble. The show highlighted Mexican design-ers and craftsman. My student, Juan Luís, covered the show, and the next day my picture was in the paper.

> *Love,*
> *Gail*

I didn't tell my mother that while wearing the costume of the matador I had the sense of being in command. Perhaps just play-ing the role strengthened my desire to kill my submissiveness.

There was no doubt that I felt a new energy when I walked down the runway, a *matadora*.

🜍

In the period between Len's departure and our summer move, I realized that Len was angry with me. I had changed a great deal during my first year in Mexico. I now earned a living and my Spanish was as good as, if not better than, his. He knew he couldn't control me, and he knew I could survive without him. Len drank his rum, went out with his friends, and prepared for final exams. Despite the growing distance between us, I still admired his dedication. And though the Green Cross still occupied much of his time, he passed his finals with ease.

Once in a while that spring, I thought of Grace Kelley. It seemed that she had fulfilled every desire from Movie Star to European Princess. A wave of envy crested and then broke. I was twenty. At this point, I had known Len for three years. I had fallen in love with him, thunderstruck by the love of a glamorous, older man. I had taken up his path as if it were my own because I knew how important it was to him. I didn't blame Len for his obsession, for he was a man bewitched by medicine. He puzzled and dazzled me. No one had sent me forcibly in a direction I didn't want to go in, and I could think of no direction other than with him. I tried to sort it out, yet all I could feel was a delicious, guilty joy that he was going away.

Part Three

Twenty-seven

The Revelation of Women

Sometimes, what separates a person from happiness is a question of timing. Had I, a staunch Roman Catholic, been introduced to a group of Seventh Day Adventists in the States, I would have kept a discreet distance. But it was all so different in Mexico. Late May, with its lovely spring days, was the season of picnics. At these outings, I met more of the American community, all "Sabbies." A common bond joined us women: husbands seeking a medical degree at the University in Monterrey. Our hostess on one particularly beautiful day was no exception. She held out her hand to me. "Hello, I'm Angie."

Angie's large, hazel eyes peeked out of the shadow of a wide-brimmed, straw hat trimmed with pink ribbons. Her summer frock, flowing pink polka dot, set off long curly blonde hair. I stared. We might just as well have been at a church social in an affluent neighborhood in California. I knew that this tall, elegant woman who swirled through the crowd of people with such poise was a teacher at the Pan-American School.

"Welcome to our little get together, Gail. I see you've brought your darling children." Angie squeezed my hand. "I've heard that you are a very good teacher."

It was a vivid day full of sunshine. She led the two children and me to a large picnic table set up in her spacious backyard. Thick, green grass carpeted the area and brightly colored flowers bordered the rich green. The yard, an open and cheerful place, could have been a setting in *Ladies Home Journal*. We sat down. From this position I watched her, puzzled that her so very blonde hair was definitely bleached. This surprised me because I knew that the Sabbies frowned upon unnecessary physical adornments. From what I had learned, they stressed temperance, simplicity in attire, and a love of humility.

All faiths have contradictions, and who was I to judge this one? I was not a spiritual robot, after all, because my mother had exposed me to many kinds of people in our days of travel with my dad. I found this community of friends a welcome change after almost a year with Len's gang. More important, they were Americans, and with them came a taste of home. Overhead, the branches of a scrub oak blew in the warm breeze, making shadows that danced on the grass. I positioned the baby's *carrito* for maximum shade.

During the next half-hour, I nibbled at the strange food: lentils made into meat-like patties, delicious salads, homemade breads, and vegetarian casseroles with unpronounceable names. *Was it really wrong to eat meat? Did Jesus ban tobacco and coffee? Were these silly Sabbie superstitions?* These questions had never occurred to me. *Do they have qualms, like I do, about birth control?*

I poured Jeanne and myself some juice and munched a biscuit. The harsh, bright landscape animated me. The heat continued unabated and Jeanne seemed sleepy, so I found a cozy place for her to nap at my feet in shade of the tree. When I looked out over the group, I did so only peripherally, fixing my gaze upward through the leafy umbrella at the bright white of the sky. I felt surrounded by a kind of benevolent tribe.

Angie passed by, and after some small talk, leaned in my direction. "There may be an opening at the school for an eighth-grade teacher. Are you interested?"

I watched Kitty striding toward the yard while carrying bowls of food. She moved quietly through groups of women and children. Her thin shoulder blades showed through the gray cotton of her dress, and her puff of hair was tousled. She hadn't given me a hint of a job opportunity, but I could sense her influence. I felt very happy, as if I were part of a harmonious family.

"Yes, I would be interested."

"If you have talented people doing the right things, good things happen in schools." Angie raised her eyebrows at me and smiled. "Don't you agree?"

I left the group that afternoon, impressed with them and their desire to serve. They took on down-to-earth projects like teaching a newcomer Spanish. Having a deep commitment to do good works for their fellow creatures far outweighed any doctrinal differences, as far as I was concerned. I had a great need to put my life in order, and I knew I could trust these women for guidance.

ॐ

In response to politely insistent queries, I finally got an appointment to meet with Mr. Tarpey, Director of the Pan-American School. I wasn't sure what to expect. His office was a spacious room, wood-paneled with a large, surprisingly clean desk. Behind it, a fair-skinned and pink-faced man with thin, red hair studied some documents. He was so appallingly homely that I found it difficult to look at him. He glanced up at me and, without saying a word, pointed to the chair opposite him. His stiffly starched white shirt crunched as he flexed his arm in my direction. Rumor had it that he was something of a priggish moralist, and I resolved to avoid any controversial subjects.

"What experience do you have?" He got to the point quickly.

"I've been teaching at the *Instituto Cultural* and I've been well received there." The chemistry between us was not good; I could feel the tension. I tried to slow my breathing.

"What methods would you use to appeal to a class—say, in history?" His watery-blue eyes peered at me over horn-rimmed glasses.

Off the top of my head, I said, "Team projects work well, as long as everyone does their share. Art work, or a little drama and music, helps to bring the subject alive."

"What about discipline? Could you maintain order?" He looked me over closely. "You're not much older than they are!" He bent his head toward me, and I noted that the shiny crown of his head was freckled. Strands of light-red hair were too sparse to adequately cover, but like so many men who lose their hair, he had made an attempt to cover the bald spot.

I couldn't help but contrast this strange, rigid man to Señor Rodriguez. For a brief moment, I recalled his desk at the *Instituto*: papers strewn everywhere, books piled high, announcements and newspaper articles tacked to the walls. I couldn't possibly mention my carefree approach to classes at the Institute with coffee at the hotel, conversations about politics or religion, or sometimes an occasional cognac and cigarette. I was sure that Mr. Tarpey would view that kind of informality as a weakness. I decided to keep those details to myself.

"Never had any trouble, so far." Hobbled by a compulsive honesty, I dared go no further except to say, "And one must like the kids. I mean genuinely like them."

"Only a few of our teachers have a college education," he said sternly. "Speaking good English is paramount at our school." His hands moved forward to a pile of papers. Each movement he made was slow and deliberate.

"I majored in English at the San Diego College for Women," I hurried to add, wondering if this was the right or wrong thing to do. "I was there for a year and a half before I married."

"Oh, really?" He pulled his chair a little closer, obviously more interested, now.

He wrote a note on a sheet of paper and nodded in my direction. Sure that I had communicated my anxiety and failed the interview, I stood up to go.

"Before you leave," he said, "I'd like you to meet with one of our other teachers, Lois Lowell. She teaches eleventh grade here. Her office is just across the hall. Go and see her."

Lois turned out to be a genial woman, eager to talk and happy to listen. It came as a relief when, in early June, I learned that I had secured a full-time teaching position at the Pan-American School for the fall of that year. I was sure that Lois had given me the go-ahead. When I brought up the subject to Len, he was pleased.

"So, you'll have a thousand pesos a month. That sounds great. I'll be away much of the summer, so you can use the time to prepare for your job."

"This also means I'll get a residence visa. The school will arrange it. Jeanne will be on it with me since she's on my passport."

"Then, you'll be here legally and I won't." He laughed, but it made me nervous. I never liked the idea of living in Mexico as we did on tourist visas.

༘

Bill and Mario—then later on, Rosemary—shared a second-story apartment. It fronted the street one respectable block from the hospital in *Colonia Las Mitras*. For this privilege, they paid thirty American dollars.

On a hot June day, we congregated there. The temperature, eighty-nine degrees at eleven in the morning, promised that the summer could break all heat records. Joining us that morning, members of the gang shared last-minute perspectives and stories about final exams. Everyone spoke at once, sharing personal agendas.

Jeanne sat next to me on the couch. I held the baby in my lap. After coffee and *pan dulces* with everyone gathered around the coffee table, we agreed that our lives had been tough—we'd all had challenges, but we'd made it through the first year. Len and Bill alternatively spoke of their hopes for the summer. Rosemary took out a camera and snapped a picture. The snapshot would reveal Len looking at Bill, me looking at the camera, and Ralph a blur in the background. He had barged into the room yelling, "I've got the final grades!"

The men gathered around, heads tiled as if they were to play a game. Len grimaced and then smiled so wide you could see the silver fillings in his teeth.

"Passed," he said. They all had.

Within moments, when it came time to collect their things, Len and Bill said, "Goodbye." We took our turns embracing them. The dry heat pulled moisture from my mouth, and I tried to think of something to say as we parted.

"Have a great summer," I blew Len a little kiss.

I picked up the baby and took Jeanne by the hand, then lifted her up so she could see. We all went to the balcony as Len and Bill trudged down the stairs.

Sounds we couldn't hear in *Vista Hermosa* reached us here—sirens, cries and shouts, *camiones*—sounds of a *colonia* that I rarely visited, all muted and mingled, mixed with a certain intensity. I juggled the two babies, one on each hip, as we looked down at Len and the departing car from the balcony. Feeling an unprecedented stirring of exhilaration, I said to Jeanne, "Wave 'bye-bye' to Daddy." Soon, he would be crossing the dust-torn desert of rattlesnakes and cactus. Laredo and then Houston lay ahead of them. Jeanne waved her little hand.

"Adiós, adiós papá."

Below us, Len turned, faced us, and opened his arms wide. He looked like a tenor ready to sing an aria. Mario raised his hand in a friendly salute. Rosemary cried and snapped a final picture. I made eye contact and simply smiled. This parting ritual, another sign of our disintegrating relationship, didn't last long. The two men below us got into the car. Bill backed out of the parking space tentatively, and the tailpipe hit the edge of the driveway as he drove into the street. Len looked at us once more, grinned crookedly, and they were gone.

To dampen the pangs of separation, Rosemary said to me, "He'll be back before you know it. Come and visit before we leave. We'll be here for a few more days."

I liked her, yet found it difficult to feign interest in her offer. I wrinkled my nose and said, "I've got to get back to work, but thanks."

I couldn't be bothered with the gang; I had only a murky conception of what the future held. I was equipped to handle my job and the move, but the knowledge that most of the Americans would be gone for the summer for some reason gave me an insecure feeling. I felt a sense of relief that Len was gone. I hadn't expected to feel quite so good. I brushed the hair out of my eyes, gathered up my children, and began walking slowly down the stairs.

That night, I scribbled a note to my mother.

June 9, 1956
Dear Mommy,

Len has a kind of family blindness. Personal relationships don't matter. Taking care of strangers always takes precedence. I have almost given up the prospects of a happy life. It's necessary to pretend that I'm interested when I'm with him. His demonic detachment to the new baby has turned into absolute remoteness. I keep hoping he will change and take to the baby as he took to Jeanne. This baby is the spitting image of him: marine-blue eyes, huge dimples. I don't understand. I've come to realize that my life is merely a footnote to his plan.

Love,
Gail

Just reading it made me feel better. Then I burned the letter. High melodrama was not for my mother. The edge of the paper curled and fell apart as the rest ignited. I threw the ashes into the grass. It was a blistering night. Grasshoppers chirped ceaselessly. Stars glittered above the horizon of luminous mountains. My intense need to be connected as a family was once again absorbed by darkness and the panorama of the night sky.

Twenty-eight

Anything Can Happen

Even when I left at dawn for work, driving along the *Rio Catarina* road, I ran into the maze of morning traffic. Dozens of shouting vendors, overburdened trucks, cars, and pedestrians hurried along the road where a thin mist still clung to the slopes of the bank. A pale sun, silver instead of gold, peaked over the Saddle Mountain. I accelerated and plunged into the thick of the traffic, weaving in and out, honking the horn at anything in front of me.

I didn't want to be late; Monterrey was full of gossip. I wanted to be the one to tell Señor Hernandez of my intention to take a full-time teaching position at the Pan-American School. He had been so kind and gracious that I did not want the news to reach him from anyone, except me.

I arrived at 6:30 to find Señor Hernandez perched on the edge of his chair in the Ambassador Hotel restaurant. He leisurely breathed in the smoke of his cigarette and smiled. He saw me and waved his rolled-up newspaper in greeting.

"You're right on time." I sat down opposite him. He motioned to the waiter, who brought my coffee and roll.

I shot Señor Hernandez a wondering look. He was entirely too cheerful to be annoyed with me. "I got your note, Señor. You wanted to see me?"

"I do, indeed. Something really wonderful is going to happen here in our city."

He was a man of ability and sensitivity, but I had never seen him quite so enthusiastic. "Marion Anderson will be singing here this weekend. The Institute has been given several tickets, and I wanted to know if you and some of your students might want to go."

"That's fantastic. Here in Monterrey?" I jumped on the opportunity. "How many students may I bring?"

"I have four tickets for you. Choose whomever you want." The hotel clock struck 6:45. Normally, he would have left by then. Today, he lingered at the table and slowly sipped his coffee. He hesitated a moment and then changed the subject. "Are you doing well? I mean, since your husband left and now that you are alone here?"

"But I'm not alone. My friend from the States will be here mext week. She's staying for the summer, and besides, I have the children."

I realized that he was staring at me. His eyebrows pulled together in a tight knot, and he leaned in my direction. "I just want to say, if you need anything—"

"Only to keep working here with you until the fall. I've decided to take a full-time job at the Pan-American School."

"That's great news," he said softly. "Of course, you may always have students here also, if you wish."

"I hope you understand why I took the job at the Pan-American School. It's not just the money; they'll get me papers, legal papers to work and to reside in the country."

"No need to explain. I'm not surprised someone snapped you up."

I sensed he wasn't just being polite, but I wondered how much he knew. I was reticent to talk with him about my situation with Len or the problems that hounded me.

Señor Hernandez maintained his reserve and a professional stance with me. Despite his natural formality, I felt a certain warmth and knew I could trust him. I couldn't help but contrast today with the uneasy feeling I had at my first meeting with Mr. Tarpey, my soon-to-be boss. I felt comfortable with Señor Hernandez and I would miss him.

"It all happened so quickly," I added. "I think it will be good for me." I feigned confidence. Inside I felt a fragile pain at the thought of leaving him.

Just then, Carlos came into the restaurant. He called out, "*Buenos Dias, Professores.*" He was a journalist and an interesting young man, but by far my best student.

"Carlos," I said, "I have a surprise for you."

As I indicated a chair for Carlos, Señor Hernandez stood. The Institute was around the corner. Our brief session was over. Just as he had done dozens of times in the past, now he would dash off. I felt he had wanted to say more.

ᚨ

The field of faces in the recital hall blinked and smiled. Many whispered. I sat next to Señor Hernandez, about midway from the stage. Three students sat to my left. We spoke in hushed voices. The curtain opened and a Negro woman of medium height walked onto center stage. The skirt of her deep-maroon taffeta gown billowed out around her and rustled as she took her place, center stage. I sensed a powerful presence.

Marion Anderson was full of mystery and, although not movie- star attractive, all eyes were fixed on her. She had a magical aura that commanded attention. During my time in Mexico, I had learned the value of light skin and European features. These qualities were necessary to "present well," and presentation could mean the difference between professional success and failure. Marion Anderson, with dark chocolate skin, heavy features, and blazing eyes, did not even come close to meeting those standards. I wondered how the Mexican audience would relate to her.

Ironically, two white Georgian columns flanked the stage—the kind one might see on the porch of some antebellum mansion in the South. A large concert grand stood midway between the columns and the artist. Otherwise, the stage was bare with nothing to distract us from Miss Anderson. A nod to the pianist, soft introductory chords, and then she began. At first, her voice quietly evoked polite attention, then compassion, and finally awe and respect. Her songs commanded things I could not put into words. All the while, the audience listened, mesmerized. A second song began.

"Nobody knows the trouble I've seen . . . " In our souls now, we were suffering with her; seeking out vast, dark expanses where ungodly things happen and not much ever changes to make it better. Her voice rose, gained in power until it thundered. Negro spirituals, melodies punctuated by ragtime rhythm, and classical favorites demonstrated the full range of her mezzo-soprano voice. At times, she sounded more like a cello or bass violin than a human being, yet her message was deeply human. She compelled us to participate, to share her sound, her vision. We let go and fell into her story. Her note was pure, loving, powerful and free. Above, from the ceiling of the large hall, a crystal chandelier sparkled like frozen raindrops reverberating with the luscious tones of her voice.

The first section ended reverently with the Lord's Prayer. Marion sang with the joy of liberated perspective. She made it clear that despite the superficial illusions of life, God alone rules and controls the universe, and His glory is everlasting.

I was profoundly moved, not even embarrassed by the tears wetting my face. The tension was palpable and I was relieved when the break came.

At intermission, we filed out to the lobby. Señor Hernandez brought our group cold drinks. "What do you think of the soloist?" His voice was thick with feeling.

I could sense genuine emotion, not only in Señor Hernandez, but also in the students and the audience. I wiped my eyes and said, "She is, of course, extraordinary."

Carlos agreed, "I've never heard anyone sound like her."

"Well, Carlos, you have a challenge to put this experience down in words. I know I would find it difficult."

"But I must find a way to do it. This is more than music. It is an appeal to the very soul, *la alma de la humanidad.*" The soul of humanity.

Señor Hernandez agreed, "The sense of loss that she conveys taps into an intimately primal place."

"Yes, but so does her will to survive," I added. The lights flickered; it was time for the second half. I turned to Señor Hernandez and told him, "Thank you for bringing us all here together. I mean it with all my heart." He smiled so that I knew he caught the depth of my meaning.

Just as I was moving to return to my seat, a woman approached me with her hand extended. It was Lois Lowell, the teacher from the Pan-American School. "Magnificent, isn't she?" she said.

"Indeed," I replied. "How nice to see you here, Mrs. Lowell." Before I had time to introduce her, the lights blinked again. The program was going to start up.

"Let's get together soon. Come for lunch next week. I live in *Del Valle.*" She handed me her card and was off. I knew of *Del Valle* from May, of course—the elite area with the plantation-style homes, stables, and thoroughbred horses—the international community.

We resumed our seats and, once again, the curtains parted. Marion Anderson stood before us again, poised between two worlds, curiously able to maintain her balance. Moments passed.

And again, her music took us to that point of tension where things seem to be going wrong in life, and only monumental effort will achieve even the slightest gain. She enchanted us for yet another hour singing of those who languished as exiles in her own country. From her gospel songs, I experienced a sense of spiritual sustenance. Her words promised protection and nourishment. Love is always there. I could certainly relate to life gone astray and I got the message: "Put your faith in God." She sang it a dozen ways until she finished with "He Holds the Whole World in His Hands."

The audience roared its approval.

After the concert, I walked with Señor Hernandez and the students around the *Plaza Zaragoza* until we came to Sanborne's. There, the students greeted familiar faces and a surge of chatter filled the room. There were questions—everyone talking at once, but no one listening for responses.

"*¡Marion Anderson, fantastica!*"

"*¡Maravillosa!*"

"*Con mi professora.*"

At last, we found a large round table. The waiter took our order.

"*Mango para mi.*"

"*Fresa aqúi.*"

"*Chocolate para mi.*"

"*Café negro.*"

Ultimately, the noise and tumult settled down, and as dishes of pastel-colored ice cream and strong black coffee appeared, the talk became serious.

Señor Hernandez looked at each one of us around the table. "Marion Anderson was a granddaughter of a slave. She reminds me that we, in México, have had our own kind of slavery. Even now, the *hacendados* are only partially succeeding, the *ejidos* require land, and the *braceros* yearn for *gringo* money."

I added, "Our countries have much in common in this regard. I've heard that here, in Mexico, there have been some attempts to redistribute land back to the peasants. After the Civil War in the States, there was a similar move to redistribute the land from the plantations. Every former slave would have been given fifty acres of land, but it went nowhere. The government felt it would lead to an even more bitter rift between the North and the South, and it never happened."

"Well, it has been a struggle down here—that is, to redistribute the land." Carlos spoke in a spurt of anger. His resentment was obvious. "It's the conquistador mentality. We bend to it."

Señor Hernandez intervened, "We can't blame everything on Hernando Cortez. Our natural proclivity toward subservience was well-ingrained even before the Spaniards came here."

Catarina, a bright young law student, broke in, "Just look at how we respond to a simple question. We say, '*Mande.*' We could just as easily say, *dispénseme* or *perdóneme*, but no—we say, '*Mande.*' The very word implies subservience and inequality." She struggled to keep the conversation in English.

I wanted to encourage her effort, but I also wanted to know more. "I still don't understand the significance of the word. It seems to be used everywhere."

"Not if you go to Spain," Carlos insisted.

"Not even in South America." Catarina added, "Although, I did hear it in El Salvador and Guatemala."

"It's not just that we are *meztizos*; it goes deeper." Señor Hernandez' voice was quiet and sober, now. "We still place value on what is outside of us—on what is different from us. It is as if our true self has been obliterated."

"Impossible," Carlos said, bewildered and angry. "Cortez came over four-hundred years ago! Are we still wallowing in our own self-inflicted inferiority from the past?"

"Not exactly," Señor Hernandez said resolutely. "We are very much in the present, but the old mentality is still with us. The

Mexican makeup is prone to self-deprecation and, until we get over it, we will never be a great nation." He said it boldly, and I knew he had a point.

"I am not Mexican," I said cautiously, not wishing to appear patronizing, "but I know that I see some very good things in this culture." I hesitated to add, "My son, Leonardo, was born here. He could be a Mexican citizen if he chooses to do so. What I like and what I respect is the tendency to share—to cooperate—and I admire the emphasis on family life."

A soft-spoken student joined in, "That, too, is part of our native background."

"I also admire the way even the poorest of people find joy in music and dance." I was thinking of Paula dancing with the baby or singing as she mopped floors.

"In that regard," Señor Hernandez said, "we are like Marion Anderson. In music, we find release and connect with something basic and human."

"We sing and dance, but that is a way to mask the real issue. The trouble with México," he said, "is that, psychologically, we see ourselves as 'The Conquered.' Even in the business world, it is a mentality that plagues us. There is a quality of self-contempt that goes with it."

"Surely, after all these years, you must be outgrowing that notion. There is a strong middleclass now. I live in a middleclass neighborhood." I thought of María Elena on one side and the doctor and his family next door on the other.

"It goes back even before the Spanish came." Señor Hernandez pushed aside the dish in front of him and looked steadily around the table at each one of us. "It's not as easy as you may think. For most of us here, there has been a servant-master relationship for centuries. Montezuma was not the first to demand human sacrifice, you know."

Catarina nodded in agreement. "Cortez knew what Montezuma and all the feudal lords before him knew: it is the labor of the Indians that is the true wealth of México. From them comes the maize, the rice, the wool, the *chili*."

"Still, things here are moving," Carlos added. "There is hope. Cortines isn't so bad."

"He's not as great as Cardenas," Catarina added and looked at me. "He was our F.D.R. With him as president, we really made progress."

"Or Benito Juarez. Cardenas and Juarez—our two really honest presidents," Carlos said.

"I agree," Señor Hernandez added, "and in the meantime, we go on within the framework of our time."

I nodded, saying, "Marion Anderson makes me believe that anything is possible. 'He holds you and me, Baby, in His hands, He holds the whole world in His hands'—the words of her last song."

"That's it," Catarina said, "Marion Anderson—she sang of a sacred world where each person can find the truth. We just need to lift the veil and see it."

Carlos broke in. "Marion is a true artist. No one else could have done it. She made me feel the hand of God. *¡La Mano de Dios, sí!* That will be the name of the article. Now I must go and write that review for my paper. *Buenas Noches.*"

An unseen clock chimed. It was midnight and the melancholy toll of the bell broke the spell. Carlos rose and we all followed his example. Over an hour had passed since we had taken our place in the magical circle. Removed from clock and schedules, and for a brief period, I felt as if I had entered another dimension. Marion Anderson and her transforming voice had created a space for us, a space where identities dissolve and reshape. For me, she opened a threshold toward what real desires are.

After Sanborne's, I walked with Señor Hernandez around the *Plaza Zaragoza.*

"I want you to know," he said, "that if you ever need anything, I am your friend."

His bluntness took me by surprise. I turned and looked into a strong, tense face, strangely enkindled, as if suffused from within. There was a pause.

"Thank you," I whispered. "I am very touched." My need for closeness and hunger for intimacy must have shown on my face, so I took a step back and away from him. "Dear Señor Hernandez, you are not the answer to my problems." I said it tenderly, yet I knew I had to be firm. I liked him far too much to lead him on.

He took my hand and kissed it: an elegant gesture.

Around the corner, I found my car, stumbled in, and drove off. The drive home gave me time to process all that had happened. Images, sounds, and ideas thrashed in my head. In my heart, I knew that Señor Hernandez's offer of friendship had deep ramifications. I knew he was a widower wih a daughter in Chihuahua where his family had a small ranch. I also knew I had to maintain proper distance with him. I pondered the word we had talked about.

Mande, "command me." It had become part of my day-to-day vocabulary. I had not given it any thought, not until that night. My relationship with Len, with the Church, with God—all pointed to a kind of dependence that I had not been able to see. And here in Mexico, I had not entirely escaped the *mande* mentality. It pervaded everything.

Nevertheless, while Marion Anderson sang of dependence and subservience, her message was also one that led to freedom and transcendence of ordinary life. She was dynamic in the here and now, yet conscious of her connection with the eternal. For my part, I wanted to shake loose of doubt and see my way clear, and it would not be in a way that was foolish, naïve, or childish. But how?

Twenty-nine

Monica

I held Jeanne up toward the high, airy ceiling and pointed to the tall, white walls that enclosed the entire house. The fortress-like shape and the large tiled indoor staircase endowed the place with a sort of regal charm.

"Our new house is like a castle, *verdad?*"

Carried away by the excitement of the moment, she followed my gesture.

"*Si, Mamá.*"

Paula came in from the patio carrying the laundry basket. Propped on top of the freshly laundered clothes lay the baby. Clad only in a diaper, he sucked contentedly on his pacifier as his eyelids began to droop.

"*¿Ya no vino su amiga, Señora?*" She was asking me if my friend had come yet.

"*No. Más tarde. A las dos o las tres. Más tarde.*" "Later," I told her.

"*Entonces hay tiempo a jugar.*" *Then there is time to play.*

She motioned to Jeanne, "*¡Vén, niña!*"

My daughter squirmed loose from my hold and toddled after Paula to the patio, a quiet sheltered area within the compound. Playpen, toys, and a gym set filled one corner. Off to the other side, a separate room, apart from the house, served as a maids' quarters. And next to this room, in all its glory, stood *la machina*, a modern electric washing machine. This abundance of material objects more than justified the move to *el castillo blanco*. Albeit, our time there would be short.

I did not call Jeanne back to me. It was only noon and she wanted to play in the shade of the tall, walled area. Besides, there were papers to correct and lessons to plan.

I called to Paula, "*Voy a trabajar.*" *I'm going to work.*

"*Descanse un poco, Señora. Una siesta.*" *Rest a little. Take a nap.*

The heat had made me drowsy as it often did at that time of day. I was no longer nursing the baby, and I had hoped this change would increase my energy. Nevertheless, I was so entangled in early-hour classes that each day, the heat and a rush of fatigue overcame me. Or maybe I was simply getting habituated to a rest in the afternoon. I marveled at how well the children tolerated the climate. A *siesta* sounded appealing.

Today, the sky was sand-colored under the scorching summer sun. There was a kind of purity in the intensity of the heat, not that it unduly concerned me, for I found comfort in the upstairs bedroom where I sat at the desk—the only piece of furniture besides the two cribs—that I had to bring with me. This house, like the one before, was furnished. The air-conditioner hummed monotonously as I reread the telegram.

> *Arriving late Tuesday afternoon.*
> *My mother may come with me.*
> *Monica*

Next to the upstairs bedroom, a balcony was sculpted into the front façade. From that height, silhouettes of colored rooftops rose and fell in tiered layers as far as Lourdes, our parish church. I peered out at a panorama of glowing hills. Dry brush stretched beyond as far as the distant mountains. *Vista Hermosa,* beautiful view.

I crumpled the telegram in my hand and moved to the bed. Lying down, I could wait for the visitors while, outside, the warm atmosphere vibrated visibly and bathed the hills in a transparency of grayish vapor.

There was a quiet hush over the house. It was deliciously cool inside, everything so peaceful that I could daydream of many things. It felt good to be alive in a space that seemed outside of time.

I heard Paula shuffle upstairs to the adjacent bedroom with the children in tow. Luisa had gone home for a week to be with her old grandmother who had taken ill, but Paula showed no signs of discontent. She had a particular fondness for Lenny and kept him close to her during the long summer days.

She crooned, "A *dormir, niños, a dormir.*" It was naptime.

Idle, I lay back on the metal bed. My thoughts meandered over the events of the past few weeks. The decision to move had proved sound, so far. The washing machine was a godsend; the air conditioner and refrigerator made living in Mexico more bearable, even pleasant. For several long moments in the cool of the afternoon, I felt cut adrift and floated into sleep. I found myself dreaming in earnest.

In my dream, I was carrying a heavy load on my back, just like the street vendors who passed every morning. With each step, the basket filled with mangoes became heavier until I was bent over, hardly able to hold up my head or to see in front of me. Ahead, lay a shivering wooden trellis. No—a bridge. Its wooden supports were broken, but I knew I had to cross it. The scorching desert lay behind me. I took three, four frightening steps as I struggled across the fragile bridge toward a field of tall sugar cane when I started. The images in the dream—with the significance of pressure, of the lack of firm footing, of the need to press on—would haunt me all summer.

Awakened by the sound of a car door slamming, I jumped up. The noise came from directly below.

I opened the sliding door and peered over the balcony. I called to them. "Monica!" She had not come alone.

Her mother, Ann Harris, stood next to the cab and haggled with the driver. Even after hours of travel, Mrs. Harris looked trim and in charge. She was a pretty woman, a full head shorter than her daughter was. Monica looked up at me, shielding her eyes from the glare, and waved.

Mrs. Harris rummaged through her purse. As I watched Monica begin to unload their bags and baskets on the street, I wondered if they had brought along their own stash of food. Many Americans did.

I called to Paula, *"Ya están aquí." They're here already.*

Together, we rushed to the door to greet them.

"You made it in one piece!" I hugged Monica. Her mother paid the driver and turned toward me. I threw my arms around her. "It's so great to have you here, both of you."

"I can only stay a few days," Mrs. Harris rushed to say. "I had to take some time off work."

I had never known her to take a day off in the ten years I had known her. An obstetric nurse at Mercy hospital, Anne Harris had kept a grueling schedule. But there was always time for her three daughters and their friends. She had always made time for me and frequently included me in their family outings.

"My mom didn't want me to make the trip alone." There was a note of strain in Monica's voice. She was just as I remembered her: tall, big-boned, smooth ivory skin, and large eyes—hazel-flecked with green. Her brown hair swirled prettily around her face.

"I don't blame her," I said, and I meant it.

We quickly established one corner of the house as their private space, and as they settled in, Paula prepared lemonade. The

visit began cheerfully as I poured lemonade and Mrs. Harris produced a surprise.

"From your grandmother—tea cookies." She opened a familiar round tin.

I almost cried when I saw the butter cookies twisted into little
wreaths. "I'm so happy to have you here." I took one of the cookies, "Yum, a taste of home." I was astounded at how something
so small could evoke such feelings of nostalgia.

"Next to my two sisters, Gail, I guess I've known you longer
than anyone."

Monica looked at me, and then, arching her eyebrow toward
her mother, continued, "We were always together in line in
grammar school. 'Tall girls to the back.'"

I sipped some cool lemonade and said, "I still remember those
family picnics you used to have—and parties, and holiday celebra-
tions. Now, it's my turn to reciprocate." I looked at Monica the
way I used to when we were on same team in a spelling bee.

Mrs. Harris balanced her glass on the side of the sofa and said,
"If it were anyone but you, Gail, I wouldn't have let her come."

I should have guessed from the way her eyes fastened on me
that something was askew, that she wasn't on good terms with
her daughter. As the afternoon wore on, Mrs. Harris insisted on
helping with the welcome dinner. She wrapped a dishtowel
around her waist and heated oil in the frying pan. In the meantime, Monica went upstairs with Paula to unpack.

"So, Len is in Houston?" Mrs. Harris tossed the steak into the
pan.

"He has an externship for the summer. We need the money
and he needs the experience." I took the rice out of the oven.

"Sounds to me like you're doing a lot."

"Our life isn't easy, but it'll pay off. Shall I make the salad?" I
brought lettuce, tomatoes, and cumbers from the fridge.

"Is it really safe to eat that? We have been warned about raw
vegetables."

"I eat everything. Even drink the water!"

"Okay, but wash the salad greens well. If you're going to live here, I guess that's what's called for." For just a moment, her face wrinkled with humor and laughed, then a hint of concern lingered.

"Pass me that large onion." She began to chop methodically, and soon there was a heap on the cutting board. She paused and pointed the knife as you would a finger and added, "Monica's been acting foolishly. Got herself a job dancing as an entertainer. I don't know what got into her." The onions sizzled as she dumped them into the pan.

"I remember all the ballet lessons we had growing up," I tried to make light of it. "Maybe those toe shoes finally paid off."

"No, it's just not right for her. Dancing in a cabaret!" Her voice escalated and she tossed a piece of meat into the hot pan.

It was a ticklish moment. I said, "Maybe she's just bored, just needs a new direction."

"Do what you can to get her interested in something new." She flipped the steak. "Dinner's ready in five minutes." She puffed at her cigarette. "The kids are adorable. Jeanne is quite the talker. I can still remember when she was born, a scrawny little thing. And the baby, so good-natured—and those soft, blue eyes." She looked at me with a steady thoughtful look.

I knew in my heart that I could not deny Mrs. Harris anything. It was she who had come in for me when Jeanne was born. It had been a difficult delivery, and with her no-nonsense compassion, Anne Harris had cared for me as if I was her own child.

"I'll do what I can, of course." Thoughts floated in my head like summer leaves on a breeze. *Why did Mrs. Harris want Monica to join me in Mexico?*

"You're very optimistic, Gail," she replied gently, "and that is good. You're adaptable." She was quiet for a while, then her forehead creased. "Supper's ready."

After dinner, we sat in the living room. Violet-colored light streamed in from the portico outside. Even when I sat relaxed by the window, I could feel the tension between the two new arrivals, two people I loved very much.

৯

The next day, I wanted to give them a taste of the city. We visited *La Purissima, La Plaza Zaragoza*, and the *Mercado* by the river. We reserved a table for lunch at the Ambassador, and after our meal we walked through the arcade of shops, then went into the coolness of the cathedral to light a candle. Mrs. Harris seemed content that Monica was in good hands for the summer.

One afternoon, I drove them by Lois Lowell's house for drinks. The afternoon get- together was a foretaste of what was to be a pleasant dinner a few nights later.

Mrs. Harris sat in the living room with Fred, Lois's husband. To my delight, he talked about life in Monterrey in such glowing terms that I thought I'd leave them alone for a few minutes. His words would do more than I could to convince Mrs. Harris that Monterrey was a safe and civilized place to live—coming, after all, from Boston as he did. I found Lois and Monica together on the large verandah, which encircled the front of the house. Large wicker chairs faced west. It was dusk. An exceptional fiery sunset left traces of flame in the distant sky. They were sipping cold drinks and their conversation, even from a distance, sounded animated and filled with enthusiasm.

"So, you also have an interest in teaching?" Lois leaned closer to Monica and cocked her head.

Monica looked up. The thought zigzagged across my mind that this could be it: the new direction. Maybe the flash of the fiery sunset was a sign. It made perfect sense. Monica was supposed to be here. I cleared my throat and their faces turned in my direction. *Pay attention, Monica,* I was trying to tell her.

Monica pondered the question and turned her shiny, hazel eyes toward Lois. "I had a rich experience as a very young child at a pre-school. There was art, music, and dance. We could hardly wait to get there every day. I wish there was more of that." She glanced over toward her mother who was chatting with Fred Lowell in the living room, chain-smoking all the while.

"I'd like to open a school like that here. There's a need," Lois said.

"Aren't you happy at the Pan-American?" I interrupted and sat down next to them.

"For now, yes. This is just my dream." She said it in such an off-handed manner that I wondered if she really meant it. I knew the Lowells had the resources to start a school if they chose to. "I spent time as a social worker before Fred and I married. So, I know how important early childhood experience can be."

Monica chimed in, "I know that my sisters and I—I have two of them—really enjoyed those early years. My mom worked all the time."

"Monica," Lois said, "there's an opening at the Pan-American for a third-grade teacher. Perhaps I could introduce you to the director."

"Oh, yes; please do," I said. "Monica, it would be great if you could stay." The thought of having my old friend in Monterrey made me a little giddy.

"I'll think about it." She looked especially pretty that night—green eyes offset by a pale pink blouse and her hair pulled back. "I really will."

§

Already, June was ending. It was time for Mrs. Harris to leave. After a cursory sampling of the city and my group of friends, it had been mutually agreed upon: Monica would stay. The three of us, all in a fairly subdued mood, ate a farewell lunch of enchiladas, rice, and cheese. We drank pitchers of lemonade until a dilapidated taxi pulled up. I went to Mrs. Harris's room. The bed was neatly made, suitcases ready and stacked by the door. We gathered everything, walked her to the taxi, and in moments she was gone.

"I'm sorry to see her go." I felt a strange loneliness as we settled in the living room. Then, at last, Monica spoke about herself, but almost as if she were talking about a person who was absent. I could understand this; I felt a sense of detachment about my own life, as if it were a stranger's story.

"Did mom tell you how angry she is with me?" Her face changed inexplicably.

"She told me about the dancing job. She didn't like it."

"Did she tell you she'd throw me out of the house if I didn't quit?" Her bitterness surfaced.

I hesitated for a moment. "She cares, Monica; she really cares about you."

"I had to find a way to pay for my class at the Old Globe. A guy at the theater—well, actually, an older man—introduced me and, well, the pay was good."

We sipped our lemonade. *There's more to the story.* I didn't press her. God knows I had plenty of stories from the last year, stories that I'd rather put behind me. Maybe Monica felt that way, too.

"Monica, it was just too hard for her to accept. Your mom just wants the best for you." I tried to sound like a woman of experience. "I'm glad you're here."

"There's another reason. One of your letters sounded like you could use some support down here. I want to help if I can."

"There've been some rough times," I said. "I remember telling you that I came home one day from work and found Jeanne crawling down the street. That really scared me. But now, Paula's come back."

She thought for a moment. "Gail, this position at the Pan-American School could be the light at the end of the tunnel." Her face flushed with eagerness. The air felt hot, heavy, and charged.

I knew in my bones that she would get the job. But would she accept it?

෬

Monica and I had the house, the summer, and the freedom to do as we pleased. That night, I found it impossible to sleep. I got one postcard from Len when he arrived in Houston. It read:

> *This was the right thing for me to do. I'm getting lots of experience here. Got to sew up at least fifty knife wounds in the emergency room this week. I love it.*
>   *Len*

After that, I heard nothing.

Thirty

Foolish Stars

Outside, horns blared and *mariachis* strummed and sang. From the garden across the street, a wedding party was in full swing, and once the songs ended, a phonograph blared for hours. I felt a sense of longing without the slightest resentment toward Len. I was still awake at dawn when a pale sun turned the sky a streaked orange—and the moon, shaped like a curved *pan dulce*, faded behind the tall mountains. Just before I left for work, I scribbled a note for Monica:

> *Be back late morning. Let's go to the outdoor movies tonight. We can take the kids and give Paula a night off.*

Sitting on the edge of the bed in my room, I blotted my face with an enormous terrycloth towel. It was part of a set, a wedding present that we had managed to hold on to. Luxurious and slightly rough to the touch, the delicious feel of the fabric gave me a sense of home. I wrapped the fluffy towel around me and sat on the edge of the bed, watching my footprints from the shower evaporate. My skirt and cotton blouse were carefully folded and draped over the chair near the balcony.

It was from this vantage point that I could see beyond the *colonia* and noticed a sea of thunderclouds in the direction of the mountains. The clouds hesitated there, teasing the jagged rocky peaks. I gazed at the craggy, now shadowy, landscape. It had a story to tell. If I could just listen hard enough, perhaps I would catch the meaning.

These were mountains that had once been volcanoes. They could be volcanoes, again. Only a few years ago, a cornfield in Michoacan had rumbled and smoked until a fissure opened in the earth. An immense stream of lava poured forth and inundated the neighborhood. In just a few days, the cornfield appeared as a huge, smoldering volcano, *Volcán de Paricutín.* Within a week, the entire landscape had been transformed; villages had been wiped out. Ever since I had heard about this event from my students, the sight of a terrified village engulfed in flames haunted me. Things can change so quickly.

The dangers, the heat, the storms could not diminish the elation I felt near the mountains. I threw on my clothes, pulled my attention back to the moment, and called to Monica, "Paula has decided to go with us, even though I offered her the evening off."

"That was nice of her. I'll go down and help her get the kids ready."

As I entered the entry room, I could hear them talking.

"*No, gracias, Señorita, toda es listo.*" Paula had bunched, folded, and gathered pillows, blankets, bottles, and extra diapers. All was ready—*listo.*

As I reached the street, Monica was standing by the car waiting for me.

Paula scrambled into the back seat with Lenny in her arms. She hugged the baby. " *¿Aye mi rey, vamos al cine, no?*" *El cine.* The cinema.

I looked at Paula in awe that she was calling my baby "her king" as she had done so many times before. I realized that there can be a positive side to the master/slave relationship. Surrender can be a sweet thing—surrender to love, and in this case, to a powerless baby.

Putting Jeanne between Monica and myself, I checked one final time to make sure we had the full assortment of necessities. Then, we headed out of *Vista Hermosa* past the *Supermercado*, around the *glorieta*, and finally down the highway toward a large, open field. The entrance to the theater lay at the end of a dirt driveway where a toothless, old grandfather collected the admittance fee: fifty *centavos*. His gray head bobbed up and down in gratitude with the clink of each coin.

A number of cars had already parked toward the rear of the field, which bordered *Colonia Las Mitras*. The air, warm and thick, smelled of dampness. There was no moon. A midnight-blue sky sparkled with stars.

The film usually started around eight and we had just enough time to find a good spot on the wooden benches, about thirty meters back from the front of the field where a motion picture screen towered over the audience. Moths fluttered on the white surface as children, play-acting, cast phantom shadows on the silver screen. A tiny, weathered stand crouched behind the rows of benches. Its counter, made of rough board and a few rickety shelves, held candy, cigarettes, and chewing gum. Below in an ice chest, chilled drinks awaited customers. A single lightbulb dangled from the makeshift roof.

Paula moved to a place in front, waving to friends, and all the while chatting to Lenny. *"Mira bebito, la luz. Es bonita la luz."* Her enthusiam for him was unbounded—a comfort to me as Paula made up for the attention that Len withheld.

Monica and I found a bench toward the back close to the wooden snack bar, and as Jeanne sprawled haphazardly next to me on a fluffy pillow, Monica bought drinks for everyone.

Meanwhile, boys and girls out for a romantic evening under the stars giggled and held hands. I was the same age as some of those girls, not a day older—a sweet, colorful existence only enhanced by flirting under the night sky.

Lights flickered. The celluloid strip of film fluttered and the show began. The film starred Cántinflas, the legendary Mexican comic. As the story unfolded, Cántinflas was mistaken for a prize fighter and, despite his clumsy antics, the agile little man managed to sway and feint his way past huge, musclebound opponents. It was only when he confronted women that his character unraveled.

Despite the fact that we could not grasp the full meaning of the dialogue—humor in any foreign tongue is hard to grasp—within a short time, his antics had us laughing as hard as the Mexican audience. Cántinflas was playful—earthy, yet devilish—with a heightened insistence on self-mockery.

I was surprised at the storyline because, in my mind, it subverted the notion of the male-dominated culture that I had come to know. This theme was underscored by the vitality and utter common sense of the full-hipped, voluptuous women, who ultimately saved the hero. A luminous, sensual glow brought out the true feminine nature, along with a tantalizing promise of pleasure. Nothing understated, here.

As the story played out, Jeanne rubbed her eyes, and soon, the intense heat mixed with the heavy night air coaxed her to sleep. She curled up next to me and hugged her bedraggled blanket. I marveled that she could sleep so soundly despite the belly laughs all around us.

Just as the first movie ended, I felt a tap on the shoulder, and turning, I saw Ralph. I had not seen him since the afternoon, over a month ago, when he hauled his piano out of our living room.

"Out for the evening?" he asked politely. "Who's your friend?"

I could see that Ralph was not alone. Roberto, the medical student from Costa Rica, stood behind him.

"Oh, Ralph, this is my girlfriend from San Diego. Monica Harris—Ralph Ochoa."

"From San Diego? That's my home, also." He sat down next to her and began the story of how he came to be in Monterrey.

Roberto said, "Pleasant to find you here this evening. May I sit down?"

"Please do," I said, with one eye on Paula, who apparently had made friends in the first row and was now chatting enthusiastically. She had covered the baby, asleep in his *carrito* next to her, with mosquito netting.

"Will you stay for the second film?" Roberto asked and sat down next to me.

"I really should go. I have classes to teach in the morning." I didn't say that I hadn't slept for thirty-six hours.

"Are you still working, then?" He asked it in a strange, almost critical, tone that I found irritating and judgmental.

"Of course. I must."

"And your husband—he is working also this summer, no?" Black eyes probed.

"Yes, he's in Texas working there." I was begining to get impatient, not sure if we should stay or insist we all go. By now, Monica was engrossed in conversation with Ralph. I could see that Paula was also having a good time.

"Why do you do it?" Roberto concentrated his look on me. "I mean work the way you do?"

"I have to. We have to live, after all."

"Everyone thinks it's a joke," Roberto added. "The way you work—and your baby just a few months old. They talk about it behind your back."

"What do you mean *a joke*? It's serious to me. It's serious to Len. We just have to sacrifice now for later."

"He doesn't sacrifice much," Roberto added sarcastically. "He's out on the town every night. Open your eyes; look around!"

I didn't speak or even look up. And I had that terrible feeling that I had at the baptismal party when I sensed how little optimism I could muster about life with Len. *What could this tall, rangy, unmarried, and childless bachelor know about anything?*

Together, we sat—Roberto, Jeanne, Monica, Ralph, and I—under the stars, foolish stars. Ralph, I noticed, kept his eye on Monica. He leaned back beside her, and I could tell he was ogling a slight opening in her blouse.

"What are you talking about?" I asked in a sedate voice, the best I could concoct in so short a time. "Len studies every night. And on top of that, he puts in long hours at the Green Cross."

"Green Cross?" Roberto laughed sarcastically. "What a joke! He may study, but he recovers at the *Copa de Oro*."

I stared at him. "*Copa*—"

"*De Oro*. It's a cantina near the center of town. Everyone there knows Leonardo. Ralph knows. He's there every night. The women are wild for him."

Copa de Oro.

"I don't believe you," I whispered, not wanting anyone to hear this outrageous accusation. "It's not true."

"I'll prove it to you. I'll take you there." He was surprisingly cheerful, yet behind his tone, there seemed to lurk a bitter sense of my frustration.

"You'll what?"

"I'll take you there this weekend. Look, don't you have family here or nearby?"

"No, besides it wouldn't make any difference." Something must have shifted in my voice.

"I'm sorry to be the one to tell you, but you ought to know," he warned.

His few stringent words blurred my feelings. I felt a rush of confusion and my heart pounded. The second feature, *Traición Total*, came on the screen.

I leaned over to Roberto and whispered in his ear, "What does it mean?"

"Total Betrayal," he answered.

Within minutes, the young heroine raged in a torrent of Spanish. I asked again, "What is she saying?"

Roberto translated, "Love is mercurial, unbridled, bestial."

Maybe I couldn't understand the Spanish words, but I grasped the meaning. After an hour or so of betrayal and gut wrenching emotional revenge, the movie ended. Lights came on. It was late, and now I wanted desperately to go home. I leaned over and tugged Monica toward me. I had the feeling that I had caught her in an unguarded moment: in a posture and frame of mind that was loaded with erotic possibilites. Ralph sensed it, too. There was no doubt; she was beguiled by him.

"Shall we leave?" It was really more of a statement than a question.

Monica gazed at me with big, hazel eyes that seemed to grow larger and greener in the light of the dangling lightbulb. Her whole face had changed. Before she could say a word, the rain came. The first drops were followed by a drenching tropical downpour. Soon, it was raining in all directions. Paula made a dash with the baby toward the car. Flustered and embarrassed, I turned to Roberto.

"Let's go!" I yelled. I cuddled Jeanne and scrambled to leave. Paula reached the car before we did. Roberto picked up the pile of paraphernalia on the bench. Ralph assisted Monica. We ran to the car, but I did not invite the men to get in.

So, Roberto stood there next to the car. His shirt stuck to his body, wet from the rain. However, he looked surprisingly composed. We settled into our seats. Roberto was flushed, his hair blown in loose dark curls. Reaching through the open window, I reclaimed the bundles of soggy, dripping blankets and pillows. On the other side, a car made a surprise turn just in front of us. Ralph dodged it.

I looked at Roberto straight on. "Len's not some frolicking clown," I insisted.

"This weekend, I'll take you and you'll see for yourself." Roberto was firm and confident enough to catch me off-guard.

"What's that all about?" Monica tuned in to the last comment.

"Roberto has invited us out, that's all," I answered her.

And then, turning to Roberto, I called out as I started to pull away. "All right. This weekend, then," my voice cracked. "Right now I've got to get us out of here."

Forked lightening struck a distant hilltop and there was enough of a flash to see the bulletin board near the entrance: *John Wayne, Rita Hayworth, Cary Grant, Grace Kelley.*

All I could think about was the *Copa de Oro.* I told myself that this was just another of those shaky moments that I had come to know in my fragile family life. It would pass.

Thanks to the storm blowing in, the hellish nightmare of Roberto's gossip had temporarily ended. *Gossip, that's all it is.* I navigated through honking cars and yelling motorists. Tired, wet, and sleepy, we headed for home. I needed to think this through. I needed to check out the story.

What I really wanted, just at that moment in the drenching downpour and muddy streets, was for time to accelerate. I wished that Len and I and the children were in some pleasant city in the States where he was a doctor practicing medicine. I wanted all of us to be living in a nice house, with enough money to buy real furniture, dishes that weren't cracked, and clothes for the kids, who would be happy and healthy. All I wanted, and all I had done in the last two years, was to enable that dream. Every action supported what I wanted to create—what I thought *we* wanted to create.

La Copa de Oro! It couldn't be true.

Thirty-one

Copa De Oro

The street entrance to the *Copa de Oro* opened down a cobbled alley, not far from the Ambassador Hotel. Never, before tonight, had I noticed the passage, much less the glaring sign on one side. The alley ended abruptly. And there, at the far end in the shadows, couples talked, squabbled, or even kissed. An unseen man snarled curses in the darkness. It must have been at least ten o'clock in the evening.

Roberto and I lingered at the stop sign, which marked the corner of the alley.

"Are you sure you want to go ahead with this?" he asked.

"Absolutely." I was determined to find out if what he had told me was true. Fear of the truth made me tense and nervous. It might be that Roberto had fooled me with his story—false words spoken, or perhaps he bore Len a grudge.

We waited for Monica and Ralph to catch up with us.

"Did you tell Ralph why we had come?"

"I said nothing. I spoke to no one about this, not to Ralph, not *anyone*."

In the interim, three other Americans overtook us, probably from Laredo and out for a wild time in Mexico. They also paused at the corner. One of them, a gangly cowboy wearing a large hat and tall ornamented boots, put his arm around his buddies and nodded down the alley.

"Down there. See it, fellas? *Copa de Oro*. That's the one."

The goggle-eyed man to his left patted his partner on the back. "Y'all say the Señoritas are great? Good as the dollies in Texas?"

"Just keep your boots on."

Behind us, an alley cat hissed. A trashcan crashed to its side, creating a cloud of dust. A shadow of an animal darted away.

The third cowboy—a thin, scraggly-looking man—said, "The mescal at that last place ain't bad, either." He whistled as the three of them turned down the street.

"Hombre, last time I was here . . ."

A ragged, potbellied child, squatting on the doorstep next to her mother, sidled toward them with her hand outstretched. The woman watched impassively and pulled a tattered shawl around her. She called the child back as the three Texans swaggered past them through the doorway.

From within, a woman's lusty voice sang a cloying, sweet melody in Spanish. Music overflowed into the street, and I felt the pounding percussion of Latin music. A large neon sign showed an overflowing shot glass. It glittered overhead. Vividly illumined by the artificial blaze, the entrance to *Copa de Oro* could not be missed.

I looked at Roberto for direction. He took my arm as our little procession entered a small, dark vestibule. Chinks of pale light from the cantina within shone dimly through a curtained entrance of plastic beads. Moving forward in the semi-darkness, I accidentally collided with an outward-bound customer. He gripped Roberto with both hands to steady himself. Roberto pulled himself free.

The inebriated man flourished his arm toward the entrance and parted the curtain. "Make way for the clientele," he lurched heavily toward the exit. In passing, he looked me in the eye and gasped, "Watch out, little lady, this place is a mantrap."

I pressed myself against the wall and the man staggered past me out into the street. Sweat ran down my spine.

Once inside, our little flock crowded around the bar until Ralph gestured to a waiter. No one paid attention. Roberto pointed off to one side and disappeared into the smoky haze. In just seconds, he whispered huskily as he found a place. "Psst. Gail, come here."

Flushed, I pushed my way through to a small, round table in a large room. Ralph and Monica followed behind. I took the chair next to Roberto. Overhead, colored lights shivered and then pulsed with the music: the rhythm of the night.

I glanced around and felt uneasy. The dance floor was large enough for ten or twenty couples, but tonight only three couples were on the floor. Upstairs, a balcony framed the second floor, and from behind closed doors came peals of laughter. In a corner just to our left, I noticed a group of American tourists. I felt better. Monica and I were not the only gringos, besides the Texans, in the place.

Small, yet creating a deafening din, the band consisted of piano, guitar, horn, and drums—nothing more. As they played, the shiny golden wood of the dance floor gleamed in the light, making the rest of the room appear dim. For just a moment, the music stopped. The piano player lit a cigarette.

I noticed that the Texans had scrambled ahead of us to get a table close to the dance floor and near the band. The tallest of the three, the one with the big cowboy hat, had sweat stains under his arms. Standing upright, he moved toward the stage and drawled, "*Tequila* for everybody," and motioned to the waiter.

The band started up again with a cha-cha. Simultaneously, the doors upstairs swung open. At least half a dozen pretty girls came down to the dance floor. They wore bright blouses, slinky skirts, or floral-patterned dresses. High heels clicked as they approached the men sitting alone or with a buddy. Some of the girls wore their hair severely pulled back; others let full, dark curls fall carelessly over their shoulders, down their backs. For just a moment, a fresh wave of strong perfume overcame the stale aroma of cigarette smoke, beer, and tequila as the giggling girls roamed the room.

An enchanting chatterbox with bobbed hair saw the big Texan. She smiled and undulated her hips at him.

Another girl with a jet-black bun pinned up at the nape of her head swooped down to a tourist at the table next to us. Her bangle bracelets jingled as she reached out toward him, "*¿Vamos a bailar, hombre?*"

The tourist grinned sheepishly and rose. With exaggerated grace, he took the *Señorita's* hand and they danced. The girl had gilded her eyelids and she blinked very slowly as she looked up at the man. Falcon-like, her black eyes grew larger.

A tray of shot glasses filled with tequila arrived at the table. Ralph stood up and held one of the glasses up toward the Texan.

"*Muchas gracias, Señores.*"

The Texan stood and tipped his hat in our direction.

Ralph proceeded to show Monica how to drink the shot of tequila. I watched how it was done.

"First salt, then lemon." He demonstrated putting a sprinkle of salt from his hand in his mouth and quickly sucked juice from the piece of lemon. "Now, the tequila!" He gulped the whole shot down. "Try it." He looked, first at her, and then around the table at me.

I mimicked him. At first, the liquid was surprisingly smooth, followed by a jolt. I almost lost my breath. Perhaps it was the salt and lemon, but the taste was not bad. I had tried Scotch once and this was infinitely better.

A rumba began. It was slow—both smooth and more sensuous—than the cha-cha.

Ralph looked at Monica. "Shall we?"

He rose and pulled out her chair. They began the slow, flirtatious dance. I watched out of the corner of my eye. I scrutinized the room, the women, and the long bar with dozens of bottles stacked down its full length.

The tourist, giggling and whispering to the falcon-eyed girl, returned to his table only a breath away from us. Odors of sweat, rum, tequila, and cigarettes permeated the thick air.

Another round of tequila appeared. Salt. Lemon. I picked up the small, smooth glass and drained the second shot. For just a second, my center of gravity was displaced, and then the room came back in focus. All I could think about was Len. My annoyance gave way to a grim curiosity. *Could it be true? Is this where he is every night?* I forced the thought away.

On the bandstand, a robust and brown-eyed tenor began to sing. Intense feeling curled around the edges of his voice.

"*Dame tu mano, Magdalena.*"

"Revolutionary Song," Ralph said. "Goes back to the days of Zapata."

I said nothing. Not a word. Instead, I ran my hand over the smooth, wooden table—now gritty to the touch from shelled peanuts and salt—and tapped to the beat of the music.

"It's about a peasant singing to his woman—they will fight together. They will probably die together," added Ralph.

The song went on—melancholy, passion, grief. Pictures came to my mind: bent men and brave women, real magic, bigger than life, and big enough to become a myth.

"But they are joined in sprit, and in soul, for freedom. She has a place in his heart, forever," Roberto interpreted for us.

Len has a place in my heart, a place that I also cherished. Sitting there, in the *Copa de Oro,* a memory of a not-so-long-ago spring evening flashed in my mind: with my arms around Len's neck, I teased with him to stay home. It had been a lovely night and I flirted outlandishly. It didn't work. He had his obligation to the Green Cross to keep, sick people to care for, and I was proud of him for his commitment. I'd stayed at home and nursed my cranky baby. I'd crouched on the floor with Jeanne and swapped gurgles. *All the while had he been here?*

"It is a fierce declaration of love," Ralph looked at Monica. As the song ended he shifted closer to her.

The audience applauded fervently, followed by yells and pandemonium. The Texans screeched louder than anyone. The singer turned to the crowd.

"*¿Amor, otra del amor?*"

"*Sí, sí Señor.*" They clamored, "*¡Canta del amor!*"

The crowd quieted down.

The tenor accommodated and sang of love, strumming his guitar as the band blended seductive rhythms with his plaintive wail.

"Another Revolutionary song?" I asked.

"No," Roberto jumped in the conversation. "This is a love song. He sings of an evening at the seashore, sun setting, bodies warm."

"Oh, the sea. I miss it so," I moaned. "I grew up by the Pacific Ocean." *If I could just see the ocean again, everything would fall in place.*

Sad-eyed, Roberto looked at me and said, "I also grew up near the sea in Costa Rica."

" . . . *Siempre amor.*" The song was a temporary tonic. Seductive.

The cash register rang. Roberto's eyes strayed toward the bar. Tactfully, he swiveled around in my direction and then whispered, "See that girl over there?"

A buxom brunette sat on a tall stool against the bar. When she noticed that Roberto was eyeing her, she whirled her legs around so that she faced us directly. She flicked her eyes back at Roberto, smiled, and nodded a greeting. Large dimples gave her a cherubic look.

Roberto said, "That's one of Len's girlfriends."

I pretended not to look. I wished we hadn't come. However, my eyes returned to look at her over and over again. She wore large, turquoise pendant earrings and a black lace blouse, cut low. A tight-fitting skirt accentuated her curves.

"Who is she? What is her name?"

"Does it matter?" Roberto said coolly.

"It does to me. I want to know," I said firmly. I could feel the tequila. My head was spinning.

"Florinda, I believe." He said casually.

"So, you know her name. You come here often?"

"No, not often. Just once in a while with friends. Why not?" I retorted, "Why not?"

"It's not really my kind of place," he added.

"Not mine, either." I glanced back at Florinda.

She had a charm—a kind of earthy, robust charm—with eyes like amber glass, a sudden laugh, and a wide smile. The combination of these details—her curvaceous, plump body; dark, curly hair; and high, glossy cheek bones—reminded me of a tourist poster with a smiling face that said, "Visit México."

"Let's dance," said Roberto. I followed him to the dance floor.

Now, the music changed. The band played a Mexican polka—a slower, smoother version of the German dance I had grown up with. I took his hand and we zigzagged easily across the floor. By now, Florinda had a partner, and when the music ended we found ourselves in the middle of the dance floor, next to her.

She recognized Roberto. "*¿Dónde está el Americano?*" she asked coquettishly with hands on swaying hips.

Roberto was playing "cat and mouse" with her. I could feel it. "*¿Quién?*"

"*Leonardo, por supuesto. Leonardo.*"

"*Creo que el está in Texas.*"

"*Aye, que lástima, me gusta mucho bailar con el.*" She glanced at me and then back at Roberto, and in a bright, saucy manner said, "*Su amiga es linda, ella.*"

He looked at me. "*Sí, ella es muy linda.*"

Over his shoulder, I could see our reflection in the long mirror over the bar. The mirror looked to be very old and created a slightly distorted image. I could see the dance hall, the band, and Ralph and Monica. Bar girls and tourists twisted in the mirror. At his table, one of the Texans waved madly.

"Somebody bring us a beer! *Carta Blanca* with lemon." He stood up and staggered around the table. "Anybody else?" A chair tipped over as he bent his flushed face down to pull a bill from his boot.

"Loudmouths, ruffians," someone roared.

The Texan waved a hundred-peso note as a waiter scurried to accommodate him. Florinda sauntered toward the band. Four-inch heels exaggerated her slow, swaying walk. Black stockings with long black seams traced up plump calves and finally disappeared under her daringly short skirt, which gave form to her undulating body. Florinda whispered something to the bandleader and then slid seductively away.

Face-to-face with Florinda and hearing her ask about Len had left me feeling outraged. Now, standing quite still in the middle of the floor, I had innocently shambled into the limelight. The Texan's faded-blue eyes spied me.

"Wanna' drink?"

I backed away awkwardly and turned away from him. I did not want to attract attention. As the lights flickered, Roberto grabbed my arm and pulled me back to our table.

It was true! It was all true.

Monica asked, "What was that girl saying to you?"

"She knows Len."

Monica's eyes opened wide. "Oh? Really?"

I felt as if my senses were honed and heightened. Survival guide for visiting *gringos*: tequila, sal, limón. Cha-Cha–Cha. Nothing made sense, yet my instincts kept me restrained and strangely composed. The music played on.

By now, the dance floor was packed. The tempo picked up; feet stomped.

"*¡La Bamba!*" someone yelled, and dancers rushed to the floor. They danced like revelers on the edge of a volcano. Throbbing movement, pulsation, drums, guitar.

My spirits crumpled. It was past midnight. Now hatless and flushed, one of the Texans beckoned to Florinda.

"C'mon over here, Shugah."

Her curves reflected in the long mirror. With a merry twinkle in her eye, she turned her back to him. "*Borracho,*" she uttered under her breath.

"Let's go," said Roberto, "I've had enough of this place." He pulled me to my feet. I was trembling. My legs wobbled as I headed for the door. I took a deep breath. *Just keep going.* I reached the door. *There were things that had to be done in the morning—the children, breakfast, other things.*

"Well, what did you think of *Copa de Oro?*" Roberto asked as we turned out of the alley into the street.

"I think it's not the Green Cross," I said.

In my mind, I had made a quick sketch of Florinda—mouth slightly open, face upturned, and liquid eyes that said "yes" in rumba time.

The streets were empty. Everything was inky black. Our car was parked down a maze of pathways, and as we reached it, a warm June breeze rippled in the air. The dark town seethed with music from the cantina.

Fumbling, Ralph opened the car door and I climbed in next to Roberto who sat behind the wheel. The others got in back. We drove for some time in silence. It was clear to me that much more than a Saturday night at the *Copa de Oro* was over.

I'll get through this. I must not cry. I must not panic.

We sped by landscapes polluted with smokestacks and steel mills. All I could think about was Len's ability to lie, fake, and perform. *Was everything a lie?*

One good omen—a sliver of a moon rose over the deep ravines and grotesque hills. Not that the evening had been a total disaster—far from it; I had learned how to drink tequila. I promised myself that I would not rationalize my conduct or feel guilty for the night's adventure.

From the back seat came the murmuring conversation of Ralph and Monica, but I didn't listen. Every turn of the river road held memories. I played the night at the *Copa* over in my head.

And the appalling rumors and the gossip. What would people think of me? Neglected yet dignified? Young and stupid?

Private betrayal was bad enough, but what Len had done was so blatantly public.

I wonder who knows.

Julie. She was trying to warn me. And Zack—he knows, too.

His remark about too much time at the Green Cross made that clear. It also meant that he probably went to the Copa, also.

Did the Sabbies know? Did they talk about these things?

Mortified, I couldn't speak. It was atrociously hot. Beyond the river, summits merged into a towering wall as the jagged, unending ridge of the Sierra Madres Oriental, a barrier of rocky darkness, entrapped my children and me in this godforsaken place.

Thirty-two

Capablanca Makes His Moves

I slept through until noon. Paula was taking care of the babies for me—my one bit of good fortune. It was too late to go to church. I could not forget the previous night. A ferocious headache, exacerbated by waves of nausea, only intensified the memory. Nevertheless, several variables warranted investigation. Most straightforward was our savings account; more complex was my relationship with Len.

Sitting on the bed, I held the old shoe box that held our important documents. And finally, having held my head and wallowed in my discomfort, I untied the black cord that clinched it all together. Light came in through the window, dusting the box and bouncing off the metal bed frame. The light felt harsh and raw.

I took out my passport and laid it to one side. I removed Lenny's elaborate Mexican birth certificate. There were some transcripts and our marriage certificate. At the bottom of the box, I found the bankbook, opened it, and checked the tiny print.

Withdrawals:
Pesos 500   *1/28/1956*
Pesos 800   *2/22/ 1956*
Pesos 600   *3/27/1956*

Pesos	500	4/7/1956
Pesos	500	5/2/1956
Pesos	700	5/24/1956
Pesos	800	6/8/1956
Pesos	500	6/12/1956

A total of 5,000 pesos, or the equivalent of ten months rent, had been taken out of our account. I was stunned. I had never bothered to check. We had agreed that those funds were for emergency only. *What could he have done with that much?*

The shock of what I had discovered rendered me incapable of feeling for some time. I knew that part of the money had gone for German medical instruments that Len needed. Another portion went for the trip to Houston.

Feeling exhausted, I held the picture of Len when he left for Texas—smiling, arms open. *The rest of our cash on the Copa de Oro? On the girls and rounds of drink?* I swallowed down my tears. The thought that Len had spent sorely needed money on Florinda and rum burned in my brain.

I had been willing to strive or suffer uncertainty and insecurity for our dream, but I was not willing to support the fantasy of the Green Cross. I felt foolish. I had not seen what was going on under my very nose.

Fear and shame gripped me, jolted me. As I thought it through, I realized that I was beginning to know who I was at my core. Instinctively, I wanted to leave, but the Church said "no." I had to stick it out.

For me, this went beyond total compromise. It was subservience. Was my life's journey a relentless struggle with the nature of power?

Technicolor pictures of the smoky dancehall—voluptuous, slightly grotesque figures of Florida and the girls—flashed in my mind. This was not why I had come to Mexico. I wanted my children to thrive and flourish, to have a father who paid attention to their needs and to mine. I threw the bankbook into the box and retied the string.

I didn't break into hysterical weeping.

Desperate and bewildered, I knew that I had to go to work the next day, put on a cheery face, and be energetic and interesting. Paula peeked in. Realizing that I was not well, she tiptoed away and took the children downstairs for lunch and later, outdoors for an outing.

As the day wore on, thoughts of home filled me with longing. I was hungry for the canyons of San Diego, the lemon groves, and the vitality of spring with the aroma of citrus blossoms. I missed the avocado trees rooted on sloping hillsides. I wanted to watch the brushfires from the porch of my grandfather's house, to abandon myself into the shiny, blue sea. I glanced out the window.

Oh, Len, how could you?

The *colonia* was curiously bright in the late afternoon sunlight. This was one of the oppressive, white-hot days peculiar to *Nuevo Leon*. Such days came in a row with sudden evening showers, which left little rivers of mud by the front door and crushed tropical leaves strewn in the verandah. My mind expanded and floated, bending and losing shape. I was in a mixed-up world of babies and students, charades and lies.

The doorbell rang. Through the window, I saw Roberto waiting on the step in front. He was neatly dressed and clean-shaven. I went down and let him enter.

"What are you doing here?" I asked.

He lingered at my front door—squinting and smiling and tapping his long fingers against the door frame. "You were not at Mass this morning," he hesitated and gestured upward with his hands. "You're always there and I wondered—"

I looked at him, surprised that he had noticed me in church. "Just a bad headache. I'm not used to drinking."

"No, of course not." He went on, "Just wanted to pay my respects."

"Well, come in, then."

I led him into the living room, ushering him to the sofa. In the kitchen, I poured two cups of Nescafé, arranged cookies on a glass dish, and took everything out on a woven tray from the *mercado*. Then, I settled onto the chair opposite him and waited to hear the purpose of his visit.

"I can see you're deeply upset," he picked up his coffee.

"Time I woke up," I admitted. Words came hard.

"So, you're all right then?"

"I'm so disappointed at the way things are turning out," I replied. "It's like a chess game. You plan, make some moves, and you miss something." I nodded at the chessboard on the side table.

"You play?"

"I try," I said. I could see he was reluctant to leave.

"Let's play, then."

It might be good to have something to distract me, even if for an hour. Paula had taken the children for a walk. I had nothing else to do. I sipped my coffee from a thick, white, restaurant-style cup I found at the *mercado*. The cup had chips on the rim, and I twisted it gently in my hand to avoid the cracks. Swallowing warm coffee, I watched as Roberto set up the chessboard. With a pawn in each hand, he held closed fists out in front of him. I tapped the right fist, feeling the slight tingling of his electricity. He opened his hand. I saw the white piece.

I groaned, "Offensive, not my best game."

We played in silence. I didn't tell him that the pictures of last night had reappeared in an endless sequence all day long. I didn't tell him that I saw my future and that of my children colored drab. Nor did I tell him how I longed to have those images cut out of my memory forever. I had done everything that was required of me, but inside, I knew a time was over. Everything had changed.

Roberto easily won the first game.

"I'd like to try again. I play a better defensive game."

"Where did you learn to play?" he asked.

"I've been teaching myself from books. All this spring, I've been playing and replaying Capablanca's tournament games from a book."

"Capablanca, the Cuban?"

"World Champion. Why not learn from the best?"

I didn't tell him about those tortured nights when I couldn't sleep or read and how chess had absorbed my attention. Capablanca had become a close friend.

Roberto set up the board again. "Ready?"

"Why do you look at me so strangely?" I asked as if he had some intuitive sense of my emotional state. I noticed that my nausea had abated.

"Let's play." He ignored the question.

"Your move," I said, feeling both watchful and wary with my body immobilized, but my mind active, stretching, and imagining.

He moved his queen's pawn.

I must concentrate. "And so," I countered with an identical move.

This time I played carefully. There was no special hurry. Evening filled the great bowl of the valley, and drifting shadows of clouds cast images on the living-room floor. My nerves were still on edge, yet I was determined not to make any hasty decisions. *Work the knights. Keep them toward the center. That's how Capablanca makes his moves. Keep centered.*

I forced myself to focus. It had grown dark since we had started to play. My throbbing headache had gone away. And this time, I won easily and with style.

"Well done," he said. As he sat there in front of me, he held his fallen king in one hand. "Admirably done, in fact."

I smiled for the first time in hours. *"Muchas gracias, Señor."*

"May I invite you for dinner sometime this week? I'd like to show you something else of Monterrey, of Latin culture."

"You mean as an antidote to last night?"

"I can see how you might feel that way," he answered and laughed softly. Then, his expression became serious. "I shouldn't have taken you there. It was a mistake."

"On the contrary," I picked up the chess pieces and slowly put them in the box, one by one. "I confess: our little visit to the cantina has clarified certain things to an amazing degree."

"Please, come to dinner with me. It will be different. I promise."

I hesitated. Matrimonial scruples held me back. And then I remembered Florinda.

"All right, then. I would like to have dinner with you, Roberto."

Paula opened the front door. Jeanne stood behind her holding an ice cream cone.

"*Chocolate, Mamá,*" she said. Ice cream dribbled down her chin and the front of her pink sunsuit. Paula looked at me, then at Roberto. I said nothing.

৯

We are who we think we are. Or so it seemed to me in the unfolding picture that summer in Mexico when I found myself alone and unfettered. Luísa returned from her visit home and I had two maids to do chores and help with the kids. Nevertheless, I was uneasy. Len had not written since the first postcard, and that was over six weeks ago. I wasn't sure if he was alive or dead.

And so, three nights later, on a hot July night, I found myself sitting next to Roberto as we drove southwest out of the *colonia*—a little farther on where the city ended abruptly and the highway skirted a stretch of green, listless countryside. Breaks of sugarcane, thorny fields, and *ranchitos* whizzed by. I told myself that, at long last, I was a free and independent being. I could be anything I wanted to be.

Where the road made a sharp turn to leave the highway, there stood a little restaurant. Concealed behind a dense, high screen of shrubbery, it promised seclusion—a quiet place to meet and talk.

We left the car. As we followed a narrow path, an old-fashioned street lamp marked the entry. We walked toward it, entered, and followed the attendant—a small man with a gravel voice and stooped back. He held a lit candle as he ushered us through a maze of narrow pathways between towering hedges that had been trimmed to form a series of charming little cubicles. Velvety, carnivorous darkness swallowed us.

At the end of a long corridor, we turned abruptly into one of the geometrical squares. A high thicket enclosed the private table, which was covered with a white cloth and neatly set with local pottery. Beneath a canopy of intertwined tropical vines, a hint of a breeze fluttered.

The waiter pulled back my seat, "*Señorita, por favor.*"

"I wonder, do tourists know this place?"

"Unlikely to find any here," said Roberto. "This is mostly a favorite for locals."

Without waiting for the waiter to say anything, Roberto gave orders. Within minutes, the dinner slowly began to unfold. Delicious dishes of Northern Mexico—*enchiladas verdes con crema, arroz, refritos*—appeared almost magically. Unseen musicians played in the background. Poignant strains of guitar floated on the night air.

I sat across from Roberto, feeling my own heart's strong, quiet beat. The dense thicket all around us gave me the impression of being in a forest castle.

He leaned over and asked me more about my life and myself. We finally got around to the topic of Leonard.

"Why did you marry him?" he asked.

"My mother introduced us and I felt that gave him the stamp of approval."

"An arranged marriage, then?"

"Oh, no; far from it. Len worked as an X-ray technician at Mercy Hospital and so did my mother. I had just won a full scholarship to a Catholic college in San Diego, and I got a job for the summer at the hospital, also."

"What happened then?" he seemed to be genuinely interested.

I was flattered by his attention and I went on, "We went out and I was overcome by the glamour of it all. Although, at one point, I remember telling him I wanted to break it off."

"Why?"

"His lifestyle was so different from mine. I was a devout Catholic and Len liked to party. He lived on the fast track. All the girls at the hospital had a crush on him."

"Why did you finally marry him?"

"I let him make love to me. I didn't want to. I was afraid, but he pressured me all the time. It was, after all, a mortal sin according to the Church. He said I was selfish. I finally gave in. And then, after we did it, I thought I had to marry him. It was the right thing to do."

"Oh, God, no. That's why you married him? For sex?"

"Not for sex. Because I *had* sex with him before marriage. I thought I had to go through with it, you see. I was raised a Catholic."

"So was I, but still—"

"Then, you know the story. The Church takes a dim view of sex—original sin, Eve, the Garden of Eden. Sex is only acceptable within the bonds of marriage. So, I gave in and I married him. Does that make any sense?"

"Some sense, but you're an American. You don't come from a Catholic country. I thought—"

"Then there was Len's personality—bigger than life—and the allure of his smile. I was always happy at the beginning, euphoric. Len can sway and inspire and dominate others with his charm. I felt blessed that he had chosen me."

"You appear so independent. Wasn't it difficult to give up your freedom?" His questions unsettled me.

"Yes, but then I got caught up in the fantasy. Len has an obsession with medicine. It got to the point that I would have done anything to make him love me and make it all work."

"Why does he stay with you?"

"I think he clings to me because my faith in him holds him together. Leonard needs love, submission, and protection. We left San Diego so he could have his dream."

"And then you came here?"

"Then I came here."

"So this thing with Len and the girl—it hurts you?"

"Yes, of course, but isn't that the way Latin men behave? I mean the way Len did? Don't they have their affairs and their *casa chica?*" I went on to tell him about María Elena and her nephews and about May Hinajosa and Pepe.

"It may appear that way to you. But Latinos take marriage seriously. They put family first. It is the husband's duty to provide for his wife and family, to put a roof over the head, to put bread on the table."

"I have all that," I said.

"Yes, but you are doing the providing. That's the difference."

"It seemed like a noble cause." Tears welled up in my eyes.

"You are very young to be both father and mother." He looked at me long and hard.

"I'll be twenty-one next week," I said.

"You deserve much more. I don't mean to be condescending. I speak what is true. If you were my woman, I would see to it that you had a beautiful plantation. You deserve more."

"The nuns at school used to tell us that nothing was too good for us."

"What will you do?"

"Stay here, at least for now. I have nowhere else to go."

"Have you ever thought of Costa Rica?" His expression was serious and mindful.

"Tell me about your country."

And so he spoke of Costa Rica, of the rain forests, the hundreds of kinds of orchids, and of the volcano that was still active. He told me he wanted to return there and set up practice.

As it turned out, the evening was a delight for both of us. It was filled with tears and laughter. Having a charming man to talk with about secret, private matters lanced the hurt inside, a little. His love of nature and of beauty resonated with my own deep love of the same.

I asked Roberto about his life and he said, "When I go home, I will be a plastic surgeon. Rich people from the States will come down for face lifts, nose jobs, things like that. They have money to spend. Then, with all that money, I can build a clinic, and with the dollars help my own people. That is my plan."

"So, you'll specialize, then?"

"Yes, I'll go to the States or to France, but in the end, I want to go to Costa Rica. I'd love to show you my country."

"I'll see it sometime. I know I will." Only, I knew it would not be with him.

"I want to live close to nature," he said. "We are close to nature here, no? I thought you would like it."

"It is a wonderful place, so exotic, so private. And the food is excellent." I felt alive again. I felt that there was still so much in the world to explore and enjoy. I would find a way to stick myself back into that world and find my place.

Roberto took my hand. He was a tall, striking man with large penetrating brown eyes. He had a careful, almost regal, bearing. His hands were beautiful with long, slender fingers. Most of all, he was an attentive. The descriptions of Costa Rica fascinated me. I could almost see cloud forests in the mountains and hear the howler monkeys in the treetops. By almost imperceptible increments, I relaxed in his company.

Hours passed. We lingered. Neither of us wanted to call it a night and we talked past midnight. Finally, the place was closing. We had to leave.

I clung to his arm as I followed Roberto through the tangle of passageways until we came to a battered, wooden door that led to the exit. The opening was narrow and I accidentally rammed my shoulder against it, and in the darkness I stumbled into Roberto. His first reaction was to catch me. I looked up and pressed my open lips upon his and twined my arms around his neck.

"I want this night to last forever." I sank into his arms; I wanted to be held.

"So do I," he said and took my hand. We drove to his place. It would be pointless to waste such a night.

៊

Over the next few weeks, my attitude about all things Latino improved enormously. Paula knew something was going on, yet said nothing. If anything, she behaved even more tenderly toward the children. For all she knew, my husband had left me.

Monica was dating Ralph. This, plus her desire to know more of the life in Monterrey, absorbed her attention. Discreetly, she never mentioned the night at the *Copa*.

Roberto and I met at his place, the outdoor theater, and once even made an outing to *Collo de Caballo*—the beautiful horsetail falls south of the city. There were mysterious and clandestine meetings in the neighborhood, or downtown coffee shops. We both knew it couldn't last.

"I never planned this," he said.

"Neither did I," I responded.

It was summer and we had time to ourselves. I felt safe with him. I was grateful to May Hinajosa for her tips on birth control and I felt strangely exuberant, liberated for the first time in my life from both physical, as well as religious, constraints.

But it couldn't last.

Thirty-three

Total Betrayal

Minutes, hours, days, weeks—the dog days of August came and went. All the while, a white heat spread over the city and into the *colonia*. No word from Len. Not a letter, not a telegram. I was kept busy by a sudden spate of new students at the *Instituto*. One morning, while I sat waiting for a student at a café, my eyes fell on an advertisement. "House for rent. *Calle Estados Unidos*." I rushed to see it. The owner who opened the door told me that he had been helping in the building project. His face looked battered and distorted; his clothes were covered with plaster. It was a lovely, big house with maids' quarters for Paula and Luísa on the flat roof, which was reached by outdoor stairs. I wrote a check immediately and began to move our few things up the hill into the almost-finished house a week later.

On my last day of teaching for the Institute, I met Señor Hernandez at the terrace of the Ambassador Hotel. It was early, but tourists and locals were rushing in for morning coffee or an American-style breakfast.

"You will be missed," he said. "If you ever want to come back, you know—"

"I know, and I appreciate your solicitude. This possibility of having legal papers, for me and for my daughter, is just too

264

important to pass up. My son, of course, is a *Regiomontano*. No problem there."

"And your husband? He is doing well?"

"Frankly, I don't know. I haven't heard a word all summer. He must be very busy."

"*Carramba*," Señor Hernandez uttered under his breath.

"He'll be home soon, I'm sure of that. School starts in a week."

"Yes, of course," he said.

"Thank you for everything." I took his hand, not caring what people might say.

"You mean a great deal to me."

I knew he meant it and that I'd been wise in keeping a distance.

⚜

Hellish heat simmered for weeks. It was on one hot Saturday afternoon early in September that I was sitting on the floor of our new home. The living room was drenched with light and saturated with the sun. I loved to work in the light. I unpacked—unmatched dishes and Mexican pottery from the *mercado*, ice chest for a refrigerator, hot plate for a stove, a few pots and pans. On the walls, I tacked a list of items to get, clippings, and appointments.

It was almost monastic, with no finery, no decorations. Simplicity, plainness. White walls and shiny, tiled floors. The house was furnished with only the basics—beds, cribs, Len's desk from the flea market. And a pile of books topped with a somber, human skull. It was there that Len found me. Heat and dust aside, it was destined to be a volatile reunion.

Len looked through the screen door and peered in. His voice intruded, "Gail?"

My heart pounded, but I didn't want to show that I was nervous. I didn't want to give him power. The door flew open and he erupted into the house. I reached for a stack of books. He barely set foot in the cool entrance hall when he saw me. His face was red; he was breathing hard.

"What's been going on here?" he shouted and walked closer. He looked around the unfamiliar space.

"Just life as usual," I replied. I picked up the skull and placed it next to one of the books. I sat back on my heels and looked up at him.

"I know all about you," Len roared. "Ralph told me everything."

"Ralph?" *He must have put it all together.*

"I just ran into him at the school. He told me everything."

"And just what is *everything*?" I tried to remain poised and calm. I didn't want to give him the upper hand. I didn't want to collapse.

"It's obvious that you're not the girl I thought you were." His voice had gone harsh.

"In what way, Len? In what way? Please be specific." I felt cool, calm.

"I'm talking about you and Roberto. Right out in the open. You never even tried to hide it."

"You mean like you hide things?" I shrugged and rearranged a book from one shelf to the next.

"How could you?" Len stared at me. Perspiration dripped from his face.

"No," I retorted, "how could *you?* I also know everything. I know about the Green Cross."

"What in God's name are you talking about?" He feigned innocence.

"I mean about all those long nights at the Green Cross. Don't you remember? Civic duty—what a joke!"

He changed his tone and growled, "Did you believe that story that I told you? You're really stupid, aren't you?"

"No," I fought back, "not stupid. I just made the mistake of trusting you. I won't do it again. As far as what you did, I consider it total betrayal."

"Do you love him?" Len leaned over me, hands on his hips, his face close to mine.

I looked up. "Who?"

"Roberto. Do you love him?"

"What nonsense. Now, you're being stupid. He was just a diversion," I lied. Roberto was my private passion and not to be shared. "Do you love Florinda? She has such adorable dimples, don't you think?"

He choked. "What? What are you saying?" An uneasy fear flitted across his face.

"I went there, Len. *La Copa De Oro.* Nice place. I know about Florinda and the girls and your nights out. I know about your bar bills. Please move." I pushed him aside. "I have to unpack." I glanced around the sun-filled room and pulled another box toward me. I wanted revenge. He needed to be punished. Only revenge would balance the scales.

"You and your religion. A good Catholic girl like you?" he asked, his eyes now popping with alarm. Apparently, he had not expected me to confront him.

He doesn't know me at all. Never took the time.

I took my time thinking deeply. "If I weren't a good Catholic girl, I wouldn't be here at all. You're probably just jealous of the fun I've been having. I sincerely hope your summer in Houston was hell."

"You certainly know how to hurt, don't you?"

"I'm learning." I wanted to hurt him. However, I wasn't sure I could. I thought he was impervious.

"You call yourself a Catholic!" he shouted and waved his hands in the air wildly.

"Why don't you go talk to the priest about being Catholic? He's just up the hill and I know he'd love to see you, at last." I automatically resumed my task and pulled some extra large books out of the box.

"I'll do just that. And I'll go see your boyfriend, too."

"*Como quieres*," I said, indifferently. *As you wish.*

"Don't speak to me in Spanish." He glanced around the house and down the empty corridor. "Where are the kids?"

"At the other house with Paula. Still too hot. We have air-conditioning there. Lenny's starting to crawl and Jeanne can get up and down the stairs. Oh, yes—Monica's here. She'll be staying with us this year."

He retraced his footsteps to the door adding, "Ralph told me more."

"More? What more did Ralph have to say?" I stood up and looked him square in the eyes.

"One night last spring he came to practice his piano and you went into the bedroom."

"So?"

"You probably wanted him to follow. You tried to seduce him."

I faced him down and said, "Ralph is a fool."

"He said you went to bed. You wanted him to follow."

"That was the night Lenny was born, you stupid man." I whacked his face with all my strength. I wanted to do more. If I were a man, I would have knocked him out. My whole body was trembling. I felt as if my knees would buckle. "Only an ignorant egomaniac would think a woman about to go into labor wanted him. What arrogance! *Sin verguenza.*" *Shameless.* My capacity for violent rage took me by surprise.

Len stepped backward. I watched him rub his face, slam the door, and leave. I hoped he would stay away a long, long time. It was his turn to suffer, to doubt, to fear.

He could have made our lives better, but he didn't. Where did my loyalty lie? With Len? With my babies?

ॐ

The afternoon sun was still high when Len apparently made his way to the refectory next to Our Lady of Lourdes. He said that Father Moreno met him at the door and showed him into the office adjacent to the church.

"So, what's bothering you?" the priest asked him. "You look like a man who needs attention. How can I help?"

Len answered, "It's my wife."

"What has happened?"

Len spoke at length and added, "I married her because there was nothing of the cheap, the common, the vulgar about her. She was so refined and intelligent. But now—"

Father Moreno heard him out and said, "You mean to say that you left your wife and two babies alone, in a country like this, *hombre*? Are you crazy? Incredible."

Backing away from the priest's accusing stare, Len stammered, "But Father, I was working in the States."

The priest raised his voice, "Your wife finds work here. Why can't you?"

"I got a good deal at the hospital in Houston, got lots of experience. Made a little money, too."

I knew that hot and windowless office. A faint smell of incense always lingered about the place. Wooden cabinets stood along the wall where tiny grills revealed that they held Church instruments—polished chalices gleaming in the dim light.

Father Moreno said to Len, "Of course, you sent money home—to her, to the family?"

"No, I was broke. For one week, I lived on crackers and water."

"Very heroic, but was that wise?"

"How do you mean, Father?"

"Your career plans are more important than your family. Don't you know what kind of country this is? It was insane to leave a young woman like your wife here alone."

Len began shuffling back and forth. He looked down at his shoes. "I went to see the man, Roberto. Do you know what he said?"

"Tell me, my son."

"He said that she never uttered a word about me. Didn't seem to care. Roberto thought it was all over between us. The guy was sweating when he told me," Len muttered. "He said she could go to Costa Rica and he'd make arrangements."

"So, you have a way out," the priest said flatly. "Then you could concentrate on medicine."

"She can't go! She belongs to me!"

Then Len waited for the priest to answer. I can picture Father Moreno positioning himself directly in front of Len and looking him squarely in the face.

"Go home to your wife and promise to be a good husband." He would have made sure Len was paying attention. Here is what reached through to Len: "This is your fault, not hers. She is very young. I've seen her at church and at your son's baptism. You have an obligation, Leonardo. Promise me you will do this."

Len was surprised at the priest's response.

"I don't know. She made a fool out of me." This would have been so difficult for Len, and I can envision his face reddening at that point.

Drawing himself up, I imagine Father Moreno looked very dignified. He insisted, "Is this asking too much for your family? For God?"

"What about her? Look what she's done."

"It's the rest of your life that's at stake. Don't you still care?"

"I care," Len answered.

"Anyone can make a mistake, Son. The highest law is to forgive and to love. Hurt feelings are the past. The loving heart is the future. There are certain things you have to let go of—when you're married, that is." When Father Moreno stared into someone's eyes, it always bored into the heart as well. Len said he felt a look of concentrated fire.

"Promise."

"I promise," Len said. Dumfounded, he left Lourdes and Father Moreno, then headed home.

₲

The afternoon melted away, and within a few hours, I was dragging the last few boxes into the bedroom. I heard the front door open. Footsteps echoed down the tiled corridor.

"Hello, I'm back." It was Len. Dejected, he slumped into a chair. The spare, menacing behavior of just a few hours ago was gone.

"You look troubled," I folded a sheet over the bed.

"So do you," he responded.

It was obvious that Len had been undone at his meeting with the priest. I listened, astonished, as Len told the story, wondering how many times Father Moreno had to give this talk to men of the parish.

Later that night, he sat on the bed next to me and mulled over the words that the priest had said. He cried and took me in his arms. Then, I cried. The room was silent.

I had never seen Len like this, a red-faced, weeping man. I was taken aback. I frankly didn't think that he cared.

"Nobody knows the right answers," he whispered. He rubbed his eye where I had hit him.

"I couldn't agree more."

"But I want to try. Give me another chance," he pleaded and put his face in his hands.

"All right," I said, "let's try again." I took a step backward.

Recovering himself, a fragile smile flickered on his face. After sharing a furtive kiss, he added, "I wish there was something I could do to change all of this."

He kissed me again and I knew there was no turning back. I didn't turn away, nor did I move into his open arms. I felt like a wrung-out sponge.

As the weeks passed, we returned to our usual routine. I wrote to Roberto and told him of my decision to stay with Len and try to honor the marriage vows that I had made, no matter the circumstances. As a token of our reconciliation, Len occasionally attended church with me on Sunday.

☙

One night after Len returned, I stopped by to see Julie Monsour. I hadn't seen as much of her since Zack got out of jail after the accident. She was sulky about something. As it turned out, she had been quarreling with Zack.

"Can you believe I lived in this place and didn't feel it? Zack has a mistress. Not that silly girl at the *Copa*—someone else. He's got her an apartment, a *casa chica*."

Julie's voice was low. I noticed that her left eyelid—puffy, bluish and swollen—had been daubed with makeup to cover the discoloration. The walls, dry and thick, seemed to push in on us as we sat in the dining room where we had been so many times before. It was a large room. But that night, hot, close air imprisoned us. "Some men are not cut out to be husbands," she said.

"*Amant en titre*," I added. "Born lovers, as the French say. Personally, I want both."

"Impossible." She looked at me with slow eyes. "Idealize all you want, but shun denial. *Mentiras, mentiras, mentiras*." Lies, lies, lies. There was a mocking bitterness in her voice.

"The balance goes too far in their direction," I said. "It's as if life says their hours are more valuable; their minutes count for more. Somebody's got to see through it."

"What's to be done?" she asked and then answered herself. "Nothing."

"Can I help you?"

"Just having you listen eases the pain." She looked down at her hands, "I'm going away."

The kitchen door opened softly. It was the maids. An elderly woman loosely and bulkily wrapped in a serape was crying. "Señora?" she whispered. The younger woman, also crying, stood behind her and glanced over her shoulder at us.

"*Déjame*," Julie said in a scarcely audible voice. *Leave me*. The door closed. We heard sobbing beyond the door. "They've been with me from the beginning," Julie whispered and paused. "You'll be all right," she said. "There's a kind of strength about you. No matter what comes along, you'll roll with it. You won't go under."

"Sometimes I feel like I've been trapped in a snare. I can't quite understand it."

"My mother used to say 'a chain of flowers is the hardest to break.' I feel like I have to tear through it," she said, "rip it apart." After a few minutes, she reached into the pocket in her skirt. "By the way, this is for you." She handed me a note. "It's from Roberto. He's really quite smitten with you. Wears his heart on his sleeve."

I unfolded the paper and read:

Querida,

    So, Leonardo is back. I saw him. I told him you could go to Costa Rica, I would take care of it. He flew into a rage. Amor, he does not deserve you, but I understand that you want to keep your marriage vows, and I honor you all the more for it. Still, I think you are making a mistake. I am here if you need or want me. Mi casa es tu casa, siempre,

                Roberto

    Never forget, nothing is too good for you.

"Thank you for this." I showed her the note.

"So, you're playing with fire?" Julie threw her hands up.

"Aren't you, Julie?"

"I'm going home to my parents. In twenty years, I don't want to say 'well at least I survived my marriage.' That's not enough." Abruptly, she turned her head, but not before I saw a look of anguish. She continued, "Empty dreams, empty words, empty futures."

I stared at her, too surprised at her words to make any reply.

"At least at home, you'll have your family. The protection of your parents."

She looked into my eyes, "Haven't you thought about it? Going home?"

"I don't have the option of going home. My Dad's broke; my mom's inaccessible. As it is, I feel I have to stay with Len. After all, I married him in the Church. If I did try to leave him while I live in Mexico, I'm sure I'd lose my children. Men always win here."

"What about Costa Rica? I'll bet a *casa chica* down there would be a *casa grande*. His parents are in coffee."

"That's not what I want," I said, "and in the end, it's not what Roberto wants. He just thinks so, now. Forbidden fruit and all that," I shrugged. I felt pity for Julie. I wished I could help her more. *How different our solutions to a common problem.* "The best thing about this summer," I said, "was the freedom. I made my own way; no one told me what to do. For a few weeks, I felt easy and released. Just the taste of this freedom makes me feel different, more alive."

꽃

When I left Julie, lightning flashed all over the mountains—maybe heat lightning or perhaps a signal of the last rain of summer. There was no moisture in the air, and the tension, electric. The heat was intense, yet I realized that I was no longer afraid of it. Roberto's words caused a stirring in my mind. The decision to stay with Leonard had not been an easy one. Perhaps the very hardness of the choice reassured me that it was right. *Was it love or a sense of duty that kept me in Mexico?* I wasn't sure.

One thing I was sure of: divorce was wrong—an unforgivable sin. My Catholic upbringing was too strong to contest that belief. If I left Len, I'd have to shuck the whole thing, and I didn't want to live in despair.

Two days later, Julie left for Detroit. She simply packed up her two children and got on an airplane. She didn't want to play a false role, and neither did I. I wanted to live without guilt, without worry, and without constant adaptation to someone else's whims.

All the while, a sense of foreboding stayed with me. *For a thrill, a little revenge, I had risked my marriage. I had wanted to humiliate him as he had humiliated me.* At least, that's what I told myself, because I was not willing to admit how much I missed Roberto, and especially missed being truly wanted, without frustration, by someone that I wanted. Yet, I felt ashamed of my betrayal.

᪣

"It's about trusting myself as well as trusting you, Len," I said. "Then love can make us happy. That is, if we really want to be a couple."

"I do." He held me tight. What he said next gave me a shock.

"I don't know if this means anything to you, but when I left you here alone, I knew you could make it. I knew you were strong enough and clever enough to do it on your own. I never doubted that." His face was shiny and open.

"Well, thanks for your confidence, but that didn't make it right. If I'm going to be with you, it has to be with trust."

Then, with an intense open passion, he said, "It's you and me."

His astonishing blue eyes stared into mine. He made no word-jokes. In my heart, I knew he would never let me go.

"Agreed. It's just you and me," I said quietly, afraid to pull away.

He was all aglow as if he had won a battle. "We'll never let anything like that happen again," he said. "It's the relationship that counts."

With the intense heat of our reconciliation, a new link sparked between Len and me. There was something irrevocable about it. Together, we chose to take the risk and forge a new agreement, a new beginning. We mapped out the future and talked about a relationship based on love and respect, although I was not entirely sure what I had committed to. I was wary. He still had a power over me and I felt, once again, mesmerized.

Part Four

Thirty-four

Pan-American School

The plaza softened the severe squareness of the Pan-American School across the street. Fall trees, flowering herbs, and prickly roses made the small, Roman-like rotunda pleasing to the eye. I walked, a little uncertain, across the plaza toward the school with gravel crunching beneath my feet. A grabbing sensation in the pit of my stomach caused me to take a deep breath. The first day of school had finally arrived. Entering the courtyard, I walked toward my designated classroom. I nodded and smiled at teachers and students.

"Good morning, Gail," a voice from an open door called. It was Lois Lowell. She advanced with a familiar, informal grace.

I waved.

She pointed to a classroom just past hers. "They're waiting for you." Her voice implied that she was glad to see me and that she had confidence in my ability. Nevertheless, my stomach lurched as I took a breath, opened the door, and entered. The chatter and bustle died and silence fell among the students.

"Good Morning." I stood alone in the front of the room and introduced myself to thirty-five eighth-grade students. Then, I told them why I was in Mexico and gave facts about my life and my family. They stared at me. The anxiety in my voice was not helping. I swallowed and, nonetheless, trudged on.

"I come from San Diego in California. And I once attended a school that looked like a castle in Spain," I concluded. "Now, let's take roll call." I slowly went through the list, scrutinizing each face as I called the name.

Just as I finished, a hand shot up. It was Cha Cha.

"Will you tell us more about castles?" she asked.

"Indeed, I will." I was glad to see that familiar face, happy that my former neighbor was in my class. "In fact, Cha Cha, we'll begin our English class today with a poem about castles. Turn to page fifty-four in your English book. 'Songs From the Princess.'" I began to read slowly, emphasizing the rhythm:

The splendor falls on castle walls
And snowy summits old in story;
The long light shakes across the lakes,
And the wild cataract leaps in glory.

A hand shot up.

"What was your name again?" I asked.

"Carlos," answered a tall, freckled boy. "Carlos Trevino. What is 'cataract'? I have never heard that word."

"Carlos, it is a waterfall. Like *collo de caballo*. Think of how that water looks," and I repeated the line. "And the wild cataract leaps in glory."

"Try the next stanza, Carlos. Read slowly."

He began.

"*O hark, O hear! How thin and clear,*

"*And thinner,*" he stumbled on the "th" sound, "*clearer, far-ther going!*"

"Thank you, Carlos. You may sit down." I continued, "The poet Tennyson was chosen as the Poet Laureate of England. That was a very special honor. His images are beautiful and full of mystery." I looked around the room. I had snared the class in the magic of the poet's web. *A good way to start the term.*

I told the students to pick one of the stanzas that they especially liked and memorize it for homework. In addition, the students were to create a list of any words that they didn't understand. I taught as I had been taught. I was available as a resource. Hands shot up; questions erupted.

"What is 'elfland'?"

"What is a glen?"

"You make it sound like music, Teacher. How do you do that?"

Time went quickly, but I was glad to hear the bell for recess. The students rushed out through the door, and I headed for the staff room—glad to have a moment to recharge and rethink the morning.

I left the sun-drenched courtyard and came into the faculty lounge and saw faces that would soon become faces of friends: Lois Lowell, Camille Coindreau, Lois Villareal de Webster. Additionally, to make things sweeter, there was my old friend, Monica. Introductions began.

"Hello, my name is Camille, and I teach fifth grade." Camille steadied herself on an ebony walking stick. A carved ivory knob at the head gave it the look of elegance.

"Very nice to meet you," I replied.

"I had polio as a child and need a little help from this." She looked down at the stick and forced a smile.

A short, slightly plump woman, she wore her silvery hair pulled back into a bun. She was dressed all in black, and I recalled that Lois had told me that Camille was a widow with ten children to support.

An athletic-looking woman with a wide smile leaned over from the other side of the table. "Hi. I'm the *real* Lois." She grinned. "Lois Villareal de Webster. High School, tenth grade.

"We call them the *tocayas*, since they have the same names," Camille nodded to the two Loises. "And this is Jim."

A tall man in a worn, gray suit stuck out his hand. His tousled hair and rumpled shirt gave the impression that he had been wrestling rather than teaching.

"I teach fourth grade," he said. "How did it go with the little monsters?"

"Monsters?" I was taken aback.

"Didn't anyone warn you about them?" he persisted.

"I didn't really have any trouble. They—why, they're charming," I answered.

"Hey, don't kid me. I have them for math right before lunch. They're hellraisers!" he huffed.

"Don't worry about it, Gail," Lois Webster interrupted. "Perhaps they only raise hell right before lunch."

Jim forced a laugh.

"Talk about raising hell," Lois Lowell broke into the conversation, "that daughter of yours got off to a fine start this morning."

"My oldest daughter is in her class." The real Lois nodded toward Lois Lowell. The easy, free chatter led me to believe they were good friends.

"She's absolutely enchanted by Fidel Castro. Says Batista's a gangster," Lois Lowell said.

The mother responded with a wry laugh, "Is that all? I would have gone much further." She looked at me. "Everyone here knows our family history. My former husband, an American, was in the U.S. Foreign Service. We were posted in Cuba for some years." Then, she looked at her friend and said with real passion. "I would have said that Batista is a real bastard."

I laughed. I liked these women.

The bell rang; recess was over. I was mesmerized by this first encounter with the other teachers. Monica and I were the newcomers, yet this enterprising group of women instantly welcomed us. I returned to my classroom feeling exhilarated.

The staff lounge was small and narrow, conducive to intimate conversation. In the weeks that followed, I loved walking into the compressed engine of their lives. They had complex households and old family ties. Laughing, talking, and arguing, we developed strong friendships. All part of a common struggle, we chatted about trivialities—birthdays, parties, books, and kids.

ॐ

In the second week of the school term, Mr. Tarpey came around to visit my class, as was his monthly custom. I had heard that he would be collecting names of those who were troublemakers, but I honestly had none to give him.

"I'd like to speak with you privately after class." His expression was grim.

I smiled weakly, sure that I had done something wrong. "I'll be there at one o'clock," I said.

Mr. Tarpey's office was cool and absolutely meticulous, just as I remembered it. He got right to the point.

"This class of yours—it has a reputation, you know."

"I'm sorry to say that I didn't know, Mr. Tarpey, but I can assure you that they are a delight. No need to worry about them."

"No," he interrupted. "I have a better idea. I'd like to put an intercom in there for a few days and try to figure out just what you're doing. That way, I can share it with the others."

"An intercom?" I was confused. *Was he going to spy on me?*

"Jim says that your class causes mayhem. He thinks you're too easy on them. Many of them really need detention."

There was an uncomfortable hush. I found his low rasp of a voice irritating.

I looked him square in the eye. "With *horas corriente*, that could be a real hardship for them and for their families. Besides, I see no reason."

We stared at each other.

"Let's just try this experiment," he insisted.

Two days later, a small gray box sat on my desk. *The silent listener!* Meanwhile, I proceeded to teach by hooking the students'

attention. I found interesting images in poetry; amusing, yet useful, projects; and fanciful team projects. They loved it and I
loved them.

If I did my part, there seemed to be no need for imposition. I
looked forward to class time and I came to enjoy and take pride
in the students. In time, we forgot the intercom and became
deeply engrossed in study.

Finding ways to adapt my teaching from the Institute's
one-on-one process to group learning proved to be effective. I
told the class to spend an extra ten minutes with me on the playground after recess. Together, we observed nature, each other,
the school. They asked questions about words for objects.

"Teacher, what is this?"

"Bench."

"And this? Please?"

"A dry leaf."

"And two of them? Three of them?"

"Leaves." I emphasized the "V" sound.

Then, we retreated back into class for composition. This exer-
cise was done on a variety of topics: *An Autumn Morning, Raindrops on the Playground, Games I love to Play*. We rarely needed
dictionaries. Experience provided the vocabulary.

History evoked group projects as students wrote and directed
short plays. Costumes and language became more elaborate as
we progressed through the weeks.

"Unbelievable," said Mr. Tarpey at one of our meetings. "You
speak to them softly and with no force." He shifted restlessly in
his chair. "But what's all this about Elvis Presley?"

"The students adore him," I said, "and *TIME* did a feature.
So, I had the students practice expository writing: one paragraph, five sentences. First sentence, introduction; second,
third, and fourth, description; and fifth, summary. We do it
together, in class. Sometimes we play music."

"Rock and roll music in class?"

"Yes, Mr. Tarpey. If three minutes of music interests the students, I believe that's how to catch their attention. The results are quite good. It also helps with colloquial expressions."

"A bit unorthodox, don't you think?"

"I went to Catholic schools all my life. That's how I was taught." I added, "And by nuns." I failed to mention that we had no rock and roll music at that time, and if we did, I doubted if Sister Mary Agnes would have brought it to class.

"And do you think you could take over the math class for Jim?"

So this was it. He wanted to take the class away from Jim and give it to me because Jim had trouble with discipline.

"Mr. Tarpey, I wish I could. But my math skills are weak. I was up front with you about that from the very beginning. These Mexican kids know more math and algebra than I do. They have a knack. It wouldn't be fair to them. Besides, I teach Jim's composition class."

Despite the success I was having, I got the feeling that Mr. Tarpey did not approve of my methods. Beyond that, and in retrospect, I was sorry that I didn't take the math class. I should have found a way to present it, and in the end, it would have been preferable to the pandemonium with Jim.

Meanwhile, Len had also returned to school, Second Year Medicine. I was cautiously optimistic. Len no longer strayed at night and never broached the topic of the Green Cross. And so, I let hope back into my life with Len. One significant change—the gang still met routinely, but now they met at our house, late into the night, with rum glasses clinking, whoops and hollers floating on the air.

I went to church on Sundays, taking the children along, and as part of my repentance I tried to be patient with the gang. My birth control foam was gone and I was reluctant to discuss how and why. As the fall term ended, I discovered that I was pregnant again. I was worried about what Len would say. *What will I do if he doesn't want another baby?*

Thirty-five

Feliz Navidad

C ome for the afternoon," the real Lois said. "It's on your way home."

Two children poked their heads out of the car that stood in the street in front of the Pan-American School. They yelled in unison, "Mommy, hurry! We're hungry!"

Pu Pucha, just out of class and obviously impatient, sat in the driver's seat and honked the horn.

Lois pressed a wrinkled note in my hand. "Directions," she said and hurried toward the waiting car as students filed around and past us, escaping for Christmas break.

"All right then, in a few moments," I called after her and waved.

Lois was a tall, large-boned, freckle-faced woman with silvery-brown hair. She wore it cropped short, framing her head in wiry abandon. Her light eyes were wide-set and gave the impression of curiosity and good humor. She was in her late thirties and carried a little weight, but instead of making her look matronly, it gave her a martial, no-nonsense air.

She lived in an old section of Monterrey, not far from the Pan-American School. All up and down the street stretched old adobe houses with their wide verandahs and high, narrow windows. Looking up, I noticed that the clouds had changed color, becoming dark brown instead of white. A flock of birds swooped low and then fanned out in the windy sky. A deep, dusty cold descended upon the city.

I parked and dashed up the front stairs to the porch of her bungalow just as an icy breeze swirled dust around my body. A strong gust whipped my face and the door swung open. Lois greeted me with a broad smile and swept me into her home. A fragrant whiff of spices caught my attention.

"What's that wonderful smell?"

"Turkey *mole*. You'll see," and she pointed to the living room. "Have a seat." Lois hurried toward the direction of the wonderful odor, calling over her shoulder as she went, "The family home: my dad built it before I was born." And she disappeared through the dining room into the kitchen beyond.

Twin green velour sofas faced each other and I sat down on one that faced the street. Pale winter light streamed through the half-closed shutters. Antique light fixtures fastened to the wall on each side of the fireplace gave off a dim glow. Very old, lace curtains, draped lazily, bestowed the room with a sense of history and permanence. Dozens of pictures covered the walls. Children yelled from an unseen room. Pots and pans rattled from the direction of the mouth-watering smells.

While I was waiting, a strong draft blew through a loose windowpane. Outside, the wind hissed and swirled dust in the barren trees. I shivered and slouched into the soft, faded cushions as dirt devils danced in the street.

On the other side of the room, I noticed a brown, faded picture of a younger, trimmer Lois, three children, and a tall, wiry—yet broad-shouldered—man.

"*Andale, pues,*" Lois commanded to someone in the kitchen and she returned.

I was drawn to Lois. She was organized and thrived in her topsy-turvy world of kids, work, politics, and family doings.

Despite tousled hair and a slightly disheveled appearance, Lois Villareal de Webster, the daughter of a prominent Mexican family, had the knack of making the world more coherent.

Lois pointed to the photograph near my chair. "That's Padre Island. We used to go there on vacations when I was a kid. My mom was American. Of course, you know how it is with families from the border. First, it was Mexican, and then it belonged to the States. "

"But you took us there every summer." Pu Pucha had come into the room.

"Hi, Pu," I said, "didn't see you there."

Pu grinned. She had an impish smile and a round, doll-like face. Her English bore staccato traces of Cuban-Spanish and she spoke rapidly, "Padre Island. Birds are everywhere."

"It's a sanctuary," Lois said. "We'll go at Easter this year. All of us. We haven't been since we got back from Cuba."

"Don't you miss Cuba?" I asked.

"We got out before all the trouble really began," Lois said. "Batista's days are numbered."

"I'd like to be there, now," said Pu. "Fidel will change everything. When he wins control, the poor people will get a chance."

"Isn't he a Communist, Pu Pucha?" I asked.

"Don't know. Don't care. Fidel is better than what they have now."

"Don't get her started," Lois said, then got up to go to the kitchen. "We'll eat in a few minutes. Wait till you try *tamales dulces*."

"I approve of revolution," Pu erupted, "and social justice. So what if he's a Communist?"

"If you knew how I was educated, you'd understand my concern," I said. "We studied communism in our religion class when I was in high school. Even watched the House un-American Activities Committee on television so that we could integrate the findings with our studies."

Pu continued as if she hadn't heard me. "This guy Fidel wants to have the whole country reading and he'll make it happen." She gave me a defiant look. "Can't say that about the States, can you?"

"Can't say what? I think—"

Pu cut me off. "I can say that because my Dad's an American. He's with the Diplomatic Corps." She reached for a notebook from amid a stack of books and magazines, "We were all together in Cuba. I've been writing poems, essays, and stories about it."

"All right, then," I jumped in. "What about freedom and personal choice?"

"Look," she said, "when we were in Cuba, do you think people had choice? Not with that kind of poverty. Not with Batista!" Her round face turned red and her eyes flashed anger. "That bastard makes deals with Bugsy Segal and Mickey Cohen. Batista, friend of the Mafia. We called him a U.S. puppet!"

"Hey Pu, *cállate tu boca.*" *Shut up.* Lois announced, "*¡Atención!* Come and get it, everyone. *¡Atención!*"

"*¿Mande?*" a young voice called.

"I wish she wouldn't say that," Pu snarled.

"Say what?" I asked, thinking she probably meant *shut up.*

"*Mande.* In Cuba no one says it. In Cuba they say, *dígame.* Makes more sense, don't you think?" *Dígame. Tell me (what you want) or tell me (what I missed.)*

Before I could reply, two younger Websters appeared from the hallway and scrambled to seats around the table. A maid carried a bowl of steaming *mole.* She leaned over and placed the fragrant stew in the middle of the table next to a heaping mountain of flour tortillas.

Lois appeared in the kitchen doorway holding a magnificent tray piled high with *tamales.* "Holiday tradition," she said, and placed the platter in the center where all could reach. She seated herself at the head of the large table. It was as if she were a general overseeing a great battle, moving the dishes into position, steadily organizing, and even conducting psychological warfare.

The younger children—a girl about eight, and a boy a little older—took their seats.

"You can't be in México for Christmas and not have *tamales dulces*," said Pu, then she abruptly turned to me and added, "Don't you think everybody should get a chance? Why should young girls have to go into prostitution just to eat?"

Lois attempted a diversion. "Let's talk about Christmas. The Tarpeys are having a party. The whole faculty's invited."

"Señora Tarpey's a prostitute." Pu continued undeterred, eyebrows pulled together, leaving an imprint in the center like a question mark.

The younger children tittered and chuckled.

"Mrs. Tarpey is not a prostitute, Pu," Lois said. "She doesn't need your approval on her choice of a husband."

"Well I think—"

"Enough! Gail came here to eat with us—not to hear your ideas about politics."

Lois then served the fragrant *mole*, ladling generous portions of the dark, chocolate concoction onto outstretched plates. I realized that this was the same exotic dish I had sampled in Saltillo. I helped myself and poured the *mole* over the rice on my plate. As we ate, everyone settled into a respectful silence. The longer I ate and watched and listened, the more I was attracted by this rambunctious, lively family.

"I've never had anything like this," I said, pointing to the *tamales* on my plate.

"Specialty for the holidays," said Lois. "*Tamales* stuffed with raisins and nuts."

Before I could finish the last morsel, Pu fired another volley. "Why would a young girl marry a pompous old man like him?"

"Old man?" Lois laughed. "He's my age, or maybe a little older."

"And his wife?" I asked.

"Your age or maybe even younger," said Lois, then she smiled at Pu. "Lets have dessert."

Pu persisted, "It had to be money. She simply sold herself." Her eyes narrowed.

"*Flan?*" the youngest asked.

"Or maybe her family sold her." Pu ranted on, glowering at her siblings.

"*Flan,*" said Lois.

Outside, the storm crashed through the trees, and explosions of thunder shook the ground, while inside, despite Pu's angry words and controversy, happy energy filled the house.

When the meal was finished, Lois and I sat in the living room. We stoked ourselves on strong coffee and shared stories. She told me that the children had been born in Cuba, their father was an American diplomat, and they were no longer together. I got the sense that he had run off with a younger woman, but Lois never said so directly.

"About Pu," she finally said. Her voice surprised me; it had a weight to it, a warning, a determination edged with grief. "She misses her father."

I knew that Lois was divorced, but I didn't know the story.

"Pu remembers the good old days. My husband was from Boston where he was recruited for the Diplomatic Corps. When we were first married, he was posted first in Guaymas, and then we went on to Cuba. It was a very electrifying and exciting period and, of course, we thought we all had a part to play in international relations. It was a time of euphoria and optimism; there was a lot of political energy in the air. Pu was—and is—utterly charmed by her father and misses the fact that he's not with us anymore. Divorce isn't easy, but then, it wasn't meant to be."

"I can understand that," I said. "I mean about Pu and her father. Jeanne is the same way and she's just a little over one year old. I don't know what would happen to her if she couldn't be with Len."

Lois nodded and shrugged. "I was much more passionate then. Life has a way of cooling you down."

I thought of the summer that just passed. Maybe Lois was lucky to have life take charge and slow things down.

৯

A week later, the faculty gathered at the Tarpey's for the Pan-American School Christmas party. The house was of modern design—elegant white stone walls, steel frames that created sail-like structures, a lush garden, and large picture windows that overlooked Vista Hermosa. Below us, town lights twinkled in the clear night.

Mr. Tarpey greeted me at the door of a large entry hall. A slight woman dressed in winter white stood next to him. "Meet my wife: Carmen." Something in his voice made me feel uneasy.

A delicate Mexican woman shook my hand. Her sullen, narrow face widened at the cheekbone where lustrous brown eyes stared at me. She smiled and then looked around, clearly anxious about her other guests. Sounds of music and laughter came from the spacious room behind the young Mrs. Tarpey and she sighed. "Nice to have you here."

We shook hands and I passed behind her into the living room. From almost any angle, the house seemed inherently unstable, as if at any moment it would fly away. Far from it. This modern architecture, a style I had never seen, was completely stable. A ledge overhanging the street was enclosed with glass and a bar stood in its center.

A baby grand piano with its cover raised stood off to one side of the enormous room. I brightened when I saw Camille Coindreau. She was dressed in her habitual widow's black and turned pages for a young man who played Christmas carols. A group of singers had already gathered around the piano and "Santa Claus is Coming to Town" reverberated through the room.

I glanced back at our hosts. Pu's voice came back to me. *Mrs. Tarpey is a prostitute.* Was it simply the voice of a scrappy, irreverent teenager? Or did she know something? Not that it mattered.

I glanced back at Mrs. Tarpey. She didn't look like the girls at the *Copa de Oro*, standing there in the entryway in her stylish little white dress. All the while, Mr. Tarpey manned his station at the door, and from time to time glanced over at the group of singers. His wife stayed close by.

The elegance of the house was apparent. Mr. Tarpey had obviously done well by starting up an English-speaking school. Rumor had it that he had been an elementary school principal in Texas.

At the far side of the room, the two Loises stood together at the bar. I hurried over to join them.

"She seems to be flourishing," said Lois Lowell.

"Who?" I asked.

"Why, the new Mrs. Tarpey. She seems to be quite happy. Newlyweds."

"I didn't know," I said.

"Who can know about anyone's marriage?" Lois Webster said. "It's not always what it seems. I think it was that way with us. With my marriage, I mean." Her words had a yearning quality.

I moved closer to her and whispered, "Why did Pu Pucha say—you know—what she said?" I couldn't bring myself to voice the word *prostitute* in the woman's house.

"You heard her explanation. Money is the big offender."

"I don't get it," I said.

"Pu has high ideals. She draws connections between social norms and her view of things."

Lois Lowell interceded, "I think we all do. The important thing is for women to make free choices and, even more important, to give meaning to what we choose to do."

"How so?" I asked.

"Whenever a woman or a girl deviates from the accepted path, she is considered dangerous, sensual, even crafty." Lois Lowell went on, "I think the important thing is to choose what we, women, want and move on, unencumbered by outside points of view."

"Even the cultural point of view," added Lois Webster.

"But I thought Pu believed in women's rights."

"She just wants to sound like her father," Lois Webster added.

"She's a teenager, an idealist. But not everyone can go it alone," Lois Lowell added, "and survive."

"Look at Camille," said Lois W. "She comes from one of the best families in Monterrey. She had polio when she was fifteen. Still, she married the love of her life. It was quite a romantic escapade. He died a few years ago, leaving her with ten children to raise." Lois W. looked at Camille. There was deep affection in her glance and she added, "Even so, her family doesn't like the fact that she works outside of the home."

"But she's a great teacher," I said.

"Yes, but she's *out of* the role." Lois W. emphasized "out of" just as Mrs. Tarpey announced dinner.

"What role?" I insisted. For a split second, I glanced at Camille.

"Stay at home, suffer if you have to. No right to any kind of self-possession." Lois Webster was adamant.

"Apparently, work is supposed to demean a woman." Lois Lowell laughed.

"I never thought of it that way. My mother always worked," I said.

"Many people think I married for money," said Lois Lowell.

"Everyone's heard of the Lowells of Boston," added Lois W.

"They don't know that I have my own money," Lois Lowell said matter-of-factly. "I work because I want to. I want to contribute and make things happen."

It didn't end there. The thought of women making their own interpretations fascinated me. As we made our way to dinner, I noticed Lois W. stopped to help Camille.

She bent over her and said softly, "*Querida*," *Dear.*

Camille looked up at Lois W.

"*¿No quieres nada?*" Lois asked.

Camille's face lit up when she heard that coaxing voice, and she stood up, took Lois's arm, leaned on it for support, and together they made their way to the buffet. The rest of us followed, filled our plates, and eventually returned to the living room where the faculty divided into small clusters.

An oval room, plenty of food, Christmas music on the phonograph, and we women made our own place. A bench and several chairs did the job.

"And Monica—where is she tonight?" asked Lois W.

"Home for the holidays," I said.

"And you—are you going home this year?" asked Lois Lowell.

"This year, I'm going to Laredo to pick up some packages at General Delivery. The family's sent Christmas presents for the kids," I said and then added "and I'm going to buy a refrigerator."

"How have you been managing without one?" asked Camille.

Then, while Lois W. folded out a tray in front of Camille, I told my story about Señor Sanchez, my move the last summer, and finding a house on *Calle Estados Unidos*. Sitting in our protected space, apart from the crowd, we four women laughed, teased, and argued. I felt myself privileged, as if I had been drawn into some mysterious world of women, and I was grateful beyond measure for the inclusion. I wondered if Mrs. Tarpey, in a way, answered Mr. Tarpey's need for submission. I knew that these women in the inner circle would never compromise and submit. I couldn't know then just how lucky I was to be in their company and learn from them.

Lois Lowell held up her glass. "Merry Christmas."

"*Feliz Navidad*," replied Camille.

Thirty-six

Away in a Manger

The car was full of purchases from Laredo. Len went ahead by foot. He stepped over the border from Texas, then walked across back into Mexico. Carrying a small suitcase, he looked like any tourist on a short vacation.

Meanwhile, I sat in the car at the border just on the U. S. side. I watched Len from the corner of my eye, and then when I knew he had made it without any trouble, I drove across, stopped at the checkpoint, and handed the Immigration official my papers. I glanced around, tense and nervous. I was now a legal resident of Mexico. Len, on the other hand, remained an illegal resident posing as a tourist. We just didn't have the money to pay for the documents.

I handed the official my passport, which had a $5.00 bill neatly tucked inside. The official opened the passport. My picture and Jeanne's stared back at him.

"¿Dónde se fue mi papá?" Jeanne asked. Her china-blue eyes held questions about Len.

"Shh, he's at home," I lied as we both watched Len walk up the street far ahead of the border point.

"No, *mamá, no.*" She was ruffled, but when the official came to the window, she looked up at him and smiled.

"*Que chula la niña,*" he said.

I was nervous. It was impossible to keep a low profile with a refrigerator sticking out of the trunk. The back seat was loaded with cans of baby food, infant formula, and Christmas packages that I had picked up from general delivery. The Laredo Post Office, a landmark for expatriates, had been crammed with holiday shoppers mailing packages, as well as those of us who lived south of the border. Sending things to Laredo was one sure way of getting packages. And with luck, we could avoid paying any duty. The official handed me back my papers. The money was gone.

"*Gracias, Señor.*" I hoped the *mordida* would work. I had never bribed anyone in my life, but Lois Lowell assured me that this was the only way to cross the border without incident. I resented having to give the official any money at all. I wasn't doing anything wrong and $5.00 was a lot for me. Still, I had bargained for the used refrigerator and got the owner to shave $5.00 off his asking price. Now that I had my resident papers, I knew I could bring goods into the country, provided the cost was less than $300. My carload of treasures weren't even close to that amount.

The official walked around the car, put the bill in his pocket, and returned to the front side of the car. He had a blank, non-committal expression. I stared into his eyes, not daring to blink.

I waited for him to ask questions, but none came. Nodding his head, he touched the brim of his hat and said, "*Pásale*" and waved me on. I finally exhaled.

Meanwhile, Len found a restaurant-bar down the street and lingered just long enough in the doorway to make sure that I saw him go in. I parked in front, and I found him finger-drumming at the bar. We located a booth and I ordered a large soda.

"Any trouble?" he asked and poured some of the soda into a glass. He gave it to Jeanne.

"*Aqúi está mi papá.*" She said it triumphantly as if I had been playing a little game with her and she had won.

"No trouble." My voice cracked with excitement.

"Your friend Lois is right. You just have to know the ropes," Len said.

"It also helps to have papers." I smiled. "How about you?"

"No problem. Dozens of people are crossing today. Holiday's coming up and all." He held up a six-month tourist visa. "See?"

"Let's get going. I don't like being here and the baby in Monterrey." Home was five hours away.

"Paula's crazy about him," Len said. "He's okay."

Still, I was uneasy. The decision to leave Lenny in Mexico for the weekend was a practical, though uncomfortable, one. Len needed to renew his tourist visa. Exiting with me and entering alone made it less complicated. Besides, the baby had both a Mexican birth certificate and U.S papers. Bringing him along would have drawn attention to an already complicated situation.

Len threw some coins on the table. "Mission accomplished," he said and shrugged.

"A good sign," I replied. We headed home.

Driving through the Sonora desert had become something of a ritual for our family, but this time an odd feeling of emptiness seeped into me as we drove toward Monterrey. After all the con- niving, there was now a sense of both victory and loss. I became increasingly aware that, despite the prized refrigerator in the trunk, small tremors of apprehension quivered through me as we drove further into Mexico. There was my marriage—knotted with doubts, fears, and fascination—there was the gray box in my classroom, and there was the fact that I was pregnant. Drained by a year's worth of worry, I found myself headed once more for Monterrey. The city of steel mills and iron works drew me just as a magnet draws iron filings.

꿁

"Jeannie," said Len. "Look at all the presents Santa left."

Jeanne walked toward the pile of gifts that filled up a small corner of the living room with eyes wide and her mouth forming a soundless "O." Her face looked so fresh, it tore at my heart. Lenny stumbled after her, carrying his bottle, also with lustrous blue eyes open wide.

"Here," said Len and he squatted down on the floor to help Jeanne open a gift. Together, they tore off ribbons and paper and ripped open the box. Inside, a rubber doll squeaked and then made the sound of a tiny cry. Jeanne handed the doll to Lenny and kept on tearing sheets of paper. With shouts of glee, she discovered other surprises.

Within minutes, the gifts were opened and scattered all over the tile floor. Joyful sounds of laughter amidst "oohs" and "ahhs" filled the room as Lenny wandered in and out of the papers and ribbons that were strewn in all directions. With a few strenuous tugs, he managed to climb into the largest box. The floor was awash with tissue paper.

"He likes the boxes as well as, if not better than, any of the toys," I sighed and leaned back in my chair.

"After this, I need to run over to the hospital. Just have a few errands to run."

I hesitated, felt a slight pinch for a moment—it was Christmas Day, after all— then nodded in agreement. Since last summer, I had developed a detached acceptance. We had gotten into the habit of arranging our lives independently of one another—he, with medical school and friends; and me, with school duties and the care of the household. In this way, we lived beside each other, close to each other, with each involved deeply in other things. A kind of armistice stood between us.

"That's good." The children distracted me. Lenny hugged the baby doll.

"What are you smiling at?" Len asked.

"Lenny seems more attached to that doll than Jeanne."

I remembered the winter before and lost my smile, the winter Jeanne had ingested fuzz from a toy animal.

One of the packages from my parents turned out to be stuffed with toys for the children—tangible evidence of their caring.

Len climbed to his feet and pointed at the children.

"Looks like they're having a great time. Guess I'll get going." He threw on his jacket.

Jeanne cried out. "Papá!" She held up her hands toward him.

He saw her face, glowing with love and admiration, tinged with pleading.

"Okay, then, come with me," he said, then swooped her up into his arms.

The corners of her ladyship's mouth curled up into a satisfied grin.

"What about Lenny? Don't you—"

Len cut me off, "Can't handle two," and they were off.

I picked up the baby, walked to the door, and watched them drive away. It was painful to see how Len ignored his son. It was hard to believe a father was capable of such coldness toward one and such adulation toward the other. I kept hoping that one day he would accept his son with the same open heart that he had for Jeanne. I held on to the idea that time would mend the situation.

Outside, the clouds were already beginning to block the sun, turning the pale morning sunlight to a dusky brown. I could hear the old car squeal around the corner.

On our porch, just beside the doorway, I had set up a crèche. Although made of plastic, it had a charming quality. The faces of the baby, Mary and Joseph, the sheep, the oxen, and the shepherds smiled back at us as if startled out of their perfect world.

I pointed to the manger. "See the baby Jesus?"

He giggled, but did not speak. At nine months, he was as big as Jeanne so that they were often mistaken for twins. Although endowed with a wistful gentleness, he was more physical than his sister. He walked early and left word making to Jeanne. Lenny squirmed out of my arms, toddled to the crèche, and tenderly touched the plastic Jesus. I squatted next to him and started to sing, "Away in a manger, no crib for his bed . . . Do you like that song?"

He nodded.

In the distance, I heard claps, then explosions of thunder, and a huge bolt of lightning flashed on the horizon.

We were living in a wild, strange place terribly far from everything I knew. Anyone who has been alone in a foreign land for the holidays knows the aching feeling I felt at that moment. It's not fair to blame the country when days like that Christmas turn out so painful, when tragedy strikes.

At about half-past ten, I began to prepare the *cabrito*. I set the portable oven on top of the hot plate, telling myself that preparing young goat was no different than preparing turkey. I just had to roast it with spices and let it cook. I immersed myself in the work and, for a while, it completely absorbed my attention. Lenny, while sitting in his high chair, chewed on a tortilla and watched with interest. The dark-blueness of his eyes followed my every move.

At some point that morning, I became aware of the pungent, gamy smell that came from the small, tin oven and I realized the impossibility of achieving anything close to a normal Christmas dinner. How I had craved that. However, the unpleasant odor had begun to permeate the kitchen and the living room. It was obvious that my efforts had been in vain.

As I waited for Len and Jeanne to come back, I had the strangest feeling. I sensed that I had somehow missed some other role in life. Perhaps like Henry James, I would write novels. Perhaps there were unknown piles of stories to be written, an infinitely better choice than cooking smelly goat.

Two thunderclaps later, Len returned. He pushed open the door with his shoulder. He carried Jeanne who was sound asleep in his arms. I was surprised to see that Luís trailed after him.

"Here, take her." Len handed Jeanne to me. "Come, Luís. Come in."

I put Jeanne in the nursery where her brother was already napping. When I returned to the living room, I noticed Len had poured two glasses of rum. I was surprised, because Luís was not a drinker. From what I knew of him, his life reflected a discipline, an almost ascetic existence. Luís sat facing the fireplace where the gas flames barely flickered. He looked distracted. He had no color. Not even a nerve reaction. He took a sip of rum. It was then that Luís started to speak as if he were reciting a monologue. In the shadowy room, he appeared to be in shock.

"I was supposed to go home two days ago," he began. "But I got word there was a message for me at school. An urgent message. It took me until yesterday to find someone."

We waited for the rest of the story. Luís choked back tears.

"Go on, *amigo*," Len encouraged him.

"Finally, I found Dr. Montemayor. He had a patient in surgery and was still in his scrubs."

Luís pounded his knee with a clenched fist. "My brother is dead," his voice cracked in pain. "You know he was in the Yucatan. He was sent there, *Seguro Social*, you know, to work with the Mayans. One of them shot him."

"Shot?" I was stunned and gasped, "Why?" I felt a quick throb in my chest and then, with some giddiness, I sat down next to Luís. He was talking fast now.

"My brother—he was delivering a baby. It was in one of the villages. The woman needed an episiotomy, so my brother made the cut. The husband was there—he didn't understand. He shot my brother, point blank, in the head." Luís grabbed my arm and then drew his hand back. His voice receded into the darkening room.

"How can we help?" Len asked.

"Need to get home," Luís muttered. "*Mis padres.*"

Traces of a story that Luís told me came to mind: the father who had gone to the States year after year during the war. He worked as a *bracero*. He had returned each year with a thick roll of dollar bills, and the family used this money to buy a gas station. Servicing American tourist cars helped the boys, Luís and his brother, to learn English.

"I'll take you to the bus station," said Len. "Whenever you're ready to go."

Luís sat with his face in his hands. He nodded.

Len motioned to me. We went into the bedroom.

"How much money do you have?" he whispered.

"Just the rent money," I said.

"Give it to me. We have to help him out." Len's voice was deep and sad.

I felt an impulse of compassion and a current of trust welled between us. I handed over the accordion type folder that kept our money separate by categories. Len reached into the pocket labeled "rent," pulled out five-hundred pesos, and stuffed the bills into his pocket.

"There's a bus at 4:00. I'll take him now."

For me, the shock of the moment was overcome with the bitterness, not just of the lost life, but of a young doctor's interrupted work. All of it was snuffed out in a split second of misunderstanding—gone in the dead heat of a tropical December in the far away Yucatan Peninsula. I was outraged at the tribal act of such brutal revenge.

And then it struck me. Len would have to do *seguro social*, social service, upon graduation. Luís's story just pointed to the precariousness of our situation. This system seemed like such nonsense, to take such risks, to be punished under a foreign code of duty.

The thought of the sweet innocence of Lenny and the manger scene crept into my mind as the afternoon persisted, dismal and rainy. I sat in the smelly kitchen in considerable dread. Life was getting increasingly hard. I was bewildered, and I had already begun to have doubts about my faith. I couldn't imagine where exactly I could get money to pay the rent. And from the oven, I was breathing the infernal mists of smelly *cabrito*.

Thirty-seven

Doomsday With a Wink

For me, the loyalty to Len's ambitions grew with each month invested. I liked to tell myself that besides us, Len had two great loves: medicine and the camaraderie of the gang. To medicine, he gave his time and almost all of his energy. From the gang, he derived the help and understanding of others with the same passion. In return, they respected him. He withstood physical hardships with humor and indifference.

It was with an intense will and Irish sense of humor that Len faced the hard task of studying medicine in Mexico. He overcame the fact that he had to study in a language in which he was not fluent by memorizing whole pages and charts until, at last, the day came when he was able to understand in both English and Spanish. No matter how bad things got, Len would say, "A real Irishman will greet doomsday with a wink."

His ability to wink would soon be put to the test.

The day came in late January. The school session had begun, and I spent afternoon hours at home correcting papers and planning for classes. I was surprised when Mario entered the front door. Behind him, Bill and Luís carried Len on a stretcher. They didn't see me in the far corner of the living room.

"Let's get him in bed," Mario said.

I ran toward them. "What going on?" I called.

"He just collapsed," Mario answered, "started shaking like a stick in the wind. Fever, chills."

"Did he see anyone?" I persisted.

"Dr. Montemayor was there," Bill said. "He said it could be malaria."

"Or even typhoid," Luís added. "The doc sent medicine."

I touched Len's head and felt the heat. His face had taken on a sullen, listless expression. His eyes dimmed dreamily.

"Here, put him in here." I pointed to the front bedroom. They placed him on the bed and, all the while, I stood by feeling helpless, trying to quiet ripples of fear. *What about the children? What if Len should die? Stay calm.*

For the next ten days, I watched Len shudder with the strange fever. It was I who made him sip water, taste meals, and rest. It was I who had to play the role of nurse, of preserver. He was burning up.

I didn't feel any panic; I didn't feel anything. I only observed him and myself as if I were hypnotized. Day after day, by stubbornly refusing to be exhausted, I managed to nurse Len in the afternoons when I came home from school. And at nights, I sponged him as his temperature rose and then covered him when it fell. I worked at the school in the mornings. Miraculously, the children did not get the mysterious fever.

As the week progressed, and as I kept my vigil, I realized how quickly men seem to deteriorate when they don't shave. At first, Len's appearance was careless. Within a few days, his normally handsome face was half-mooned in red whiskers and his eyes were pale and listless. He looked like an unkempt bear. But he never deserted his belief that he would pull through; his vision never left him.

Meanwhile, the gang came and went, bringing news. One afternoon, Len tugged at my arm.

"I've got to present this afternoon," he whispered. He was still very weak.

"You can't mean it," I replied. "Just raise your head and I'll turn your pillow."

"No, I have to go," he insisted.

"You're much too ill," I said. "Why do you have to push yourself so much?"

"If I don't, I'll be at a disadvantage. Must go; have to." Len's face was young and hard, and despite the illness, he still had the will to fight. Already, there were rumors that he had dropped out of school. I wondered if he had heard.

And so, it was arranged that he would go that afternoon. Len had lost weight and looked frail. The sight of him—usually so bubbling and spirited—now, so vulnerable, made me feel like someone had kicked me in the ribs. I could feel the pressure of tears welling up and struggled to keep them back. The light was harsh and it made Len's eyes shrink into his skull as Mario and Bill carried him out of the house, once again on a stretcher.

Mario told the story when they returned.

"We took him to school and found a place up front in class. It was Anatomy," Mario said. "When Len's number was called, he tried to get up. He couldn't make it, so we had to prop him up. He insisted and he knew the material cold. The professor said, 'To my knowledge, this was the first time anyone has presented from a stretcher.' Everyone cheered. Len got a standing ovation from the students."

And then one day, as rapidly as he had taken sick, Len was well. He seemed to have some protection around him, some Irish luck that had a way of kicking in just when I thought he was finished. Len had a touching habit of covering his illness with humor, making himself ironic and whimsical. Chicken broth and plenty of rest improved his strength, and he began to gain weight.

By the end of January, when his strength returned, he jumped out of bed and headed for the kitchen. "I could eat a whole pot of *frijoles!*" he yelled.

I looked at him and smiled through tears, then crumpled into a chair. He'd managed the wink.

It seemed like the New Year, 1957, might begin to go smoothly at last.

꿎

During those days and in the weeks that followed, my association with Lois Lowell and Lois Webster grew. They were, in a sense, my adopted mothers, and I can't remember a time when their understanding of my youthful problems was lacking or their practical advice withheld.

I was married, but I had not yet learned the ways of life. I shouldn't have been surprised. I knew when I took a certain initiative that I was taking a risk. During Len's illness, I fell into a thoughtful quietness. One day, musing over our problems and the loss of our rent money, I had written to his benefactor, a Mr. Johnson in the States.

Len had worked for Mr. Johnson at the Health Department for six months, and it was there, under Mr. Johnson's supervision, that they became friends. Len had won his support. In this regard, Len was unique in the way that he could know someone for only a short while and was able to gain their wholehearted interest. Mr. Johnson was not a wealthy man. He was close to retirement and had children of his own. But I wrote to him and asked if he could advance us the monthly contribution. I needed to pay the rent; it was that simple.

I was lunching at home. Paula cooked as usual and served as usual—rice and beans, fresh tortillas. Lenny sat in his highchair; Jeanne sat next to me on a chair. Len had just come home: a rare occasion, for he usually stayed all day at school. Before he could join us, I heard the postman's whistle.

Len opened the door and leaned forward. The mailman handed him a single envelope. Len opened it, and as he scanned down the lines, his face turned beet-red. Then turning, he came towards me, waving the letter in his hands, and hovered over the table where I was sitting.

"You wrote to Mr. Johnson? You asked him for money?" His blue eyes flickered with anger and suspicion.

"Yes," I said. "I know he helps you with tuition and fees."

"That's between him and me. It's none of your business."

I blundered on. "We needed rent money. I gave you all I had in December. Remember, for Luís?" I felt something inside me shrink.

"Did it ever occur to you that you could ruin everything?" He breathed hard.

"No, it didn't."

"Don't ever interfere with my private affairs, again!" he screamed. "Never again!" He threw the letter in my face. "Here's your damn money!"

Paula grabbed Lenny and uttered something in Spanish under her breath. Jeanne, eyes open wide, looked from me to her father. She bit her lower lip with tiny, white teeth while watching every movement as Len stormed out the door.

Jeanne cried, slid out of her chair, and ran to the window. With hands pressed against the cold glass, she watched her father get into his car and drive off. Her pale, blonde hair curled at the nape of her neck. Lenny straggled after her.

I took the check from my plate where it now lay atop a mound of refried beans. I felt a peculiar mix of relief and humiliation.

Thank you, Mr. Johnson.

"*¿Dónde se fue mi papá?*" Jeanne asked.

Her innocence in the moment contrasted with my pain, and I gave attention to the love in her voice. Why couldn't I love Len that way: with complete trust?

All I could think of were the disturbing memories of the last month, quick storms sweeping dust downward from the hills, dysentery, malaria, typhoid, and strange, unknown fevers, and nursing Len who had turned on me with such outrage.

I thought about Luís and his brother and was overcome with a sense of loss. I shook my head and tucked the check, a temporary painkiller, into my pocket.

And it was then that I felt the new baby move—the quickening. It kicked and stirred, impatient to live.

How would Len be with another baby?

Paula held a needle on a thread in front of my belly and when it spun counter-clockwise, she said, *"Es un hombre."*

Another boy? Len didn't pay any attention to the one he had. Did he see a mirror of himself in the blond-haired, blue-eyed, one-year-old? Did he feel competition? What would he do if another male entered our family?

I knew there would be trouble.

Len appeared in the doorway. "What are you two doing?" he asked.

"I didn't see you come in." I grabbed the needle from Paula's hand. "We've just been playing."

Len frowned at the needle. "Playing at what?"

I couldn't think of anything to say but the truth. "Fortune-telling. The needle's direction can foretell the sex of the baby."

There. The secret was out.

Len rubbed his eyebrows as if the news tired him.

"So . . . ?"

"A boy."

"Oh." He didn't blow up. He just shrugged it off.

"Well . . . time for class."

Len turned and walked out the front door. He'd just gotten in. Now he was leaving again. I was relieved that he wasn't angry but heart-broken that it didn't seem to matter. He was too caught up in his private world.

☙

I went into the airy nursery and watched with pleasant curiosity what my little boy was doing. Two cribs arranged at right angles, one empty, and Lenny in the one closest to the door, shaking the rail and whining to be picked up. Words eluded him. He was a child of action—sturdily made, plump limbs, and skin like velvet—a tow-haired miniature of his father. He held his arms out to me and I lifted him.

"Do you want to see Jeanne?" I asked. No reply. I repeated the question in Spanish and his eyes lit up. *He needs to be held, to feel wanted.* But he would have none of it. He squirmed out of my arms and scurried down the hall to find his sister.

We found her in the side verandah where thick grass and shrubs all around made a perfect playground, or so I thought. Jeanne splashed the cold water and exploded in gales of laughter. Compared to her brother, she was dainty with an impish restlessness.

Paula, hair tied back with a flowered scarf, was protective and watchful. She laughed, and when she saw the boy, she said in a soft, reassuring voice, "*Vente, mi rey.*" *Come, my king.* They had a special connection.

Lenny, at first timid, soon scurried toward her and summoned the courage to test the water. He made a lunging gesture and mimicked Jeanne. A water fight ensued.

I went into the house for the camera. It was just when I found the 45mm Zeiss that I heard a crash from outdoors. Paula screamed.

She hurried into the house with Lenny in her arms, blood flowing from his hand. Jeanne fearfully held to her skirt.

Paula, alarm in her dark eyes, explained what had happened. Lenny had run to the corner of the verandah where workmen, unbeknown to me, had left a plate of glass. In his hurry to run, to play, to tease, Lenny stumbled and fell on the glass.

I gasped at the sight of the blood, then grabbed the toddler, left Jeanne with Paula, and rushed Lenny to the hospital. Repair surgery was done immediately.

Afterwards, the doctor told me that Lenny had cut a tendon and assured me we were lucky; it could have been worse. My eyes moistened as the doctor explained that he had done what he could to lessen the damage; he'd sewed up the wound and put a cast on the tiny arm. I heard the professional timbre of his voice when he offered the explanation, a matter-of-factness that quite suddenly made me feel cold. The doctor emphasized that the boy really needed a good hand surgeon. There was no such specialist in Monterrey.

I took Lenny in my arms. He smiled up at me with his disarming dimples. I was shocked, depressed, and angry at myself for letting it happen.

Feeling reflective and heavy, my mind moved in slow motion as the days passed. I couldn't focus on my work. The light dimmed in the usually bright living room while I worked.

Where would I find a hand surgeon?

For the time being, Lenny would have to heal as best as he could. I pestered Len to make inquiries and we learned that there was no hurry to do the procedure.

Len's professor told him, "Better to find the right doctor than to rush into anything."

※

Three weeks later, I came down with the fever. Just as with Len, it hit hard and fast. By Sunday afternoon, I was too weak to get up. Alone in the house, I curled up with every blanket I could muster and tried to sleep. It was a cold winter afternoon. I shivered with a sudden chill. When it passed, I reached for a glass of water. By mistake, I knocked it over.

At that moment, to my surprise, Lois Lowell came into the room.

"My God! What's wrong with you?" She raised her brow at me.

"Don't know. The fever, I guess," I muttered. I was ashamed that she had found me in this state.

"Where's Len?" Lois asked.

"He went to see someone downtown. There's a sick man; he said he had to go."

"But you're sick," she replied. "You need help, too."

Perspiration dampened my hair. I had a parched, burning throat, cramped muscles, a pain in the gut. "How is it you came by?" I asked.

"I was in the neighborhood. Something just tugged at me, and I turned the corner and ended up here." She paused and looked around the room. "Where are the kids?"

"Monica took them to *Quinta Calderón,* to the park for the afternoon," I whispered. "Paula will be back tonight."

I began to cry. I was furious with Len. *How could he care for strangers and be so unfeeling about his wife?*

My anger made me feel heavy. Lois had found me out. It was a humbling experience to have my friend Lois see how easily Len neglected me. To make it worse, he was the one who brought the fever into the house. Yet, despite my embarrassment, at that moment I felt very close to Lois, grateful to have her as a friend.

Lois righted the overturned glass and poured water from a bottle. "Here. Drink this." And she put her hand behind my head to help me.

"I must have caught Len's illness. To make it worse, I'm pregnant."

"Yes," she said, "I thought as much. Does Len know?"

"Yes," I said, "he's known ever since I found out. He's so absorbed with his classes."

She lingered for some time. I couldn't judge how long she stood at the foot of my bed. Windows admitted a cold light.

Contours of trees fringed with the sun's pale glow stood out sharply, making weird shapes.

"Listen," Lois said, "you get well and we'll go to Texas for a few days at Easter. We'll see a movie and do some shopping. The trip will be on me. I insist."

I felt a rare pleasure shoot through me. The thought of going to the States for just a few days gave me something pleasant to hold on to.

"Don't say anything," Lois went on and smoothed the covers. "We're going to San Antonio."

Evening approached and the room darkened. I heard footsteps. It had to be Len; he had a ringing voice when he spoke, like laughter. Lois rose, left the room, and I could hear mumbling in the corridor, then the rustle of departure. Len came in to see how I was.

With a sly smile, he gave me a devilish wink and said, "The old man was really sick, but he's better now."

Flushed and excited, he sat on the edge of the bed, patted my hand, and told his story. When Len first talked, it seemed so natural and familiar. Something clicked in my mind as he constructed his tale, and I knew it was a lie; there was no old man.

In that moment, I realized that Len tinkered with reality, and that his lies were not lies for him, but roles that he would like to live out. Instinctively, he plunged into invention—I was sure of it now—the way he plunged into an evening of rum or tequila. It was his way of escape. I didn't press him on the story because I knew he hated explanations, seduced as he was by his own fictions and romance.

I listened silently and twisted my mouth in ironic agreement as he spun his web. If I listened hard enough, perhaps some clue would surface to something in his life that lay behind it all. He had no scruples, no guilt, no conscience. *What was behind it all?* I wanted to know the secret. His total lack of interest in my health no longer came as a surprise. I'd had a good taste of that when I

was in the hospital with Lenny. He wasn't happy that I was pregnant again, and maybe this was one way of dealing with it.

My heart beat rapidly. I could feel it thump in my temples and
fingertips. At last, I fell into a feverish sleep. I could hear Len's
words swirl through my head like a tropical squall as his exuber-
ance pursued me into my dream.

I saw myself on an ocean liner. Len stood on the dock, and
wherever he gazed, he made the ocean boil. Wild, unpredictable
storms crashed over the ship. The captain approached me and
said, "The food on this ship is extraordinary. We fish the seas and
bring up strange animals—baby octopus, mollusks, and slimy
animals. I hope you will like it."

Before I could reply, I found myself in the ocean, diving under
the ship. I swam through many shades of blue, levels and levels
beneath the ship, amazed at my ability to hold my breath.
Finally, I breached the surface. I saw Len's face everywhere in the
breaking waves. I was at sea for ten days.

When I awoke, the fever had broken. I was not angry with
Len. Overcome with great compassion, I wanted to help him. I
wanted him to face himself and be real. I loved him.

"Len," I called. When he entered, I said, "I'm going to go to
Texas with Lois for a few days. While I'm there, I'll make some
calls about Lenny's hand. Get me some names to contact."

My voice came out calm and strong.

Thirty-eight

Semana Santa

I leaned back in the seat and gazed out the window as Lois drove her wood-paneled yellow station wagon through the flat desert highlands. Off to the right, one lonely spiked dust devil collided with a large Saguaro cactus and dissolved on impact. The gritty dervish didn't have a chance with so great a giant.

It was a warm spring afternoon and the desert hinted at color to come. I had never been there at this time of year before the intense heat of summer baked the whole surface into sullen gray. My health had improved in the two weeks since we decided to make the trip. Today, I felt completely well. The road started to climb, and we headed up a slight pass.

Lois was a blonde woman with an easy face to look at—in no way extraordinary—yet open and honest. She did not appear capable of hiding anything. She was focused and personable, yet curiously detached.

"Look ahead. See? There." Lois pointed to a wall of sediment about twenty yards from the road.

"It looks like the land was turned on its side and came down right there." I replied and pointed to a dramatic layered area.

"They say it's a sign of an ancient earthquake," she said. "Some scientists believe that this part of the Sonoran desert was once connected to Southern California."

We drove past the huge rift in the earth's surface. Two great tectonic plates had been stretching and yawning until, at some distant point in the past, they settled into this present resting place. The shift seemed complete, revealing no sign of subterranean tension.

I took a deep breath. I had never been *al otro lado*, to the border, in weather like this. The sky was flawless, the air warm, and a soft breeze caressed my face through the open window. A mile farther down the road, two cars with Texas plates passed us from the opposite direction. The driver of the first car honked and waved. The second car, filled to capacity with young people, sped by with "hoots" and "hi's" trailing in the desert air.

"Looks like college kids going to Monterrey for the break," Lois said while she waved.

"I'm glad to be going the other way this time," I said. "At least for now."

In every direction, I saw unspoiled hills, rocks warming in the sun. Lois looked at me and smiled; I responded in kind. The day went by very fast.

"I'm glad you decided to come along," she said.

"Me, too. It's really good to be here, Lois." I was grateful to her for this unexpected treat—a shopping spree in Texas.

After driving for nearly four hours, we drove into the border crossing. Few people were traveling north, and within seconds, she and I breezed across. Two hours later, we were settled into adjoining rooms in a comfortable San Antonio hotel. Lois called room service and soon I enjoyed the luxury of iced tea along with a bacon, lettuce, and tomato sandwich—a combination that would always be a special treat.

I immediately made telephone calls to check out contacts for Lenny and soon learned that there were no such specialists in San Antonio.

"You have to go to a really big center, probably one with a medical school, to find that kind of specialist," the doctor's assistant told me.

When I gave the news to Lois, she told me, "It sounds to me like Lenny's hand isn't urgent. You'll resolve that problem soon. In the meantime, we're here to have fun."

The next day, Lois showed me the Alamo. Our guide, a graduate student from the local college, told the tale of brave men who fought for Texas—Davy Crockett and the Tennessee volunteers, Jim Bowie, and Colonel Travis.

A stroll through the Alamo Gardens led us to the *Paseo Del Rio*. Just as in San Diego, Spanish words punctuated the landscape. The river flowed through a tangle of hotels, bars, and restaurants. And there on the bank, a cobblestone trail charted a meandering course for city pedestrians and tourists alike. The smell of roasting corn and cold beer drew us forward in the direction of a tiny café.

"In a few days, this place will be teeming with tourists. We just made it." Lois motioned for us to sit at a table perched over the river.

Mexican pottery stacked in rows at the shop next to us formed a partition to the side of our table. Bright serapes in the shop doorway fluttered in the light breeze.

"How're you doing?" Lois asked and glanced down at my swollen feet.

"I'm fine." I tucked my feet under the chair. "I just don't want this bubble to burst. I feel like I'm in a picture postcard."

The next morning, our last in San Antonio, Lois took me shopping. She was as enthusiastic as I was when she bought me a pair of shoes and several maternity outfits. I so loved Lois and being pampered and made to feel as if I mattered. *Love is a Many*

Splendored Thing was playing at the Cinema near the Hotel, and we found time to see it that afternoon. I cried when Jennifer Jones lost her true love, William Holden.

He had the same erotic aura that Len had. Despite everything, I wanted to see my husband's smile again. I had to admit that I looked with awe on Len's impulsiveness and his primitive strength. I couldn't stop thinking about him.

As I settled into the passenger's seat for the long ride home to Monterrey, Lois chatted excitedly. She was consoling and understanding, someone with whom I could share things. We passed a field down the highway parallel to the riverbed.

"Those baskets for the children should be safe on the back seat. I always put the packages where customs can easily see them," she said.

Easter baskets for Jeanne and Lenny, along with bags and boxes of household goods, were piled almost to the window of the car.

"Do you think we'll have any trouble getting across?" I asked.

"I have a hunch it will all go smoothly," she said.

Lois took my passport along with hers and slipped a ten-dollar bill into each. The official, with apparent indifference, glanced into the back seat, checked our papers, and—tucking the bills into his pocket—smiled, then touched his cap and waved us on. Within a few seconds, Lois and I breezed across the border.

As we drove, the old concerns and worries came back to me. *What would Mr. Tarpey do when I strolled into class wearing my new maternity clothes? How would I pay the bills if I lost my job?* I was desperate to talk.

"I haven't mentioned my pregnancy to Mr. Tarpey," I said.

"It seems doubtful whether he even realizes the situation, you're so very thin," said Lois.

"I hope I've concealed the fact by wearing loose clothes."

"Well, you're going to have to tell him. I've just got a hunch it will turn out fine."

Lois and her hunches. The way she talked, it all sounded so reasonable. It was a relief to have someone to confide in. I felt a great warmth toward her because I felt understood, therefore known and accepted.

"So, Len's doing well in school?"

"He is, for now," I said. "The condition with his heart scares me, though. I think he does too much."

"What ever brought you two to Monterrey?"

As the afternoon wore on, I broad-brushed the story of Len's ambition, of his inability to get into school in the States, and of how Mexico seemed the perfect solution. When I came to the end of it, I said, "You apparently enjoy life in Monterrey."

"I enjoy living in an unfamiliar world, somewhat disoriented and uprooted. It's refreshing after the restraints in Boston. You'll get used to it."

"Right now, I just see new possibilities for problems," I said. "Do you think I'm crazy for believing in Len's dream?" I knew this wasn't a fair question. Lois didn't have all the facts, but I asked it anyway because I wanted to be reassured.

"Not at all. He's shown a lot of perseverance. I don't know him very well. However, the few conversations we've had lead me to believe he's right on track."

"I think so, too. I hold a vision of Len practicing medicine in some nice town. I can feel it."

The solace of open spaces full of weeds and thistles put me at ease. On top of that, Lois's bright optimism made me see things in a highly positive light. I considered the situation. Despite his lies, I had faith that Len could do it. Besides, lies weren't really lies to Len. They were little fictions, or "blarney," as the Irish say. For some reason, he needed a disguise. His friends were always awed and charmed by him and his stories. I just wanted to help him make his dream come true. It was so simple.

꧁

Semana Santa away from home had a therapeutic effect. The short break and Lois's encouragement managed to calm my nagging anxieties, but it must have been a cue for many new ones. Easter break ended all too soon. I had to deal with Mr. Tarpey and my pregnancy.

Three days after my return from San Antonio, I discussed the situation with Monica.

"Lois is right, Gail," she said. "You have to tell Tarpey."

"He's always disliked me. I know he'll jump at the opportunity to get rid of me. Even in the States, pregnant workers—much less teachers—have to leave their jobs. It's as if pregnancy were contagious."

"What if he does fire you? Lois Lowell wants to start up a new school next year. I know she'll want to bring you along. She's told me so. She's just waiting to get things lined up before she tells you."

Conversations like this with my friends—the two Loises, Monica, and Camille—gave me heart. Swept along by optimism, I imagined how I would walk into Tarpey's office, look him in the eye, and announce my condition. This decision brought me relief. It was time the secret was over.

By the end of Easter break, I was ready. Wearing my new maternity clothes, I returned to class where my students greeted me with applause and cheers of support. My spirits soared with such an ovation.

At the end of the first day back, I went into the office and made an appointment for the following day. All that week and the next, Mr. Tarpey avoided me. I told myself that things were going well, and therefore worked with more assurance and enthusiasm. I found myself able to work with great energy as my abdomen began to bulge more and more by the day.

It was toward the end of April that I got the message: Mr. Tarpey wanted to see me. It was a Friday, and as the day moved toward one o'clock, my apprehension increased. By the beginning of the last hour, the reaction to my recent days of work had set in. I should have told him before I marched in here wearing maternity clothes. I should have said something.

I walked across the courtyard and up the steps into the office. Mrs. Tarpey's large brown eyes watched me come toward her. That day, she was the secretary. Outside in the hallway, students were swirling noisily toward the street, toward freedom. Mrs. Tarpey's eyes fixed on me, then left me to scan uncomfortably the students outside, and then looked back at me as I approached her. Her small, sallow face took on a pinched expression.

"Good afternoon, Mrs. Burns." Her voice was soft, but agitated. "Go right on in." She rolled her eyes toward the open door to the principal's private office. Her face looked resigned.

I followed her direction and found Mr. Tarpey sitting behind his desk. As I came into his presence, I knew I was not out of the woods. His head bent over the desk, utterly engrossed in work. I noticed a shiny bit of scalp; his hair was thinning a little on top and he'd combed it over to try to cover the baldness.

"Close the door." His eyes did not flicker in my direction. With a slight jerk of the head, he motioned to the chair opposite him and carefully selected a paper from the stack, read it, then signed a document.

I sat in the chair opposite him, remembering the first time I had sat in this office. The same uneasiness came over me. The feeling grew into a dark, downward pull.

The office reeked of precision. Neat rows of books stood at attention in dark, mahogany bookcases. Except for a tidy stack of papers to Mr. Tarpey's right, the desk was bare. Its bright surface reflected light from the desk lamp.

"Of course, I'm going to have to let you go." He looked up. "Dismissal is in the best interest of the school."

"Why?" I sucked in air, knowing I couldn't hide my round belly, which almost touched the edge of the desk. It was viscerally painful to hear him.

Pale-blue eyes, magnified by large, gold-rimmed glasses, fixed on me. "Why? Why indeed." He added, "You've broken the contract. We don't hire teachers in your condition."

"I just want to finish the term. The students aren't bothered. In fact, they're happy for me. Many of them have moms at home in the same condition as me."

"Look at you! I watched you walk past the other day; you waddle like a duck. What gives you the absurd idea that we want you around here?"

"The students do," I argued as I felt my face flush red. I rose to leave and my knees trembled. I took in a breath and backed toward the door.

His eyes swept over me, judgmentally. "Your employment as of now is terminated. Get your things and get out. Mrs. Tarpey will take over from now on." His large, red face took on a stony contempt. "By the way, I know all about the *Copa de Oro*."

My breath quickened. His sarcasm hit the mark. I felt guilt pour through me like a stream from a cold underground source. *Did he know about Roberto?*

"What a disgrace that one of our teachers should be seen there." He picked up his pen. Icily and efficiently, he signed a document.

I turned my back on him and my eyes overflowed with tears. As I pushed the door open and stumbled out, I knew I would never see Mr. Tarpey again. He had wanted to hurt me, to humiliate me. His harsh words and frigid manner had done just that. I wiped my tears.

When I got to the counter outside, I noticed that Mrs. Tarpey had left. I leaned on the counter, flicked the hair away from my eyes, and grabbed a piece of notepaper to scribble a note to the real Lois.

What do you think? Tarpey fired me. I know I can still do the job and he knows it, too. He told me to get out on the spot.
Gail

I put the note into Lois Webster's cubbyhole. At the same time, I noticed a piece of paper in my cubbyhole. I took it out, opened it, and read.

Mr. Tarpey would like you to return your work documents immediately. Upon receipt of those papers, the school will return your passport.
Mrs. Tarpey

❦

On my return home that afternoon, I felt shattered. I realized that not only was my income gone, but—more important—my status as a legal resident. My papers were tied to my job at the Pan-American School. I told myself that life goes on and some-how mine would, too.

The next day I received a note from the real Lois.

Gail:
Your note reached me at a very bad moment. For the past few days, I have not been well and have been unable to take care of anything, except the basics. I'm asking you not to panic and to keep yourself as calm as possible. Things will turn out for the better. Don't hand over your documents to anyone.
Lois Webster

I sent a note back with Monica. She was, of course, still employed. I prayed that Mr. Tarpey had not heard that she, too, had been at the *Copa de Oro*.

My Dear Lois,

You are a good friend. Your note brought me hope. I am most concerned about my resident status at this point. I also need to make arrangements at a maternity hospital. La Muguerza, where I went last time, is too expensive and not an option. Isn't there a hospital near your home?

Gail

The following week, Lois came by the house.

"Let's go to the hospital and make your reservation. It's a public hospital, not private like *La Muguerza*, but very nice."

"Thanks, Lois. I'm sure it will be fine." I trusted her judgment. After all, she was from Mexico and knew the ins and outs of life in Monterrey far better that anyone else I knew.

"By the way, Gail, they don't fire women for getting pregnant in my country. This is México, and we have our own laws. Even Mr. Tarpey has to obey them. It's illegal to fire a pregnant woman. I've never heard of such rubbish. The women got together and issued an ultimatum to our fine principal. If you go, we all go." Lois was an intense and fiery woman. I knew that, yet I had never seen her quite like this.

"You mean you'd quit?" I stared at her in amazement.

"No, I mean *Huelga*! Strike!" She sounded offended and outraged. "This is our country, and he's going to have to abide by the rules."

"I can't believe it. You'd do this for me?"

"For you and for the principle of the thing. We all agree—Lois Lowell, Camille, Monica, me—all the other women on staff."

"I can't believe it," I said.

"He'll try to dig up all kinds of things against you. He would do the same to any of us and that's the point. Motherhood is a big deal in México and Tarpey doesn't get it. Pregnancy is cause for celebration, not termination. By the way, your class is having a shower for you next week, Saturday. They miss you."

༘

And so the table turned, somewhat. It was the end of April. Mr. Tarpey had his hands full having to deal with an angry faculty and an impending strike.

The real Lois took me for coffee. "Look, he's trying to extricate himself from a bad situation. He's told the bargaining committee that he's willing to give you a little something: severance pay."

"Like what?" I moved closer to her.

She sipped her coffee. "Mmm, good. Pay for a week or two. Not enough."

"Better than nothing," I said.

"The truth of the matter is that the severance is illegal, and he's just beginning to get it. No matter what, don't hand over your papers. Not yet— not to anybody. And Tarpey really wants them."

My heart beat rapidly, but I felt protected. The script of my life was being re-written by a group of women who refused to cave in.

༘

Shortly after the negotiations had begun, Mexican Immigration Officials showed up at our house. I saw the government car through the window and went to the front of the house. Len was home that day. He had a break between classes and came home for an early lunch.

As I opened the front door a crack, I heard Len rush out the back door. The official nudged the door open and came in.

"Señora Burns?" they demanded.

"Yes, how may I help you?"

"Mr. Tarpey needs your documents for the new teacher."

Lois was right. Tarpey really wanted the documents. The senior official asked to see my papers and passport. Then, he made the point that I needed to leave the country immediately. In fact, that very day.

I presented my resident papers. They clearly stated, "Valid until July 1959."

"As you can see, my papers are in order. I understand that Mr. Tarpey wants them." I snatched back the papers. "As for my passport, Mr. Tarpey has it. We have some unfinished business."

The senior official took a step closer. "Give the papers, Señora." There was a look in his hard-nut eyes that said he meant business.

"First, give me my passport." I remembered what Lois had told me and tucked the papers in my bra.

"*¿Mande?*"

I repeated, "If you don't give me my passport, I refuse to go. Besides, I'm due to have the baby at any time," I exaggerated and added, "any minute."

The officials hesitated.

"Bur Mr. Tarpey said—" said the junior official.

"If you force me out today, whatever happens to me and to this baby will be on your conscience."

One of the men clearly understood English. He winced.

"I will complain to the U.S. Consul, if I have to." By now I was shouting.

"We were ordered to escort you out."

"You can escort me to the Consul General of the United States of America," I screamed. "I'll tell them Mr. Tarpey has my passport and refuses to give it to me. That's bound to be illegal. How much did he pay you to do this?" I was choking with rage and my body trembled.

"Okay, okay," said the senior official. "*Más tarde.*" Miraculously, they backed off.

When the officials left, I was still shaking. I was angry with Len for sneaking out and not standing by me. Once again, he had left me in the lurch. *What if they had tried to force me out?* I knew his reason: if they had caught Len without proper papers, he could be pulled into the tangle of red tape and probably expelled from Mexico. Given the circumstances, I would have liked him to take a chance. Just once, I wanted him to risk something for me. But, of course, he didn't.

Thirty-nine

Frederick William

My trouble with Mr. Tarpey had begun in the spring. And now today—the first day of summer—there was still no resolution. Officially, nothing had happened. Everybody knew that there had to be an end to it. After all, we had all agreed.

The drama moved into its final act that May. All of us, with our different points of view, had come up with a solution. The faculty insisted that I be paid for the entire year. In return, after the birth of the baby, I would go to the border and exit the country. Once in the States, I would relinquish my resident papers, then pick up my passport and a check for my full pay from a neutral party in Laredo.

"It's your choice," Lois Webster had said. "Just sign the agreement and Tarpey will send you a nice check and your passport. Then, you can return the work permit and all will be in order."

All this had come about because the strike at the Pan-American School succeeded. It had been a real coup, all engineered by the "*tocayas*," the two Loises who, as it turned out, were my two guardian angels.

It was late June. I sat on the porch in the shade with a bowl of white grapes in my lap. Crystal juice ran down my fingers. The tiles felt cool and soothing to my swollen feet. Everything about me was swollen by now, since I was due momentarily. I could hear Paula singing a Mexican love song in the kitchen with her accompaniment of the clang of pots and pans as she scrubbed and polished.

Lenny sat on the floor next to me. He reached up and I handed him a grape. At fifteen months, he kept up his growing pace and was still as large as Jeanne. Something about his mouth and dimples hinted at the man he would be.

Every now and then, without looking up from his toys, he reached out to touch my foot. Every now and then, I reached down to stroke his head.

From our house at the top of the little hill, I looked down the tree-lined street toward the main avenue past little one-story homes, new additions to the neighborhood. I waited for the postman. The first subtle sign of his arrival was the sound of his bell, and even from this distance, I could hear the tinkle long before he turned into *Calle Estados Unidos*.

"Trring, Trring."

There it was, soft and inviting. A little tinkle of hope drifted in on waves of hot air. From a distance, the little sound was nearly lost in the bustle of the *colonia*. A million *cicadas* the size of hummingbirds hummed rhythmically.

Within three minutes, the postman appeared around the corner. He was pumping hard up the hill past the vacant lot immediately below us. I felt a little pain, but not much.

Not now. Not yet.

The postman pulled up to the front of the house. He wore heavy, old-fashioned glasses and a blue uniform with a little cap. When he saw me, he smiled and stopped just long enough to stretch forward and hand me a single letter, calling out, *"Buenos dias, Señora, adiós,"* in one fluid movement. He waved at Lenny and pedaled away.

I nodded gratefully, and my heart pounded when I saw that the envelope bore the Pan-American insignia. I ripped it open.

The porch went silent. The air was dusty and still. The letter read:

> *Your passport is waiting for you in Laredo. Please turn your work visa over to Mr. Jacoby at the designated address and he will give you your passport and check.*

I stared in disbelief. I needed more time. Now, I was really sweating. I tried to relax. An address with a map of Laredo, Texas was enclosed. On the map, a big, red circle highlighted the address where, presumably, I would meet up with Mr. Jacoby. I felt another pain and this one could not be ignored.

How could I get to Laredo now? Laredo was four to five hours away and across the barren desert. And I would have to go with Jeanne. She was on my passport and I couldn't return to Mexico alone.

I leaned on the wall with a view of the street in the late morning light. I stifled a cry and went inside. I allowed five minutes to pass from the time I received the letter to calling Paula for help. There was to be no trip to Laredo that day. An hour later, I was at the hospital where Dr. Salas Garza met me. Fortunately, he also served at the public hospital.

"*Buenos, buenos,*" all around.

The staff hustled me onto a stretcher, and I was rushed into the delivery room with a mask placed over my nose and mouth. By now, I knew the routine. Before any serious pain brutally bore down on me, I was drifting in the glorious "twilight sleep." Falling, falling, falling. Dreaming, dreaming.

From far away, I heard, "*Es un hombre.*" Then came waves of darkness followed by nothing.

Despite intervals of light and movement, I slept. Something seemed wrong. So much sleep. An image of my doctor ordering people about flickered in the distance. He seemed impatient.

I heard voices followed by a woman speaking, almost whispering. She asked what the problem was. Doctors and nurses came and went. If Len came, I didn't know it. I awoke one morning noticing that the deep-green curtains had been drawn. Dr. Garza and a nurse entered the room.

"You are fine." The doctor nodded to the nurse who gave me an injection and I slept again. In this very drowsy state, I saw the baby. He was blond, wiry, and also very sleepy. More blackness. In rare moments of lucidity, quietly gathering concerns began to surface. I felt hours slipping by. Time distorted.

It was light. Breakfast came and went. And then, in the corner of the room, I noticed Kitty. Dear Kitty—she was not by nature a vibrant, voluble woman, but this morning she appeared to be.

"They say you are fine." Her statement sounded more like a question.

"Yes, all went well, very fast. I remember nothing."

"The Mexican doctors are really very good. And your doctor is the best, they say."

I nodded in agreement.

She briefly went on about news in the *colonia*, and endlessly chattered about the medical students, final exams, and—of course—the heat. Kitty rattled on. This was not like the Kitty that I knew. Finally, she became settled and drew in a long, deep breath, then asked, "But what is wrong with the baby? Will he be all right?" She emphasized "wrong with," and had an uncanny evenness to her voice.

Wrong with the baby? The words slowly penetrated my awareness, but with a kind of delayed reaction, and not knowing exactly what she meant, I answered, "Oh, he's fine. I believe he is fine. I've heard nothing contrary."

As soon as the words were out, I knew it wasn't true. Some sort of creative disagreement with everything around me surfaced. I was confused. *And where is Len?* I had not seen him since the birth.

"Have you a name for the baby?" Kitty didn't sound alarmed.

I responded calmly to her words. "Yes, I'll call him Frederick William, after my grandfather. In Spanish—Federico Guillermo."

"Sounds impressive. He is adorable." Kitty squeezed my hand. "Count on me to help in any way I can." She nodded to emphasize her words of support, then backed out of the room.

Why do I not feel anything? I seemed to hover in a twilight space where feeling did not exist—a place of pure mind. I began to wonder, *What was wrong with the baby? Why had I been kept sedated?* I would have felt frightened if I could feel fear. I wanted to see the baby.

Fortunately, I did not have to wait long. The nurse appeared with babe in arms. She placed him next to me, and as soon as she moved toward the door, I raised myself up. I'd done it too quickly and winced from the pain. Still haunted by Kitty's words, I propped myself on the pillows and began to undress the baby. I checked his fingers and toes. All there, he seemed fine. Then I turned him over and discovered what looked like a little finger at the base of the spine. I touched it. He didn't move or seem to mind. I dressed him again and waited. The disturbing discovery made me angry. *What presumption of them!* To have to learn about this by accident—I shuddered not knowing what it could all mean.

Dr. Garza appeared about a half an hour later. He glanced around, as if good humor should prevail in the room, and approached me. He took my hand.

"Well, you have done very well."

"Tell me what's wrong with the baby," I directed.

"Well, you see, he has this little problem," he coughed nervously. "It is like a little growth at the tip of the spine. We will just put it back inside. All will be well."

"What is it? Tell me what this means."

"Something very slight. Now, rest."

"No, I want to know what it means." I worked to fight back tears.

He reseated himself, and with a stern look said, "Make your-self comfortable. Get strong. Don't jump to conclusions." His gaze held me for a few moments. Then, he rose and left. It had been a brief, bitter visit.

Hours later, I pried information out of a nurse. I discovered the issue was spina bifida—not a little problem.

I was not angry with Dr. Garza for not telling me the truth. He was trying to protect me. He wanted me to recover and heal so that I could nurse my baby. In the end, I felt nothing except com-passion for him. I trusted him.

It was only much later that night that Leonard finally made his appearance. As soon as I saw him, I told him, "We have to leave Mexico."

"Yes, I know you have to go to Laredo to get your passport and your money. I can't go; I have finals. I'm in the middle of finals," he repeated.

"I don't mean that; I'll handle that. We have to leave here for good. I mean it."

He would not look at me.

"I want to leave here, Leonard, and I want to go soon. The baby needs attention. Have you seen him?" I tried to keep my expression neutral, reasonable, although my tone of voice might not have been.

Len's face was impassive. "Of course I've seen him. Just listen to Dr. Garza and do what he tells you." In other words, submit.

Standing before the windows, with his frame backlit, he declared that he had to focus on the present, on the exams. Too much was at stake to panic now.

Forty

The Mountains

As soon as I arrived home from the hospital, I made plans to go to Laredo. I had to go; I needed my passport. I arranged to have Lenny and the new baby cared for, then loaded the car with water and canned milk for Jeanne. While planning the journey, I experienced conflicting feelings: excitement, because the trip would be both hazardous and necessary, and sadness at leaving a tiny baby who was so dependent upon me. For his sake, I wanted to speed up the departure. At the same time, I feared that something awful might happen on the journey.

Leaving at dawn, I planned to be back the same night. I had to be; I was nursing a baby and my breasts would start to overflow before too much time elapsed. Besides, I didn't want to put additional strain on the newborn. He had been through so much, already. Incredibly resilient, he rarely cried and seemed normal in every way, except for the finger-shaped growth at the base of his spine. The road was rough. I calculated that it would take about six hours to get to Laredo.

All was ready. I put Jeanne into her car seat and drove out of Monterrey into the hot, dry desert of Northern Mexico. Jeanne slept during most of the trip, and for this I was grateful. For the first few miles, I thought of the tasks at hand. My mind moved

335

mechanically, ticking off items that had to be accomplished: money, gas, lunch, bank, Mr. Jacoby.

I headed out of Monterrey, past the airport cut-off, and eventually proceeded down the long, hair-raising stretch of highway between Monterrey and Nuevo Laredo. From there, it would be just seconds to the other side—Laredo, Texas.

Crossing the flatlands, we occasionally drove through villages. At one of them, shops were just opening. I carefully made my way through the town center full of milling vendors as Mexican commerce yawned into life, colorful and aromatic. Through the open stalls of the bazaar, I could see stoic faces.

We passed a woman on a tiny, gray donkey. In her arms, she held a child wrapped in a faded blue cover. A man in a green, scarlet, and yellow serape walked beside the woman. He wore a large sombrero on his head. Farther on, we passed a procession of women carrying baskets on their heads on the way to market. If I'd brought Len's camera, I could have snapped classic shots of Mexico, worthy of postcards.

To the far right, masses of mountains became clear, backed by white, thread-like clouds. As we climbed the foothills, village life disappeared. Not a soul in sight for miles.

The road twisted and turned through the canyon rims, plunging downward. I guided the car around endlessly winding curves—butterflies fluttering inside me at the edges of steep drop-offs. Below the many escarpments and gullies lay rusted or charred relics of trucks and cars that had missed a turn. The burnt-out remains offered warnings.

This place, so far from civilization with no sign of human life anywhere, held a stark beauty, yet it also terrified me. The trip was not an enjoyable summer drive. I steeled myself, not knowing what awaited us at the end of this potholed road, marked with crosses commemorating the loss of lives in countless accidents. I glanced back at sleeping Jeanne, sorry for having to put one so young, so vulnerable, at such risk.

The early hours had been cool. By midday, a severe sun flashed an unendurable glare. Shimmering heat wove the yellow, gray, and brown tones together. Pale, stagnant air and a fearful wasteland enveloped us. Jeanne, her blonde head drooping to one side, alternately dozed or watched the passing scene, all the while contentedly sucking her thumb.

To one side in the yellow sandstone mountains, I noticed dark caves and pointed them out to Jeanne. The approaches must have been worn away by the elements.

"*Mira, las montañas.*" I made up a little story about a giant who lived there, in great, high caverns long ago.

Jeanne pointed to the mountains, her eyes now wide with interest. As I spun tales, she listened to me in a way that she never did when Len was present. Soon, the warm breeze and movement of the car lulled her back to sleep.

High above, like aeries of winged gods, the isolated caves remained protected, the sandy haze elevating them high into the sky. I slowed down as the imposing view of the mountains tempted my gaze upward. I shivered a little despite the heat.

A *power emanates from these mountains*, I thought.

Despite everything, a sense of fearlessness came over me. I recalled a line from the Bible, "I lift mine eyes unto the hills whence cometh my redemption."

In that moment of peace, I said a prayer.

I had not far to go; I knew I would get the job done.

With Fred's arrival, the problem of life in Mexico had taken on new dimensions. I had to forge ahead, and I knew I had the will to do whatever needed to be done.

※

At last, the brown adobe building marking the border appeared not far ahead. The walls and portico were broadly constructed, and as I pulled into a gigantic shadow, the guard simply glanced at us and waved us on. *A miracle.* I felt tremendous relief and headed toward the American flag, flying high a few yards away.

We drove through Laredo, looking out the windows at restaurants, stores, and theaters. An unpretentious little Texas town, it possessed an uncluttered calm. I parked the car, took out the map, and after a few wrong starts, located the designated office. I found Mr. Jacoby alone sitting at a desk. With Jeanne in my arms, I approached him.

"Mr. Jacoby?" I said.

He was a small man with white hair, a gray mustache, and a fastidious manner.

"Yes. Who are you?" Gray eyes peered over half-rimmed glasses.

"I'm Gail Burns. You have a package for me, I believe?"

"Yes," he said. "But first—"

"Here, I think this is what you want." I handed him my package. I wanted to cut through any complications. He nodded and, in return, handed me the passport and the check.

"Thank you." I turned and left with a sense of relief. I wanted to be out of the office as soon as possible. The exchange had the uncanny feel of espionage.

Once back in the car, I got my bearings and took Jeanne to a clean, cool restaurant where I ordered scrambled eggs and toast for her. I had an American hamburger and French fries, which tasted better at that moment than any meal I had ever eaten. I drank American coffee and Jeanne slurped orange juice.

We did some essential shopping, mainly for baby food and infant supplies, and headed back to the border. Everything was going as planned. I turned on the radio and there was the voice of Elvis with a tight, driven beat. "You're right, I'm left, she's gone," the boy from Memphis wailed.

Staring straight ahead, I drove out of Laredo with Elvis singing of unclouded youth. To the south lay the border crossing. Minutes later, I pulled into the portico and my heart began pounding. Guards milled around—some faces smiling, some gloomy. I flashed my passport. Another miracle: we passed with no problem. What a wonderful sensation!

It was cool in the clear evening. The moon had not yet risen. Ahead of us lay the sandy flats and behind them the blue mountains in all shades from midnight to purple.

I began a story, "Once upon a time, there were three little pigs . . . " Reaching over toward Jeanne, I placed a protective scarf over her head. Flies, mosquitoes, earwigs—Mexico offered them all.

Jeanne turned her head to listen to my words. "Then I'll huff and I'll puff . . . " together we blew and blew. When the story ended, I gave her a bottle. As I leaned over, I felt the pressure building in my breasts. They began to throb.

In the evening light, we drove through an opal desert. To the left, there were rolling hills. In two days, it would be the fourth of July, the day of our American Institutions, the day of the founders. We'd be home in Monterrey to celebrate with the other U.S. Citizens. I looked forward to what I hoped would be a moment of regeneration for all of us.

We followed a broad plain southwest of Laredo. By now, it had become very dark, and just ahead lay the fifty-mile checkpoint. I had completely forgotten all about it. As I approached the stop sign, the road was enveloped in clouds of dust. A large bus passed me then pulled in ahead and to the right in the station designated *Camiones.*

For a moment, a trail of yellow-gray dust obscured everything. The mountains disappeared. And then, out of the cloud, the guard approached me on the driver's side.

"*¿A dónde van ustedes?*" He shined his flashlight in the car. The beam fell on Jeanne who, in her tousled state, looked like an angel asleep on the backseat full of baby toys, blankets, and pillows.

I answered in English, "I'm going to Monterrey." I gave the gringo pronunciation of Monterrey. "To see friends," I added. I could feel the painful pressure in my breasts, aware that I was beginning to drip milk.

"*¿Sólita?* Alone?" he asked, switching to English.

"Yes. I'm in a hurry to get there tonight." My heart raced.

"But *Señora*, you cannot travel this desert alone. There are *banditos* at night."

"I must get there." Tears welled up in my eyes.

"But thieves and robbers are out there, *Señora*. Wait a minute." He turned and went to the bus.

A minute passed, then more minutes. I was nervous and afraid. It had been a tiring day and I had not counted on this. Obviously, the official wanted to do the right thing, but I didn't know. What cash I had was concealed in a money belt around my waist. Maybe he would make me take the bus, but that didn't make sense.

The official finally got off the bus with a young man in tow. He had his arm on the man's shoulder. The man was waving his arms about in anger or frustration. Meanwhile, the official—who by now had a firm grip on the struggling man's arm—was obviously cajoling him into accompanying me. They both glanced my way. These well-intentioned efforts to help me were beginning to have a maddening effect.

Hurry up, hurry up, hurry up. Decide. Let me go.

The officer disappeared for several more excruciating minutes. The Mexican man, dressed in a nice suit and tie, staggered under apparent intoxication as he walked over to a post and leaned against it.

The bus pulled out, leaving the three of us to figure out what to do. I was in no position to argue with the official. After all, I was entering his country illegally and I think he knew it.

The officer appeared again, carrying something, and accompanied the stumbling drunk to my car.

Some escort! I couldn't believe the official intended to put this drunk in as protection against anything at all.

"Look," said the officer, "this man is from Monterrey. His father owns the big brewery. Good family, very good family. He will drive you."

Drive me? What kind of insanity was this?

The guard opened the door on my side, took the keys, and ordered me to sit in the passenger seat.

I had no choice but to comply.

"It will be better this way," he added.

Then, he shoved the strange young man into the driver's seat and yelled at him for a while in Spanish. The gist of it was that he was telling the tipsy fellow to be a gentleman and help a lady in distress.

"*Sí*," said the official, "he will be your escort."

The official handed the man a cup of coffee from a thermos he'd carried over and watched the man drink it down.

And then, at long last, the official handed him the keys to my car.

All this had eaten my traveling time, and I was panicky about getting back.

"All right," I said, "and thank you for being so concerned."

The guard focused on the young man saying, "*Ándale, pues.*"

The stranger started the car and we drove off into the night. I was astonished at how the events of the day had piled up. I had planned everything, but how could I have planned for this?

"My name is Gail Burns," I said, wanting to keep him awake.

"Jorge," he hiccupped. "Jorge."

The summer moon had moved far into the blackness of the western sky. We sped off. Before me was the possibility of night in the desert, in the heart of a most dangerous terrain—and on top of everything, a strange, inebriated man in command of my automobile.

I decided to keep him awake by talking and we chatted until past midnight. I learned about his father, the brewery, and his drinking spree in Laredo with American friends. We had not completed half the journey before he reached his hand over and began to paw at my swollen breasts. Milk poured in great profusion.

I took his hand and firmly pressed it back in place on the steering wheel.

"Look," I lied, "is that a coyote?"

He squinted his eyes to see the phantom animal. Finding nothing, and as if by instinct, his hand groped again in my direction. I slapped his wrist and, once again, placed his hand on the wheel.

"For God's sake, keep your hands on the wheel." I reached in back for a diaper and stuffed it into my bra to stench the flow. "Don't you want to get home?" I was cold, my entire bosom sticky and wet.

He nodded. I fought back fear—fear of him, of unknown robbers, and of the winding, dangerous road. I told myself to keep focused. I glanced at Jeanne—safe, at least for the moment—in the back seat.

"Slow down," I begged. "Más despacio, por el amor de Diós."

Throughout the night, we wound our way through the shadowy desert as the road seemed to writhe. Maybe it was better to have a man in the car, even though he seemed useless to me. Here and there, I recognized sights seen earlier in the day, now contorted in the moonlight. My memory flashed on sights of the burnt-out wrecks that we had seen earlier. Sharp curves and precipices lay ahead.

Jorge's foot weighed down on the accelerator again, and I insisted again that he slow down. Crawling was better than careening. To make things worse, his pathetic assault on my breasts persisted. Finally, I'd had enough. I insisted that I drive.

Grinning broadly, he agreed and we switched seats. His head promptly fell on my shoulder. He threw his arm around my waist, and in a short time, passed out. Gray masses appeared on the distant horizon. At last, flat land.

I sped through the squatting little villages. A rooster crowed in the distance. While it was still dark, I passed the airport road and finally drove into Monterrey as pale lemon yellow lit the sky. The Dos Equis brewery was to my right. I slammed on the brakes, shook Jorge, and pointed to the door.

"You're home," I said.

Puzzled, he rubbed his puffy eyes. His grin hovered next to me. I pointed to the brewery and said, "*Adiós.*" I heard myself laugh, high-pitched and half-strangled. "*Adiós.*"

Jorge heaved himself out of the car and stumbled toward the brewery. I began to tremble and couldn't keep my hands still on the steering wheel. What should have taken no more than six or seven hours had taken twelve.

I arrived home just as the household was waking up. Lenny ran down the hall to meet me as I approached with Jeanne in my arms.

"Papá?" she said and bit her lip. I put her down to seek him out.

I sponged my breasts, then found the baby, sat down, and immediately put him to the breast. He sucked away content, as if I had never been gone. At first, the pain was excruciating. After a few moments, it subsided. I watched my baby nurse, his dimples popping in and out.

Len came out of the bedroom rubbing sleepy eyes. "Did you have a nice trip?" he asked.

Part Five

Forty-one

Independence Day

"Look, Mamá." Jeanne pointed to a large American Flag flying high in the summer breeze. Lenny followed her lead and went wide-eyed with pleasure.

The flag flew from a large pole on a point within the compound, a stately and prosperous-looking square of buildings that lay ahead of us. Leonard turned into the drive and we were on the property of National Steel, a U.S. owned concern outside of Monterrey. A corridor of cypress, like a walled fortress, led toward the plant. There was a distinct serenity and privacy about the place.

"The red, white, and blue," I said.

Jeanne repeated, "Red, white, and blue."

Every year, the U.S. citizens in Monterrey come here to celebrate the Fourth of July. We went because we wanted to reconnect with a sense of home, and for just one day, be with Americans. The whole event was a wondrous ceremony with a big, exotic show of patriotism that celebrated Independence Day in a way that never meant so much to me at home.

We made our way toward the entrance, which was festooned with red, white, and blue balloons. As I stood by the gate, several families from *Colonia Vista Hermosa* passed by. Women wearing silky, flimsy dresses and men in crisp, short-sleeved shirts nodded "hello." Many of the children were waving small American flags in greeting and someone handed one to Jeanne. Dressed in a white sunsuit with red ribbons in her hair, she looked like a poster child for U.S. Travel.

Jeanne, in a nearly perfect parrot-like imitation of the words she heard, called out "Happy Fourth of July." Growing up in Mexico had sharpened her ear. She quickly responded in either Spanish or English, gauging by accent which one was most appropriate. In contrast, Lenny spoke no English at all. Usually, that made no difference, since most of the people we knew were bi-lingual. But today was the day of English and of Americana.

"Let's go, Papá." Jeanne tugged at Leonard's arm.

He catered to her and let her have her way. Meanwhile, Lenny helped me push his new brother in the *carrito* as we strolled through the compound.

Inside, there were hamburgers, corn on the cob, cotton candy, and lemonade. There were sack races, watermelon-eating contests, and music. I loved the flags, the games, the kids with ice cream, the music in the bandstand. I loved the soft air, rich with favorite aromas. I loved everything about the place.

The sun was hot and white, and the trees cast a blurry pattern on the sidewalks, which wound through the promenade. At some point, a booming voice announced over the loud speaker, "Ladies' beer drinking contest! Two o'clock! Bandstand! "

I have a chance at that, I thought, since many of the families in attendance were Seventh Day Adventists and were teetotalers. None of them would participate, I guessed. That would limit the field.

Len's mouth fell open in surprise as I shoved the *carrito* with Lenny in it to him, handed him the baby, and mounted the stage. The Master of Ceremonies, a tall man with very black eyebrows, greeted me and explained the rules. Then, he placed a familiar bottle of *Dos Equis cerveza* in front of each of the contestants. I had guessed correctly; there were just six of us. I was thirsty and I was a nursing mother. Maybe I had an edge. Besides, beer is good for nursing babies.

"Go!" yelled the man. My heart rate quickened and I drank without bothering to breathe. I slammed the bottle down and emerged the winner.

"Congratulations," the man said and handed me a blue ribbon. The crowd cheered.

I had not had any alcohol during, and since, my pregnancy, so the beer flooded me with an exhilarating sensation. I felt a flush lingering on my face and neck.

We spent the remainder of the afternoon visiting with friends and listening to speeches given by company officials and the Consul General. Gradually, the sky darkened.

When the sky overhead was sufficiently dark, the fireworks began. We found a place on the grass, sat down, and watched the shimmering explosions above our heads. Lenny squirmed closer to me while the baby slept on a blanket spread out beside me.

"Ooh! Ahh!" I could hear voices around me.

Jeanne cuddled in her father's lap as luminous showers of color cascaded down from the night sky. My attention was held upward as if some artist were guiding my eyes. The fireworks added to the experience that I'd had when I had gazed on the mountains during my trip to Laredo. I wanted to surrender to the power that made such beauty—the red that glowed ruby, then shimmered into silver. I watched for a long time—burst after burst of glimmering color. I felt as if an angel folded me in arms of light protecting me from all harm.

Kaboom. A gold and green explosion.

"How beautiful!" I cried.

Fluid light overhead drizzled down slowly as if in a dream. *I have so much to be grateful for.* In that light, the blades of grass appeared luxuriant. The far mountains stood like a protective purple wall. Even from so great a distance, I could feel their power.

We left at half past eight, before the crowd. We crossed the grounds strewn with red, white, and blue streamers, napkins, and cups—magical remnants of a magical night. As we drove home by the river, all three children fell asleep.

"I did well on all of the final exams." Leonard's voice broke the spell.

"Great." There was a new edge in my voice. All day, I had not once thought about Leonard, medical school, or his obsession with it. I'd just returned from a wild trip to and from Laredo. And there was Fred's condition to consider. I could no longer relate to Len's agenda. The baby's condition was not a fairytale; it was a catastrophe and no one would talk about it. No one.

"Well, you won't have to take another exam for at least six months," I said flatly, not really interested.

"Thank God! Next year will be easier. You'll see." His voice expressed the relief he must have been feeling.

I shrugged. "Sure."

Our house sprawled at the top of a quiet street lined with porches and gardens. Tonight, there was no traffic from the busier street nearby. We reached home by nine-thirty and proceeded into the house in the cool stillness under the moonlight. The living room was dim and we carried the sleeping children to their beds.

As I came back to the living room, I noticed a letter on top of the desk. Paula must have put it there before she went to bed. I picked it up, aware of an official letterhead that read: "University of Tennessee." Above me on the bookshelf loomed the skull. On the desk was a small pile of medical books, a bottle of rum, and glasses.

And then I recalled that Leonard had written to the University of Tennessee to inquire about a possible transfer. However, that was months ago in the winter and we had all but given up on the idea.

"Leonard," I called out, "there's a letter for you."

The bedroom was at the other end of the house and he came down the long hallway. He approached me and, with a quizzical look, took the letter.

He hesitated for a moment. I watched his face as he read. I saw comprehension of good news and had a vision of us moving to Tennessee. He poured himself a drink of rum, then read the letter again. He set it down on the desk. He stretched, reached for his drink again, and gazed blankly at the shelf of books. And then his face flushed.

I stood, watching him within a hazy bubble of expectation, terrified at what he might say. I took a few steps toward him.

"They want me to take a test," he said.

"What do you mean?" I wanted to learn more.

His eyes went wide. "They say they'll send me an exam and, if I pass, they'll accept me to their second year."

"What do you have to do?" A clammy layer of perspiration had built up on my forehead.

"If I agree, they will send the exam here—to the American Consulate—and I'm to take the test. It will be sealed and sent back. Then, we'll see."

At the mention of the test, he appeared tense and ashen. I knew that he hated tests. The darkened room was empty and I sunk into a chair. The words came out sounding cold and automatic.

"Curious. We saw the Consul General today," I said. "You'll have to go to the Consulate tomorrow and call the University."

For a moment, he gave the impression that he was a man on the point of death. The exams in Mexico were oral and Leonard had been able to work this to his advantage. He knew how to leverage his garrulous personality, his facility with language, and his quick response. I realized that now, with this new opportunity, he felt helpless. In our personal world of ever-changing borders, he would have to submit to an extensive exam—the kind of thing that had beaten him in the past in the States.

Oh, how I wanted this opportunity.

Forty-two

Adiós, México

Eleven days had passed since Fred's birth. From doctors, books, and friends, we gathered bits of information. That night, it all came together, at least for me. The realization that the new baby had a serious birth defect destroyed all pleasantries and trivial conversation. No one knew for sure what effects the spina bifida would have, but I knew: it would be devastating. I was his mother.

Paula brought scrambled eggs, *frijoles*, and handmade tortillas to the table, but I could only pick at my food. Dinner conversation faltered badly. I couldn't revive it and the meal ended in awkward silence. Attempting to collect my wandering thoughts on Len or his new opportunity was impossible. My attention was elsewhere; it was on Fred.

I couldn't help but wonder if the baby's birth defect had been my fault with so much negative energy around me during the pregnancy. I wondered if the physical body of my offspring had been affected. The conditions of life had been trying, even harsh. I had been ill and exposed to fever. Dr. Garza had assured me that this was not the case. "It happens," he told me the day I left the hospital. I kept hearing that in my ears.

"You're daydreaming." Len broke the silence.

"No, I'm just thinking of Fred."

"I've made arrangements," Len replied.

"For what?" I thought it had to do with the exam. I was happy for him, but I was preoccupied with the baby.

"One of the professors at the school will operate on Fred. He's a Board Certified Plastic surgeon. I think it's best that we do it soon."

Listening to him, I felt a terrible tension build. I nodded slowly and shifted uncomfortably in my chair. At last, a specialist would see my baby, but the idea of surgery on so tiny a person terrified me.

Two days later, the Mexican doctor undertook the difficult task of operating on our pint-sized baby. Fred looked small and vulnerable on the huge stretcher. I looked down at him and my gut wrenched as they rolled him away from me, down the hospital hall and into surgery. I gathered my resolve. After they took him away, I leaned on the railing of the balcony, which overlooked the quad and I stared out the window toward the *colonia*.

Life was so unfair. This tiny baby, trapped in a disfigured body and by family problems, too. The smell of hospital scents hung in the air as a reminder of the place and the event. I lingered in the hall and paced back and forth between the door to surgery and the hospital window. Len sat by the window smoking one Camel cigarette after the other. Several hours later, the door swung over and the surgeon, still in his green scrubs, came toward us.

The doctor spoke to Len in hushed tones. I sighed with relief when it was over. A big hurdle had been overcome; the operation was finished. The doctor told us that the little piece of spine that looked like a finger of skin was now tucked inside the baby's lower back.

When we came home from the hospital, Leonard sat me down in the living room and took my hands the way he had done when he told me about my grandfather's death.

Len looked up with a worried frown. "There's more. They say Fred will never walk. I'm so sorry. The lower part of his body will be affected, you see. It lacks proper enervation." There was a new kindness in his voice.

This was the Leonard that I loved—the man who could make me feel awash in a love that destroyed all barriers. I closed my eyes, searching for a way to express what I was feeling, but words failed to come. Anguish washed over and through me, and then came denial.

We have to go to the States, I thought.

One part of me wanted Leonard to succeed, to have his dream. Still another part, even stronger, wanted refuge from the chaos and trauma that life in Monterrey had brought. And now, a new conflict had emerged: anguish for Fred against Leonard's dream. It drained me.

The new baby must have had his father's resilience. He bounced back from surgery with amazing speed and vitality. A quiet joy came over me when I held him as if there were a private secret between us. The baby squirmed in my arms and looked up with wide, innocent eyes. His mouth turned up at the corners in a crooked smile that stirred me deeply. His tiny, wiry body brought up haunting memories and a sense of familiarity came over me. I'd seen a look of amused tenderness when his eyes met mine.

ᛉ

The exam from the University of Tennessee arrived sooner than we'd thought, and Len received notification from the Consul General to arrange a meeting a week later.

It was another blazing summer day when Leonard presented himself to the U.S. Consulate at the appointed hour. He spent two grueling days taking written exams in basic physiology, anatomy, and chemistry. Then we waited.

The days dragged by. Lois Lowell invited us to her home for dinner. When we arrived, she took Len out to the verandah. Through the window, I saw them together—Len and Lois, talking. He gestured with his hands in excitement. Lois bent her head down and listened. From time to time, she nodded. They rose and she gave him that same maternal smile that had given me so much reassurance.

The second letter from the University of Tennessee came the first week of August. It read:

August 20, 1957
You have passed the examination and have been accepted to the second year of Medical School. Classes begin the second week of September. Congratulations.
Dean of Admission

Len waved the letter like a flag. He screamed, "I passed!"

With that scream, I knew we'd be going to the States.

The exam had covered those very subjects that Leonard had learned by heart during the past two years in Mexico. All he had to do was translate that knowledge into English. He was elated. I was, too, but for very different reasons. Mainly, I just wanted to go home.

That evening, the announcement of Len's huge success was followed—of course—by a rowdy, drinking spree with Leonard and his friends celebrating on the rooftop. There were whoops and hollers of congratulations and amazement.

Leonard found support and connection through the gang, but I never found that kind of support or understanding from him. Listening to the party above me, I thought about the women I knew: the ones who were helpful, the ones who stood by, even risking a strike. They had taught me so much. Friends, sisters, and guides—those women were the ones I could share things with and laugh with. I loved them. Most of all, there was power that came from the connection, like an electric magnet that drew us together, like batteries recharging us. And that—for me, at least—compensated for Len's coolness.

I had already said "goodbye" to each of them alone, privately. Lois Lowell had said, "I want to help. I'll talk with Len." The real Lois just hugged me and told me to enjoy every minute of my new life. I knew I'd never see them again—such a staggering loss.

I was tired, but not exhausted. I read for a while, then tried to sleep. I had come to suffer the insomnia of uncertainty. A whole new galaxy of concerns whirled in my head as I heard the laughter and cheers seep down from the second story above me.

"*Salud*" followed by the clink of glasses.

I lay in my bed with Fred nursing beside me as a small breeze came through the open window. The night was hot. I could almost feel myself in Tennessee. It was strange to think of Tennessee—a place I knew nothing about—just as once I had known nothing of Mexico. I felt a twinge of regret at leaving the city of steel, the city of my friends, the city of successive misunderstandings and illuminations. After all, two of my children were *Regiomontanos.* The baby looked up and gave me that look of recognition.

"You will walk," I whispered.

Innocent blue eyes looked up at me.

The noise of the party above continued for hours, lit only by starlight and the little kerosene lantern. What if one of them toppled off the roof? Ah, they were all so tipsy, it probably wouldn't have hurt.

"You did it hombre! Bravo!" someone shouted and the gang roared.

I could hear their words, but they barely registered as I felt the plot of our lives being turned round and round. Acceptance at the University of Tennessee had actualized part of the vision.

Now, a new path—dismaying, yet hopeful—lay ahead. Eagerly, I turned toward that new path.

With help of Mexican friends, I sold the old Packard in Mexico, having learned the value of American cars from my old landlord, Señor Sanchez. With the bundle of cash, Leonard rode the bus to Laredo and bought a new car. Albeit a more recent version, it was still another gas-guzzling Packard.

We found two American students who recently arrived from the States. They wanted to rent the house and buy the little furniture that we had. Paula agreed to stay with them. Meanwhile, a conversation that Len had with Lois Lowell somehow prompted her to lend him several thousand dollars so that we could make the trip, pay the tuition, and begin a new life in Tennessee.

"You can pay me back whenever you can," she said. Lois Lowell had gone out of her way to help people in need. Apparently, she had faith in Leonard and now wanted to help him.

We began to see that change was possible. Len could go to a States-side medical school, one that was fully accredited. Behind my eagerness to take on life in Tennessee, there was also a thread of a connection that reached back several generations. I had learned that my father's father had roots from Virginia, as far back as 1830, and I looked forward to exploring life in the South.

As we drove out of Monterrey, a blinding sun sent long shafts of light down through enormous formations of clouds to a parched earth. When we reached the Texas border, I leaned out of the window and whispered, "*Adiós, México.*"

Jeanne echoed me in perfect Spanish, "*Adiós, México.*"

It was a long trip with three small children. From time to time, I experienced occasional passing spasms of frustration and impatience with screaming kids, but I dismissed it and tried to keep my focus. Through the fields of Texas, Oklahoma, and Arkansas, then finally crossing the wide Mississippi, we arrived in Memphis. We had survived hardship, but there had always been a roof over our head, food to eat, and a car to drive.

We cannot live through some of the things that we lived through in Monterrey without being affected, without being changed. In retrospect, everything was a lesson. I'd learned that I could earn a living in a foreign country. We'd discovered that Len had a serious heart condition, and also the will to surmount it. I'd learned about the power of women and about taking risks.

The speed with which we faced the new challenge in the States was a reflection, not only of our respective talents, but also of an improvisational approach to life. And improvisation was something that grew out of Mexico, the country where I learned the word, *"Mande."*

When we first went to Mexico, we'd struggled with the language, with the culture, with the events. For me, a young woman of nineteen, there had been the additional struggle to find myself, to learn to understand that submission comes in many forms.

I'd made progress, but what would this new life do to our family, to Len and me? Was my increasing understanding of independence and the refusal to submit to the intolerable now changing me into a woman incompatible with what Len needed in a wife?

Forty-three

Bluff City

Overlooking the Mississippi, Memphis is frequently referred to as "Bluff City." Like its Egyptian namesake, it was a Mecca for art, culture, and music. The Egyptians believed in magic that could revive even the dead. I yearned for magic. I hoped that the move there would revitalize our lives.

We found a little duplex next to the railroad track. On the far side, the Black neighborhood provided an abundant source of household help. Just as in Monterrey where the poor clustered in the *Colonia Independencia,* in Memphis the same pattern held and the poor clustered on the far side of the track behind our home. I hired a young woman named Jewel and set out to find work for myself.

I was surprised one day when the phone rang and a call from Monterrey came through. It was the young man who had rented our house on *Calle Estados Unidos.*

"Can you tell me how to find Paula?" I could hear distress in his voice.

"What's wrong? What happened?"

"She's gone. Taken all our money. Passports, too."

My heart sank. "I'm sorry. She was so honest and forthright with us. I don't know what to say except that she lives across the river, in *Independencia*."

Had my confidence in her been totally misguided?

I suppose I shouldn't have been shocked; Paula had no future with the Americans. A Mexican family would take a servant, and, in a way, become responsible for her. When she was sick, they'd send her to the doctor. If she was young and got married, they'd arrange it. Paula stayed with us because she liked me and she loved Lenny. Now, there was no reason to stay with some Americans she hardly knew and who, in a few years, would be gone anyway. They weren't worth her time. She'd made her move—taken their money, their papers, and was gone. I was sure the Americans would never find her.

The culture in Tennessee was different, as different as Mexico was to me at first from what I had known in San Diego. The approach to medicine at the University of Tennessee was different as well.

All the while, I was beginning to understand what it's like to face a mountain of petty decisions when faced with the tragic problem of Fred's condition. Unquiet ideas about Fred's condition dragged and pleaded, one lonely worry at a time. His disability could not be denied or ignored. I needed to investigate every possibility.

I also hoped that once in the States I could find a hand surgeon for Lenny's hand, which was eventually repaired with reasonable results at the University of Tennessee Medical Center by a skilled specialist.

In those days, people knew little about what to do for Fred, however, and the outlook was not good. Amazingly, he was able to walk, albeit with a limp, and in every way appeared normal. The doctors warned me that various symptoms could develop over time. They did. But later, rather than sooner. I told myself that to be effective I needed to take a clinical attitude toward

Fred's history, and I tried to do that. Sometimes the pain of it overcame me, and only Fred's smile saved me from giving in to despair. Gradually, I learned more about spina bifida and I was able to add facts to the uncertain story. Many spina bifida patients died very young, some developed hydrocephalus with enlarged heads, and many were incontinent. I had to accept the facts. Once again, I had to submit.

The summer in Tennessee was just as hot as in Mexico, except that where Mexico was dry, Memphis—on the Mississippi River—experienced high humidity. One steaming day, I gathered the children in the kitchen for breakfast. I was wearing a gauzy, cool dress. The room felt warm and close. My forehead was damp.

The morning started, as usual, with Fred in his highchair and me spooning oatmeal into his little mouth. Without warning, his head fell to the side, tiny arms went limp, hands trembled from wrists, and eyes rolled upward until only white showed. I rushed his listless body to the hospital. Hours later, the doctor approached me.

"Your son's had a little seizure and needs to be on medication." He handed me a prescription. "We don't know if this is part of his condition, or just the heat," the doctor said. Luckily, it turned out to be the heat. Events like this kept me on my toes and I was reluctant to return to work.

"Just stay home," Len said.

"We can't live on $50.00 a month," I responded. "The money Lois gave us is gone—tuition, the car, the furniture."

So, once again I went job hunting. I secured a position as a medical assistant and found the work was tedious and the hours long. One good thing about it was that I met Elvis Presley's mom. She was a patient.

"Elvis still drives around town on his motorcycle," she said. "Now that he's a big movie star and all, he shouldn't do it. Maybe someday you'll see him go by, Honey."

I came to look forward to her once-a-month routine visit. Mrs. Presley never came empty-handed; she always brought produce from her farm—corn, okra, tomatoes.

"Here, Sugar. You fix something nice for those kids of yours."

Even Mrs. Presley's kindness wasn't enough to keep me. I could not ignore the fact that close association with a random company of sick people had a severely negative effect on my health. I became subject to colds and flu. I dreaded going to work, and when another opportunity came along, a healthy instinct for self-preservation made me grab it.

The Supreme Court's desegregation decision in Brown vs. Board of Education came down in 1954, and it was during the integration at Little Rock that I secured a job teaching seventh grade in our parish grammar school. Many students fled across the bridge that spanned the Mississippi River from Arkansas—the center of the storm—to Memphis. The Civil Rights movement exploded all around us; the South would never be the same.

Our parish, Blessed Sacrament, needed a seventh-grade teacher and I was promptly hired. I said "farewell" to billing statements, putting up with cranky patients, and typing letters. Once again, I plunged into teaching. Although I had never been formally trained to teach, my girls won a blue ribbon that year for a science project at the county fair.

I learned from the nuns who gave no slack to bad behavior. Sister Clotilda found a stink bomb on one of her sixth grade students.

"Want to stink?" she said with her Irish accent. "Okay, then," and she poured the rank mess all over him.

One day, Tony Cortino shot himself in my class.

I had been keeping him up front where I could keep an eye on him. He had a wild streak, and I tried to keep him busy with schoolwork, but that day his attention strayed to another topic. Tony had fashioned a zip gun out of clothespins and a thick rubber band. He'd found a bullet in his Dad's drawer, brought the concoction to school to show off, and zip—he pulled the trigger in my class.

"Ayee!" he screamed. He held his hand and stared at the bloody wound.

"He shot himself!" someone cried out.

I grabbed the boy and rushed him next door to the rectory. Tony was a little thing, so wiry and thin. I knocked on the heavy door while holding my breath. Father Murray opened the door, showed us in, looked at me with the zip gun in my hand, then focused on the boy. No words were spoken. When Tony approached, the priest hit him with the back of his hand so hard that the boy went flying across the room, spattering blood as he went. When I saw the poor child slumped down—back against the wall, head lolling as if stunned—my heart constricted.

Father Murray grabbed the gun from my hand and waved it in front of Tony. "What makes you think you can bring this trash into this school?"

The boy picked himself up and stood, holding his bleeding hand. I was terrified, sure that Tony was badly hurt and that I'd be fired. After my experience with Mr. Tarpey, what else could I expect? Nothing could exonerate me from this mishap.

"You've scared your poor teacher half to death," he yelled again at the boy. Then to me, "Go back to your class, Mrs. Burns. I'll take this rascal to the hospital."

I turned to leave. Father Murray took me aside and whispered, "Don't ever let a kid like this get the upper hand." Then, he turned to Tony and gave him a big hug saying, "We'll get you fixed up, Son." At last, I saw tears in Tony's eyes.

I had some knowledge of teaching, now—hard-gained over three years of my life, but Tony was a challenge I didn't know how to handle. I didn't know what to make of Father Murray's cuff-then-cuddle approach. Maybe I didn't know as much about teaching as I thought I did.

When I returned to school, Mother Superior told me that Tony's dad was in the state penitentiary. She said that the family looked to us—the school and the Church—to help rear the boy. The next day, Tony's pale and apprehensive mother brought her son to school. His hand, covered with thick gauze, soon became the object of intense inspection. Mrs. Cortino tarried at the door, and when I went to speak to her, she apologized for her boy's outrageous behavior.

"Please take him back," she pleaded.

"Of course," I said. Out of the corner of my eye, I saw the boy waving his hand in the air in case anyone had missed seeing it.

I was gratified by the trust that Mother Superior, Mrs. Cortino, and Father Murray continued to show me. Nevertheless, I felt terribly guilty. I wished I had done better. At the same time, I realized more than ever the grave responsibility that lay in teaching.

🙟

We had survived hardship in Mexico, but our life in Memphis was equally difficult with Len's attention still narrowly focused on medicine. So much of what I was learning and experiencing was through Len. In a way, the shooting incident woke me up. I went through a period when I felt it was important to look into my own soul. Tired of myself, I began a back-and-forth process of inner debate. I suffered from self-doubt as a result of my subservience to his ambition and ended up angry with him—and with myself.

That winter, Leonard's heart condition manifested as heart failure. He was rushed to the hospital. This encounter with death frightened both of us. After many anxious days, his fantastic resilience and ironic sense of humor pulled him through and, once again, he was able to bear down on his studies. Graduation day was not far off.

In early spring, I became critically ill from infectious hepatitis. I think the nuns believed that Tony Cortino had pushed me over the edge, but that wasn't it. I had an infection and it was serious. When the bilirubin tests consistently failed, they thought I had cancer of the liver. The doctors told me there was no hope. I called my mother with the unhappy news that I was about to die.

She said, "Don't pay any attention to it. You've always had a pain in your side."

Now, I can smile at her words. By trivializing my condition, she did me a favor, though I didn't know it then. I ceased putting attention on the problem and did what I had always done: keep on keeping on. I told myself that the only way to improve the situation was to take a few steps at a time. I held on to life. Len seemed to hardly notice.

As in Mexico, he was a charming rascal who lived entirely by his whims, desires, and rhythms—oblivious to the needs of the family. He was enormously popular with his classmates, almost winning the award for "having endured the greatest hardship" in the process of his medical training. He lost to Joe Talley from Nashville. Joe and his family lived in their car while in medical school. I heard a few years later that Joe had learned to fly, crashed into the Smokey Mountains in Tennessee, and died instantly.

The day we had longed for, strived for, and sacrificed for, finally came. Leonard graduated from a bona fide medical school in May of 1960. He immediately left to go to Indiana where he had secured an internship.

The Greeks used to believe that the liver is the seat of the emotions. Maybe that's true. I had come to hold so much resentment toward Len that I believe I made myself ill. The day he left Memphis, my liver function tests improved. Perhaps his absence shocked my liver into a strong reaction. I was going to live.

When I returned to my job, the whole class—including Tony Cortino—cheered. I completed the school year. The family joined Len in June of that year. He began his life as a doctor—an intern at St. Joseph's Hospital in South Bend, Indiana.

Forty-four

A Stop, or Two, Along the Way

The very day I arrived in South Bend, Len said, "We're going to a party on Saturday night: a cocktail party. Don't worry; I've got a babysitter. One of the nurses has a kid sister . . ."

I wore an expensive little black dress, one that Alice had sent me. Every so often, she'd pack up a box of clothes that she didn't want anymore and send them to me. The most recent box came with a note:

> *Can't use these any more. Hope you like them.*
> *Alice*

So, even when we were flat broke, I had costly, stylish garments.

The dress was the clingy kind—but not too tight—with the skirt draped to the right, creating a little flounce. I piled my hair on top of my head the way I did in Mexico when I went to church.

"You really look great in Mom's clothes," Len said.

"Thanks," I replied. I felt strangely uncomfortable with his remark.

We got to the party a little late. No sooner had we arrived than a very handsome man in a black suit and Roman collar approached us, then extended his hand in friendship. He was in his mid-sixties with wide-set, brilliantly intelligent eyes.

"So this is the beautiful Mrs. Burns." He winked at Len before whisking me away. "I'm Father Cavanaugh. Father John. Used to be president of this place. Let me buy you a drink." He took my arm and led me to the bar.

"I'm pleased to meet you, Father." I sensed his over-powering personality. "I'll have club soda."

Father John told the bar man, "Make it tall and put a cherry on top."

"Too bad Joe's not here; he'd really like you. Since his kid is running for president, he's too busy to do anything. Otherwise, he'd be here. You've probably heard what Joe said. 'We'll sell Jack like soap flakes.'" The smile that he turned on me was bold and demanded attention. "Len tells me you went to school with the Sacred Heart. Joe sent his girls to their school: the one in New York."

"Manhattanville, you mean?"

"Yes." He handed me my drink. The smile momentarily faded. "I had a heart attack a few months ago." He waved at a person across the room. "Len helped take care of me. He's a great guy." Father Cavanaugh moved easily with grace and decorum. He guided me around the room, here and there acknowledging an acquaintance. All the while, he gave me the impression that I was the most important person in the room.

"Tonight's an opportunity for the faculty to meet with leading citizens, to hear the Notre Dame story," he said. "Let's meet some people. It never hurts to have a pretty woman on your arm."

Len looked at me sharply several times, and more than once indicated for me to join him. Father Cavanaugh kept hold of my arm and introduced me to various friends. The evening was a fundraiser; the school needed a new science building. Looking out the window, Father indicated with his arm. "See all those buildings? See that golden dome? Football. The Fighting Irish did all that."

Father John revealed himself to me in many small, intimate ways. He wanted to win me over and he did.

"Look," he said, "I know about Len's heart condition. I want him to stay here, join our staff, and take care of us old guys. We're quite a bunch—arthritis, strokes, heart attacks, and like me—retired priests. Holy Cross Order. When Len finishes his internship, I can arrange it. I'll get you and the family a nice place on campus like that." He pointed to a large sprawling frame house. To me, it looked like a mansion.

I'm sure Father Cavanaugh divined my desire for a settled life, a desire which fit his own, that Len should join the staff at Notre Dame and become the resident physician.

Over the months that followed, we accepted Father Cavanaugh's invitations as often as we could, but not as often as he would have liked. Len's schedule was grueling. Sometimes, he worked forty-eight hours straight.

Occasionally, Father Cavanaugh would arrange his weekly schedule to drop by for dinner or a quick drink. Once, he brought me a metal shingle from the golden dome. "They're redoing the covering. Thought you'd like a souvenir. Make an ashtray out of it."

And he loved to talk. "I never met Hitler, but once I met Mussolini. He told stories of days spent with the Duke and Duchess of Windsor.

"Is there anybody you haven't met?" Len asked.

As for Len, it was so obvious; Father John felt a special bond with him.

"Len, this is the perfect job for you. We're just a bunch of old fogies. Don't need much. You'd have good hours," he chuckled. "And I'm sure that we could ensure that your family would get a nice pension. You know—if anything happened to you."

Life in South Bend suited me well. I was content having every reason to look forward to a pleasant, comfortable existence—

security, position, good company, and a Catholic environment. For a while, I entertained the idea that we had found a home. In the end, Len turned down Father Cavanaugh's offer.

"I don't want a practice of old priests," he said.

"Why not? They need care and attention like everybody else."

It was then that Len lavished all his persuasive skill on me, arguing that he wanted to be a radiologist. "I'll tell Father Cavanaugh tomorrow so that he can start looking for someone else. He's in a good mood, now that John Kennedy has won the election. I wouldn't dare tell him I voted for Nixon."

"That's okay. I voted for Kennedy. Guess I canceled out your vote." It was the first time I'd ever voted in a presidential election. I felt good that my guy won.

Len did as he had promised and told Father Cavanaugh that we would not be staying in South Bend. This depressed me, for I had grown quite fond of the old priest, and life at Notre Dame offered many benefits. Len's life expectancy was not good. The idea of a pension for the family was very attractive. However, it was not to be. It never occurred to me that I could actually demand to have a say because the old *Mande* mentality still controlled me.

1960 had been a big year for us. Len sent out letters seeking a residency program that would train him to become a radiologist.

🦗

"How'd you like to go to Spokane, Washington?" Len asked.

"I'd rather go to Hilo, Hawaii." The hospital there had advertised for a general practitioner. I could imagine swaying palms, trade winds, the family living near the beach—the good life. I bought a muumuu, wore it around the house, and played Hawaiian music. Just to pacify me, Len wrote to Hilo, though he was never serious about going there.

"I really want to specialize," Len said. "I started out in X-ray. I love it."

"So, you'll be a doctor's doctor?" In a way, I thought it was a waste. He had such a perfect bedside manner—so much compassion, so much empathy. Patients loved him. Even though radiology meant three more years of training, it would be physically less demanding for him and I agreed to it.

Spokane offered a pleasant opportunity for Len to pursue his specialty. And with minimum stress, he plunged into his residency. While there, I resumed the career as a professional model that I had started in San Diego as a teenager. I even did some ancillary work in television.

Once again, I found myself in the midst of creative, dynamic, and caring women. I formed very strong friendships with doctors' wives and with the models. The women were the guides, the ones who stood by me, the ones I could listen to, and the ones I shared things with.

Chris, our fourth child, was born at Sacred Heart Hospital in Spokane. Our marriage was never peaceful or secure, except for the interlude in Spokane where a semblance of normalcy settled over us. I gave up on trying to change Len. I tried to love him as he was. Out of compassion, I chose to remain imprisoned in his dream.

We rented a home with a lovely garden, a place built by a Mormon family who had moved on to a grander lifestyle. When I signed the lease, the owner told me that his beliefs led him to the conclusion that some kind of reckoning lay ahead for all of us, and that there was a bomb shelter in the basement. During the Cuban missile crisis, I stored the shelter with water and supplies. Missile silos ringed Spokane. There was a Strategic Air Command Base not far from town, and I knew we had to be a potential target. The Holocaust never came, but President Kennedy was assassinated.

Toward the end of the three-year residency, an opportunity came our way. Len was greatly liked, due to his own efforts—his sociability, boundless energy, and hard work. I had become a minor celebrity. I loved the attention. People liked us. We were considered an asset. Len and I had integrated into the community.

"They've offered me a permanent job in the department," Len said.

"At Sacred Heart?" I asked.

"Yes."

"I could live here," I replied. "It's a lovely city. Snowy, sunny winters; beautiful residential areas; and good schools for the kids. The gardens in the spring are magnificent."

"I think I can do better," he said.

Len left on a search mission. After ten days, he returned.

"I've found the perfect place for us."

Forty-five

Someplace, at Least

One morning in June, I piled Jeanne, Fred, and Chris into the Volkswagen bus. The engine sputtered and started. I backed out slowly. We waved "goodbye" to Lenny. He had become an unruly, wild boy. I knew I could not manage him, along with the three other children, and make the drive. Father and son would join us in two weeks. Lenny held our Siamese cat, Minnie, in his arms. Soulful and sad, the little boy nodded "goodbye." We waved back.

§

"California, here I come." We sang it together past Moses Lake, along the Columbia River, over the bridge into Oregon. When we got to the California State line, I whooped. "Home, at last!"

"Tell me again, Mom, where are we going?" Jeanne asked.

I caught the forward, eager thrust of her profile out of the corner of my eye. "Eureka, California."

"Why?" Jeanne persisted.

"Your Dad's going into a practice there. He says we'll love it."

"What's California like?"

"It has warm weather, palm trees, wide sandy beaches. We'll swim, play in the sand and . . . "

We rounded a bend and came upon the coastal town of Crescent City. The kids looked at me, wide-eyed. A few months before, the Alaskan earthquake triggered a huge title wave. It had swamped the little fishing village, leaving only destruction.

Fred yelled, "Look at that!"

I peeked at him through the rearview mirror. Fred's pale, intense face, with innocent blue eyes, looked back at me.

My jaw tightened when we passed an overturned railroad car thrust nearly a mile inland. "Less than one-hundred miles to go," I called out, trying to sound upbeat.

Shortly afterward, we crossed into Humboldt County. My first impression—harsh, windy, cold—didn't change as we got closer. Sixty miles down the road and, at last, we reached our destination: Eureka. The town was wrapped in fog, sea smells, and the overwhelming odor of the Georgia Pacific pulp mills. The stench permeated everything. It smelled like boiling cabbage.

In that moment, I saw my life dissolving into despair and bitterness. Living here—swallowed up in the drabness of broken-down Victorian houses, gaudy bars, shabby store-fronts—would require total anesthesia of my senses. I knew it was the opposite of everything I had hoped and worked for.

I hated it there from the start. Eureka lacked the charm of Spokane, the culture of Memphis, and the color of Mexico. Nothing except rain, day after day. The sky never glowed pink at dawn; the sun never shone.

Len arrived with Lenny several days later. He found us at a run-down boarding house in Fortuna, twenty miles south of Eureka. Here, at least, the stench of the pulp mills did not reach us.

"Welcome to Appalachia West," I said as Len walked in.

Lenny peeked in around the door, hesitant at first, holding the cat in his arms. I smiled at him and he ran to me, then clasped my legs. The cat squirmed out of his arms. Gingerly and wary, she rubbed up against me and purred.

"Honey, the kids are in the kitchen. There's lemonade and cookies." I hugged the boy kissing the top of his head. He took off down the hall; the cat scampered after him.

"Looks fine to me. Small town, a golden opportunity," Len said.

"This place is hell." I tried to fight back the tears. "Impossible. Why have you done this, Len?"

"You're being shallow about my choice." He lit a cigarette and looked up. "The countryside is beautiful."

"It is. But we can't live in the Redwood Forest. The town is seedy. And besides, there's no housing. I've rented this whole place for a few days until we can sort things out."

"Looks like fun. I'm perfectly comfortable."

By this time, Lenny had found Fred, Jeanne, and Chris in the kitchen. At first, I heard whispers, then giggles. The kids ran up and down the hall, exploring various rooms, laughing, hooting, and jumping up and down on the beds. Each room had a number and there were twelve of them. The sheets smelled of mildew.

"I'll take number three," said Fred

"Two, for me," from Jeanne.

By now, I was really agitated. "Why have you done this, Len? Why did you settle on this?"

"This is great," he said. "I love it."

I collapsed into an overstuffed armchair, sat down, and faced him. We talked for a long time. I told him the decision was "harebrained," "hasty," "divorced from reality." I saw only his superb recklessness and utter contempt for the family.

"I've already signed the documents. Besides, I like it here. You know how I love the rain." He turned his blue eyes toward me. "You'll get used to it." He flashed his knowing cat-eye look—the look that promised, teased, yet never delivered. "You'll find us a place to live. You always do."

It was late. Len went into room number 10. "Can I undress in here?" he asked. A naked light bulb dangled on a wire over his head.

"Why not?" I replied.

He slept while I packed the bus. Early the next morning, I loaded the kids into it and drove away.

"Where are we going, now?" Jeanne asked with an insecure and doubtful voice.

"To San Diego," I said and added, "and to Disneyland." I made it sound strong, confident.

I left a note.

Len,

You can live here if you want. If you think this is the gold ring after all these years, wake up; it's nothing but brass.
> *Gail*

Fury drove me until I got to Mission Beach in San Diego where I rented an apartment on the beach. The children and I spent two glorious weeks in the sun by the sea, the surf, and the sand. Hot days, cool breezes, and palm trees. We went to Disneyland. I wrote checks from our joint bank account. *A golden opportunity.*

Leonard flew to San Diego. Cleverly, he mustered all the forces he could; he brought in my mother, his mother, my grand-mother, and the Church. They pressured me and spoke of responsibility, duty, and dogma. I knew the real reason that Len wanted me back; he thought I was his possession. I was useful to him. I helped his image and, without me, his pride would take a blow. In the end, I succumbed—not to his charm, but to the necessity of having the children grow up in the same home as both their parents.

"I'll never forgive you for this," I said.

He shrugged and brushed it off. "You'll get used to it. You'll see."

I found Eureka to be a stifling, chauvinistic, smelly town with one hundred or more inches of rainfall. My vow to break away—the major theme of my twenty-ninth year—was met with many obstacles, not the least of which was the future of my children. I relentlessly thought of ways to escape.

How could I have known?

The decision to live in Eureka precipitated more experience, more adventure, more life, and more drama than I had ever imagined.

To escape suffocation, I found a way to rebel, protest, and clarify. Redemption lay in a small liberal arts college: Humboldt State. Located in an adjoining town, Arcata, the college would become my refuge. I rented a temporary place near the campus for us to live in, immediately enrolled myself in classes, and put the older children into the college elementary school. Chris would attend Aunt Bea's daycare, just across the highway.

Our first year in Eureka was the winter of the big flood. Swollen rivers overflowed their banks by thirty feet. Towns were destroyed, bridges leading to and from Eureka were washed away. The devastation of highways marooned us for weeks. I'd wanted to create a home, a more sincere life. However, the tighter I held onto my dream, the more it shattered.

Eventually, we bought a house on the outskirts of town. Actually, it was on the road to the dump. However, the land contained seven acres of second growth redwoods, tiny fern dales, a pasture, and a little orchard of apple trees. We acquired animals—a horse, ducks, goats, a German shepherd dog, and—for a short time—a raccoon.

The children found the College Elementary School both fun and challenging. Jeanne particularly thrived in an environment where no grades were given and where art and music had high priority.

I made the best of the situation, plunging ever deeper into my studies: a bachelor degree program in English, a minor in philosophy. Excellent professors. They came from Stanford, Berkeley, Michigan, and the University of Chicago. Many found sustenance and solace in the craggy, harsh seacoast. "So like Cornwall," one of my professors told me.

Leonard resented my seeking out an education.

"Why do you have to do this college thing?" he asked me.

Had he forgotten the pact after my affair with Roberto? "We made a deal. You have to live up to it," I answered.

He did, though reluctantly, and my deviant behavior was soon noted. Apparently, a woman who had independent thoughts and ambitions was a threat to this narrow-minded enclave of tradition.

At a community banquet, one of the doctors came up to me. I had never met the man, but that didn't stop him. "Why can't you just stay home and take care of your kids like you're supposed to?"

"Because my husband has two holes in his heart and can't get life insurance," I snapped.

"I'm sorry, I didn't know."

"There's a lot you don't know." I wanted to be rude.

Nevertheless, my intention to get a degree provoked opposition. I soon got used to being scorned socially by the medical community. The resultant discrimination only aroused a new anger and strengthened my unwillingness to accept their judgment.

"You need therapy." Len pushed me to see a psychiatrist.

I did.

"I want to face my acts and feelings. I want to know my true reality," I told the doctor.

"What would happen if you gave up going to school?"

"Self-annihilation," I answered. "Is that what being a doctor's wife requires?"

Three weeks into therapy, my psychiatrist ran off with his nurse.

The rejected wife called me, and I urged her to join me in pursuing a college education. She did. Fortunately, the wayward husband provided for her generously.

One day she said to me, "It takes one kind of woman to get a man through medical school and a very different type to live with him afterward."

"You may be right," I answered.

Several weeks later, I saw Ellie at Daly's Department store. Ellie was the local tennis star; not a pro, but she played every day that it didn't rain. Her wide cheekbones and tan, roundish face with sexy brown eyes looked a little Latin. She told me she was Polish and from Pennsylvania. Her light brown hair was cut short, and she wore soft, fluffy curls all over her head. She had the habit of wearing bright red lipstick, which made her look a little scary. Ellie was married to the local anesthesiologist, Tom Brody.

"Gail, I can't tell you how glad I am that I ran into you. Come for dinner Saturday," she said. "Nothing fancy—cracked crab, artichokes, and vodka."

"Sure, but count me out on the vodka. I don't drink," I said.

"It would be wonderful if we could just have some drinks and dinner. Just the four of us. Get to know you and Len better. He's so handsome—like he just stepped out of some advertisement." At the mention of Len's name, she became a shining woman.

"Got to run," I said, "but we'll be there."

Life in Mexico had taught me to keep an open mind. Here, at least, was someone who didn't criticize my going to school. She seemed genuinely interested in us. We arrived at their house, which I found to be a little stark. There were no rugs or drapes in the living room.

"Need to get this place fixed up," Ellie said. "Someday. Tennis takes all my time." Since there was nothing to absorb the sound, her voice had a harsh quality.

For the occasion, the dining room table was covered with newspaper. Large bowls of crab, cracking implements, artichokes, melted butter, and shot glasses stood in place, ready for action. First, we had cocktails. I asked for a club soda.

"I thought you were just kidding. Got a problem, Honey?"

"I had hepatitis about a year ago. One drink actually makes my liver hurt." I was annoyed that I had to give an excuse for why I didn't drink.

Ellie mixed a double martini for Len. Then, she asked probing questions to find out more about him. Ellie obviously took great pleasure listening to Len when he talked about his early life in Wilkes-Barre, Pennsylvania. I noticed a vacancy in her rapt, almost delirious, focus—as if she were not so much listening, as appreciating. Her eyes devoured his outrageous smile.

"I'm from Pennsylvania, too. Pittsburgh. Can you believe it?" Her eyes sparkled with mischief. "We're both from the Quaker State."

I can't say she was pretty. Attractive in an athletic way best described Ellie. Her hips were wide, breasts large. Her face was covered with freckles. While Tom had the same mischievous quality, his level of intensity never quite matched hers. He looked at the crab piled high on a bed of ice, then smiled as if in anticipation.

"Shall we?" he asked and looked at me.

Dinner entailed a physical workout. Cracking crab turned out to be messy. Energetic, but worth the effort. Melted butter dripped on the newspaper. Shot glasses were filled and re-filled with vodka. We cracked crab and sucked its succulent meat from secret hiding places.

"Eureka custom." Bill pointed to the crab and the newspaper.

"Don't you want some, Honey?" Ellie held the Vodka bottle toward me.

"No, thanks."

When there was nothing left except empty shells and scraped artichoke leaves, Ellie rose from the table.

"I'll just get the coffee." She looked at Len. "Wanna' help?"

"Sure," he said. They disappeared.

"So, you've been here ten years," I said. I smiled politely and the host returned my cheery expression with a hungry look.

I felt uncomfortable. Len didn't come back. I kept my eyes on the newspaper. Minutes passed. I pretended to suck on the empty crab leg as if I had missed something. Tom looked at me, still staring with that look. He pulled his chair closer and put his arm around me and puckered up. I pushed him away and stood. I walked away from him around the table, glancing in the direction of the kitchen to see if Len and Ellie had returned. No one in sight.

Tom followed me around the table. "You're a real cutie," he said and reached out to touch me.

I picked up the pace. After I had circumnavigated the table twice with him behind me, I realized the absurdity of the situation. I stopped, turned around, and faced him square on.

"Take one more step and I'll flatten you, Buddy." I was a good head taller than he was. And I was sure I could do it.

Tom started to giggle. He'd had a lot to drink. "Okay, okay. What do you wanna' do?" He was a vague, dithering drunk.

"Well, let's watch television." I could think of nothing else. "Wait here. I'll go see about coffee."

I went into the kitchen. There was no sign of Ellie or Len. The coffee was ready. Soft laughter came from down the hall. I poured two cups and returned to the living room.

"Let's watch *Star Trek*," I handed Tom his coffee.

At least a half-hour passed when Ellie returned to join us from the dining room. "So, what have you two kids been up to?" She winked at me.

"Captain Kirk," I said.

Out of the corner of my eye, I saw Len enter from the hall door. "Ellie's got great pictures from her school days." He ran his hands over his hair, smoothing it down. "Remarkable. You've got to see them."

How he could lie!

"It's been said that the unexamined life is not worth living," Captain Kirk said from the television. *Did he really say that or did I just imagine it?*

"I agree with that," I said.

"Why don't you two kids join the tennis club?" Ellie asked and looked at Len. "We have lots of really great activities."

"I don't play. Let's go." I looked at my husband. There were slight smudges of red lipstick on his face.

"But Len hasn't had his coffee." She kept her eyes on my husband as if he were some kind of prize.

"Next time," I said and turned to Tom. "Bye, Sweetie Pie. Dinner was great."

When we got in the car, Len asked, "Did you have a good time?"

"I don't know when I've had a better time." I started to laugh. I saw the images—Len, butter dripping down his chin; Tom looking at me, then sucking on his crab leg; and Ellie consuming Len with every breath. I laughed so hard tears came to my eyes.

"Why did you call Tom 'Sweetie Pie?'" Len asked.

"He's so cute! Good enough to eat, don't you think?" Then I burst into hysterical laughter and said, "Maybe you should think about examining your life. But first, wipe the lipstick off your face."

All through those months—October, November, fall, winter—I thought the rain would never go away. I tried to forget the incident at the Brody's, telling myself it was a fluke, until a similar event occurred at the home of another friend. I'd met them at church. He was a lawyer and she, like myself, from Southern California. We went for dinner.

The hostess prepared a magnificent meal—roast pork, mashed potatoes, baked apples—and the table setting included fine china and crystal glasses. She was a tall woman, thin and quite lovely with hair pulled tight on top of her head in a neat,

neat bun. Her dress was fawn-colored to match her hair. She was carefully made up with pale pink on her lips and cheeks.

When we had finished eating, as before, Len made a pilgrimage with the hostess to some hidden spot in the house. Astounded, I sat across from the husband on a love seat in front of the fire. Minutes crept by. It felt like hours. I bit the inside of my mouth and tasted blood.

"So, you're going to school?" he asked. He was a lawyer, nice-looking.

"Yes," I replied, "I'm studying English, but I have a double minor—philosophy and theater arts. Right now, I'm involved in some production work." I didn't know what I was supposed to do. *Was he waiting for me to make the first move?*

When I didn't, he asked, "Isn't that time-consuming?"

I wanted to ask him if this game of hide-and-seek was a local custom, but I didn't. Instead, I answered, "Time consuming? Yes. Next week, we'll be doing *Carnival of the Animals* with the Humboldt State Symphony. I'll do the narration. Ogden Nash wrote it. We're going to videotape it live." I struggled to keep up my end of the conversation.

"We'll get tickets." He was absolutely calm, showing no concern. There was a long silence. "What do you like about performing?" he pushed on.

"I like the whole thing—the creativity, putting things together." I forced myself to sound unperturbed. "Last month, our group wrote and produced a puppet show based on *The Man from La Mancha.* We made our own puppets and a stage. We performed for local schools." I paused, agonizing to find words. "I'd do more if I could. We have four children."

"So do we," he said. "We've got a lot in common."

Our conversation limped along in this way. I kept trying to respond to his questions until the fire had all but died down. The host tossed a middle-sized log in the fire, which sent out a shower of sparks.

"Let's have dessert," the hostess said, all of a sudden coming into the room as if she'd been gone only five minutes instead of nearly an hour. Her eyes were cast down demurely. She carried a tray with china plates, cups, and saucers. Len followed behind, holding a chocolate cake. He reminded me of an altar boy at Mass. I felt like Alice in Wonderland.

Her eyes had a softness, a childlike quality. "Len tells me you're doing some theater." Her gray eyes stared straight into mine.

"Yes, I've been offered the lead role in *Desire Under the Elms.* I'd like to do it." I hadn't said a word to Len and wanted to see how he would respond. Sure enough, it broke him out of his altar boy façade. I twirled my cup in the saucer and waited to see what he would say.

"The hell you will!" Len's face turned bright red. He was petulant and irritated. "No wife of mine is going to be in a play like that. We saw the film last year. Sophia Loren. Remember? Ran off with her husband's son. Disgusting." He sat down next to me.

There was a moment of silence. Our hostess cut the cake and served it. Something twisted inside of me.

"I rather liked it," the husband said. *"Desire Under the Elms."*

Coffee was poured.

As we drove home, once again, I noticed lipstick on Len's collar. This time, it was pink instead of red. That night, the temperature dropped. The next morning, there was snow—snow in coastal California.

On these occasions, Len never offered any excuses for his actions. There was no point in asking questions. He'd only accuse me of being "dirty minded."

I decided not to take the part in the play, not because of the theme, but because it meant too many hours away from my children. I would have liked to play the role because it was so different from my image of myself. However, it wasn't worth the strife it would have caused for me at home.

The very idea that I would think about being in a play aggravated Len. He held to some pre-conceived pattern to which I, as a good wife, was supposed to adhere. The prevailing culture in Eureka only strengthened his notion. He needed to mirror himself in the eyes of an adoring woman. But I could no longer reshape myself according to his needs, his pattern, his vision. Instead, I became accustomed to the change and havoc brought about, not only by his growing alcoholism, but, as it turned out, also by my mother's.

 She visited us in Eureka at that time. When I met her at the airport, she walked down the stairs singing, "Hello, Dolly." She was wearing a gold leather jacket, hat, and boots. Nobody could miss her. She reeked of liquor.

Later, she'd made a scene in a restaurant. I felt ashamed that the children should see her drinking so much and told her to quit. That only enraged her. On the way home, she had jumped out of our moving car in a wild spree. It was obvious that she liked to drink, disintegrate, give in to whims, and be careless. These escapades had a strange hold on her.

Meanwhile, day by day, Len reverted to the old pattern from Monterrey. I watched him retreat from life while he practiced radiology all day and came home at three or four in the morning—puffed, worn, and intoxicated. He cast us aside for the love of his work, which brought him praise, power, and money. He ran away from us—his home and children—and I felt, once again, abandoned.

He had the necessary elegance to make women notice him. Careful grooming, suave manner, and he was a good dancer. At the country club, eyes of doctors' wives followed him. In return, he could not resist the pleasure of charming and flirting. He'd flush. He carried the look of rascality, of one who loved to tease, yet loved no one.

Moved by his energy, enthusiasm, and generosity, his colleagues sought him out. Escapades, dramatics, and insincerities escalated. He collected guns. He took up golf, a game that brought into relief the grace and agility of his movement.

Making the best of the situation, I completed my B.A. and launched into a Master's program in English. During these months, I relied more and more on my intuition and instinct. With intellectual nourishment, I felt air, space, vitality, and movement. I read D.H. Lawrence and Jean Paul Sartre. I took a lover. I discovered sex, and with it came a promise of a bond that never happened with my husband.

Forty-six

Home at Last

A wintry night, a shattered night.
Len came to my room, woke me from a deep sleep, and looked at me with a strange curiosity.

"I have to talk with you," he said and pulled me to my feet. His eyes flashed.

He led me gently by the hand to where he had been sitting in front of the roaring fireplace. A nearly empty bottle of vodka lay on its side next to a needlepoint footstool and a pistol on the floor. Len sat on the stool. He forced me to sit at his feet.

"Tell me the truth," he slurred. "Tell me what you really think of me. I'm an asshole. Free me. I don't want to hang on to someone who thinks I'm an asshole."

He took the gun and put it to my temple.

"I don't think you're an asshole," I looked him straight in the eyes. "I think you've had too much to drink." I kept my voice calm and strong. I could feel my heart pounding in my ears.

"I know you're lying." He gave me a long, cool, demonic smile. "Tell me what you think or I'll kill you."

I faced him down. "I'd rather be dead than married to a bas-tard like you!" I screamed it with fury. The fire of my anger made

386

me strong, and I pushed down his hand with the gun. He began to sob.

"Asshole, asshole . . . " He banged his forehead with closed fists then wept uncontrollably.

I saw the boy who craved love, but could not give it—a man incapable of responsibility, restraint, or self-denial. There was tragedy at the bottom of his deep-blue eyes.

"I just want you to be honest with yourself." I led him to bed while he sobbed.

In that minute, the magic faded away. The veil fell. Realizing that I didn't love him, I felt an extraordinary release. That night, I gave up pity. I no longer wished to be pitied and I could not conjure any more for him. I didn't care if I abandoned him to his narrow, cramped world.

The next morning, I sat at the breakfast table. Light from the little kitchen window poured through glass slats making gray-green lines on the table. I leaned forward on my elbow, swallowed my coffee, and glanced at my watch.

Len came out of the bathroom shaved, bathed, and dressed to perfection. His shirt, stiffly starched under a blue tweed jacket complemented his curly, short hair, which he had smoothed back. No hint of the night before clung to his appearance, except for a left eyelid that drooped lackadaisically. *The perfect professional. Chief of Staff.*

There was no hope of setting things right. Nothing held me, except the frigid bonds of the Church, of duty, and of custom.

"About last night—"

I interrupted him. "I have to get the kids to school. Let's go." Jeanne, Len, and Chris made the morning dash to the car. Fred trailed behind. He walked with a slight limp, which made a little thumping sound that I could always recognize. I followed them and Len followed me. I turned to close the back door. His eyes pleaded and begged for attention. Before he could reach us, I slammed the door and got in the car.

"Hooligan!" I shouted. I'd reached for one of my grandmother's favorite words. I didn't want to swear in front of the children.

That afternoon, he sent me a dozen red roses. The card with it read:

> Don't give up on me. I have a need of loyalty, of understanding.
> A.H.

It took me a moment to figure out that A.H. stood for "Ass Hole," but I failed to see the humor. I felt nothing. I spent the remainder of the day housekeeping, cooking, and writing a paper on Sartre, who said, among other things, "You don't need a hell. Hell is other people." I used that quote in my paper.

I saw how I had built up a relationship with sacrifices, lies, and deception. Sartre insisted that one can be free of all that by saying "no." Yet, it was not so easy for me to say "no" to the marriage. My children depended on me. Nor was it easy to say "no" to the church, which insisted I stay in the marriage. My first understanding of God came from the Catholic Church, and I was grateful for that. The very thought of disobeying my religion had left me feeling bereft.

I had no vision. Just to get through one day at a time was all I could do. In the weeks that followed, a sense of emptiness washed over me. At school, with friends, during the whirl of activities, or even on stimulating days, I couldn't shake a permanent sadness.

I found myself in the center of the drug culture. Eureka had become the marijuana capital of the country. I smoked pot, hashish. I even tried LSD. Surrendering all need for control, I refined my receptiveness to beauty. I opened my heart. John Lennon sang, "All you need is love." I got the sense that unconditional love was the answer—love that embraced a wider and wider circle, love that dissolved all barriers and obstacles. I wasn't up to it.

All the while, there was no end to Len's needs. He required unquestioning faith, indulgence, adoration, a home, children, a mother, a bookkeeper, a secretary. He had to be the center of the world.

I needed a new center. I learned transcendental meditation.

The teacher said, "It isn't a belief or a religion. It's a simple, mental technique. Just follow the mantra and let it take you past thought."

And it did. I went deeper and deeper past thought, past the panic, terror, and desperation of Leonard's alcoholism, past the endless rain and foggy days. I entered a pool of profound silence and peace—a home, at last.

Back in waking state, I could savor the ancient redwood forests, the misty mountains, the sheer beauty of the shining sea, and the splendor of my children. I forged a link with Maharishi Mahesh Yogi and Eastern thought. I knew he was right when he said, "Drugs are a counterfeit reality."

Meditation activated my thinking. Gradually, I discovered my lost self. Simultaneously, I encountered an awareness of creative flow, a fresh process of becoming. The process depended on me and nothing else, except my own effort. Maharishi shared an important aphorism from the Bhagavad-Gita: "It is better to die than to take up another man's dharma." That statement really hit me. "Dharma" means path. I had taken up Leonard's path and it was wrong of me. And, ironically, he resented me for helping him. I was the living reminder that he so desperately needed help.

I left the marriage under strange—one could say "karmic"—circumstances. The Children's Orthopedic Hospital in Los Angeles called.

"We have developed some new approaches to spina bifida that could help your son. I think you should come down."

"I will."

"We'll do a work-up and determine a course of action," the doctor replied.

I hired a kindly, capable woman as a housekeeper to care for the children. It wasn't easy to leave them behind, but it had to be done. We had to take advantage of this offer from a prestigious doctor from a prestigious hospital.

It was spring. The trillium bloomed in the forest and wild rhododendron burst in color when I set out with Fred in my Dodge Station Wagon. He was a good companion. I fell in love with the image of him, the one before he donned the mask of pain. The little face next to me asserted itself with humor and an agility of mind. Eyes soft, mouth gentle and half open, not yet thinned by the tightness of pain. We laughed and joked as we drove along the coast to Southern California.

So it was that after thirteen years with Leonard, I found myself alone in Los Angeles with my son. Despite the seriousness of our mission, I was enormously relieved to be away from my husband. I rented a small apartment in Westwood Village. Fred was admitted to the hospital where he underwent a series of excruciatingly painful operations.

There is no emotional torture worse than watching a beloved child suffer, and I credit meditation for saving my sanity and my stamina during those months. I don't know what saved Fred's sanity. I stayed with him all through the summer of '68.

At first, Fred had an ankle operation. They took bone slivers and fused his ankle to prevent it from rolling over on its side when he walked. Then, they put a cast on his foot. Still in the hospital, he had the second of three operations where the doctors took metal pins and screwed them through his hips to prevent them from constantly dislocating out of the hip sockets. Then, he was put into a body cast. After weeks in the body cast, they cut him out and operated again. This time, they removed the metal pins from his hips and then put Fred back into a new body cast for about six more weeks. This was to make sure that the hips had calcified to the pelvis; thus, fusing both hips.

A pleading, yearning—or sometimes belligerent and wary—gaze met mine when I went to visit him. I thought my heart might break. Sometimes, he got a pass for the weekend. For most of the time, he was in a cast from his waist down, so I devised a way to prop him up in the back of the car. With his head raised, he could see out as we drove through Hollywood, Santa Monica, and Griffith Park.

I tried to lessen his suffering. I was shocked and sad to see his youthful face change so much. The unfurrowed eyebrows and the innocent face I loved were disappearing. The full horror of Fred's suffering numbed me.

"Mom's always here," he told the nurse.

They gave him morphine to dull the pain. I'd find him flushed, eloquently drunk on his own words. He feigned callousness, perhaps afraid to show his true feelings and his fear. Born under the astrological sign of Cancer like me, he built up a shell to protect his soft inside.

As he recovered, Fred became bored, restless, and irritable. I gave him all my life, all my energy. When his cast was reduced, we ventured further and made trips to Disneyland, my little apartment, the Hollywood Bowl, or anything I could think of to divert his mind from the pain of his condition. We were very close.

Hours upon hours, I maintained a vision of Fred healed. Thought is the builder of forms. I meditated and gave energy to building a body that would work for him. There was so much waiting. I had to wait for doctors' reports. Wait for decisions to be made. Wait for Fred to come out of surgery and out of therapy. I spent hours in the chapel meditating. *With each new thought, we create the world anew. We are responsible.* The summer dragged on and I signed up at U.C.L.A. and managed to complete two classes toward my degree in-between visits to the hospital or forays into the Los Angeles area with Fred.

A disabled child does not necessarily bring a couple together. Quite the contrary. Leonard came down only once during the entire summer. He insisted that I come home, but I would not be pried away from my brave, and sometimes angry, little boy. Bobby Kennedy was killed in Los Angeles one unforgettable night while Fred was with me at home in our little refuge. We watched the tragedy unfold on television, not believing our eyes. That was the summer of dissolution.

My mother died there, quite suddenly in Los Angeles, one evening after visiting Fred. Certainly, it is fascinating and painful to speculate what might have taken place if I had given in to her wishes. She and Alice Denny arrived early in the day. They took a room at a hotel across the street from the Orthopedic Hospital and arrived in time for afternoon visiting hours.

Edgy and provocative all afternoon, my mother laughed as one dangerously balanced at the edge of a cliff. But Fred loved her teasing nature. She quickened the liveliness and sparkle in him. Before she'd come, his face was mask-like, but when she arrived her words charmed him with the skill of an expert magician. That day, her last day, she spent with Fred.

She took a loose pearl from her pocket and tied it to his toe. "Now, you look great, Kid. Alice broke her string of pearls this morning. I've been carrying this around all day. It belongs on you."

Fred laughed with a surprised look in his eyes and wriggled his toe.

Quite suddenly, she said, "Let's go party."

She'd caught me off balance. "Not tonight." Utterly drained and weak, I couldn't lose any more of what strength I had.

"I want to go to Don Ho's." A stubborn, fierce glance in my direction told me she meant to do it.

"I just can't go out tonight." I knew what nights out with her could be like. The visit in Eureka still haunted me. I knew that I couldn't handle her. Little nerves at the pit of my stomach tingled at the thought of it.

"This is my vacation," she said. She was beginning to breathe hard.

"No, you came here with Alice to see Fred."

"Still," she said, "I want to play." She had died her hair red and the color accentuated the blue of her magnificent turquoise eyes.

I knew she'd find a way to tangle herself up if we went out. Hard to believe that this woman—so devoted, loyal, the perfect Catholic wife who never ate meat on Friday—could be so capricious, so contrary.

A little wrinkle appeared between Fred's eyebrows. I rubbed his forehead.

"I just can't," I said. "I'll take you back to the hotel."

"You're against me," she hissed, outraged that I would not accommodate her.

I'm usually so sensitive; I pick up on everything, everyone. I'm never disinterested. But that night, I failed to pick up on the scent of death.

༜

A sharp ring broke the silence in my apartment. It was Alice. Her breathless voice said, "Gail, come at once. I don't know how to tell you—your mother, she's dead."

I felt like I was standing on quicksand about to sink.

I found her in the hotel room that she shared with Alice, her body crumpled on the floor and an empty bottle of gin next to her. Her once beautiful eyes stared blankly at the TV as if someone had eyes unplugged them from the current of life. I couldn't speak. Alice called the police.

A fresh pain came over me, a pain that was new. The loss of my mother shocked my old pattern of thinking. After all, she had always been there—my convert, Catholic mother—always wanting me to be better than she. The sudden anguish and emotional strain of her passing, as well as Fred's intense suffering, triggered

something in me that severed forever my tie to Leonard. It happened in an instant—the instant that I saw my mother's corpse. I
had offered my whole life to my husband, yet it did not belong to
him. I would not be the corpse one day of a woman who ruined her
life the way my mother did. I would not ruin another second of my
life by enduring Len and all that conspired to bind me to him.

The specter of the watchful parent disappeared. The heavy
straining cord of the Church could no longer stifle or strangle
me. I was bereft of a sponsor. I had to be my own. Duty, Church,
family—nothing could force me to go back. I was risking everything that I had worked so long and so desperately for: children,
home, and a kind of security, bizarre as it was.

Because of the peculiar circumstances of my mother's death,
the coroner in Los Angeles held the body for a post mortem.
They asked dozens of questions.

"Did you know that she drank?" the police investigator asked.

"Yes."

"Anything else?"

"She took prescription drugs. You probably found some in her
bag."

"What for?" He wrote in his notebook.

"To calm her down. She was like a time bomb waiting to
explode. It began when I was five."

"Her relationship with Mrs. Denny?"

"Friends." *My God did they think that Alice did it?*

In the end, they kept the remains for two weeks. The coroner
stated the reason for demise: alcohol poisoning. I told my grandmother that she died of a sudden heart attack.

At the end of August, I sent Fred home by plane and planned
my mother's funeral. A peculiar release had come with her
death: a sleeping power awakened. I felt a greater flow of love
than ever before.

Alice Denny had found a lacy white dress.

"She always lamented that she didn't have a proper wedding."
Alice was right.

"So, we'll bury her in white," I said. "This is a way to make it
up to her."

The day of the funeral was somber. Everyone was weighted
down and depressed. My father who sat defeated and passive—a
tragic figure in a dark-blue suit that hung loosely on his thin
frame—sobbed out loud. We sat in an orderly fashion in front of
the open casket. I listened to those who were weeping. *Did we all
feel our own death approaching?* My grandmother screamed, "My
girl! my girl!" *What could I do to comfort her?*

I looked lovingly and intently at the face I would never see
again. Perfume of roses floated upward from my mother's body. I
knew her spirit was there to shield me, to protect me. Part of me
died. Another part was freed and I felt lighter.

After the funeral, I filed for divorce. Len counter-sued, claiming that I had abandoned him. All through this time, the rhyth-
mic activity of daily meditation increased my energy and shored
me up. I felt my mother urging me on, and I planned my return
to Eureka. I knew I had to confront the issues and finish my
Master's degree.

On a hot, smoggy morning in early September, I set out for
San Francisco, which I reached at sunset. I drove over the
Golden Gate Bridge. It was still light and gulls dived into the sea.
I wound my way in moonlight many miles north, over the bridge
that spanned the Eel River, past curves in the road shadowed by
groves of ancient redwoods. I rolled down the window and listened to the rush of the river. It was alive, vital, and turbulent.
There were sudden shadows, sudden ravines. The perfume of my
mother enveloped me.

From one end of the state to the other, I felt the vagaries of climate, the colder airs of the north winning out over the hotter currents of Los Angeles. During the long drive, I discovered that all
my thoughts of turmoil—a frenzied succession of images of loss,

catastrophe, and disaster—began to dissolve. *I can't save my world.* There was no time for remorse, regret, or contrition. The fact of my mother's death forced me to see clearly that Len's whole life pattern was destructive, and I could no longer play a part in it. I could see a similarity between my mother and Len. Like her, Len was an imprisoned child with unspoken, unfulfilled desires.

Still, Fred needed access to health care. That worry nagged me and I couldn't shake it. With Len, he'd have it. With only me, he wouldn't. What could I do?

Arriving in Eureka after midnight, I found a dome of fog enveloping the town—a misty atmosphere that distorted the lampposts, street signs, and landmarks. Damp, cold, and tired, I installed myself in a modest hotel room with a low ceiling. Two windows looked out on the nightmarish street. I felt dazed and lonely and my heart tightened. I was not afraid of being alone. However, the knowledge that my children were just miles away, and I was not with them, was excruciating. The room made me feel altogether remote and unfamiliar. I finally caved in and slept.

Face-to-face the next morning, I began the negotiation process with my lawyer. His desk was strewn with legal pads and the debris of my life: broken dreams, broken promises, and broken hearts.

He said, "Leonard can provide health care; you can't. Be realistic. You have to leave the children with their father. After all, he's a doctor. The community is on his side."

"He's not a good father," I said.

"Can you prove it?"

"He's taken from me and never acknowledged it."

"That was stupid of you, wasn't it?"

"He held a gun to my head."

"Do you have witnesses?"

"He's stalking me, now."

"What do you mean?"

"Outside my bedroom, there are piles of rocks so he can peer in. Around the piles are stubs of Camel cigarettes, his brand."

"Did you call the police?"

"Yes, they said it could be anyone. And he follows me. I can see at night—out of the rear view mirror—a silver Jaguar. It's the only one in town. If I go in somewhere, he parks. I'm afraid." I screwed my mouth into a sarcastic smile. "No, I don't have witnesses."

"He doesn't want you to have anything."

"I don't want much."

"If you made him sell the shares in the business, then I could get you a cash settlement."

"Then, there would be nothing for the kids," I said. "They've been through a lot, years and years of poverty."

"Tell me about it."

As I told my story, giving places and dates, it all seemed so trivial. Just numbers.

When I finished, he said, "I'll do my best for you. But there's nothing in the law that says that you're entitled to compensation for putting him through school."

"What I want most is minimum inconvenience for the children."

In my divorce settlement, I relinquished all interest in Len's business and put my share of the business into a trust fund for my children with the condition that Leonard had to do the same. *Insurance for their future.* I got four hundred dollars a month in alimony and a property settlement of four hundred dollars. This, for four years.

I was at the end of my strength. I thought of taking Jeanne with me, but I knew she would be reluctant to leave her father. She was still Daddy's little girl and was in for a lesson that she would have to learn the hard way, I feared.

In the end, I chose to leave the children with Len for the time being, which was the harshest sacrifice I've ever made. Jeanne was thirteen; Lenny, twelve; Fred, eleven; and Chris, six. I had concluded that leaving them was in their best interest, at least for the moment. I wanted them to have as much stability as possible. After all, we had been on the move for many years. In Eureka, we had established what little roots we had. True, we had joint custody, but Leonard had a house, a housekeeper, a profession, and an excellent income. For a long time, I didn't cry. I told myself that I had my memories.

I had built all of this with Len. Surely, I could build something on my own. I could do it again. First, I had to rescue myself.

The war in Vietnam dragged on, and rather than give in to despair over it and over the loss of all that I worked for, I chose to leave the United States and move to France. I believed our national karma was monstrous and that it would come back to punish us. I wanted to emigrate and find means to get my children away. I wanted to live in a country that appreciated women.

All the while, I thought it was about me. But weren't we all caught up in a whirlwind of social change? Feminism gained widespread influence. The anti-war movement swept across the country.

It was my hope that I could leverage my Master's degree in English into some worthwhile skill. I didn't want to live in constant conflict. I had a right to experiment with my life, to strip myself of all non-essentials. Through meditation, I learned to release the outworn. I discovered the great creative power I had in determining what lived and died in me at any time.

When I went to France, I couldn't speak the language and I had no friends. From the beginning, I loved the streets of Paris, the little cafés, hidden bookstores, and the escape from the taboos and restrictions of my past life. I found delight in everything. I could see and feel my connection. The force of life, my love of it—pure joyousness—transformed me.

Slowly, I began to emerge. I taught courses in Transcendental Meditation and gave a lecture to the Paris Chamber of Commerce on "Higher States of Consciousness." I'd sit at the

Les Deux Magots, sip *espresso*, and fantasize about bringing my children to France. Never did I dream this would come true in a matter of months.

Paris signaled a change from a closed, crystallized state and set my life spinning off in a new direction. At night in my room at the Alliance Francaise, I would lie in bed and replay the themes of my life—sex, money, children, health, religion, birth, death. I had acted according to the light that I possessed, yet I felt a longing swell in my chest. Below, sounds from the Boulevard Raspail in the Latin Quarter hummed, honked, and screeched. I'd slip out of bed and look out the window. The view was spectacular: Paris, the city of light.

I could not accept letting Len play a role for me. I needed freedom, but not merely from him. I had to create it for myself. Now, the answers come more easily. Sometimes, I felt my soul stumble. Some threads have doubtless unraveled. Yet, in pleating my story, I found a magical power through entering into language that clarified what happened and transformed my baffling reality into something with meaning.

Jeanne graduated from Case Western Medical School in Ohio. She and her husband are both psychiatrists in the Bay area. They have three children. Jeanne still has the skull that her father annotated.

Lenny married and changed his name to Lynn. He has three children and umpires Little League Baseball in Springfield, Oregon.

Fred became a stand-up comic and performs at the Icehouse in Pasadena, as well as around the country. He has made movies and written a book, *Handicaptions,* and is the oldest surviving spina bifida patient on record at the Children's Hospital in San Diego.

Chris lives in Atlanta with his wife, Cindy. He works in the software industry and, like his father, enjoys the South.

I completed a Ph.D. in Leadership, Human Behavior. My topic, *Kindred Spirits,* explored the dynamics of female bonding. I focused on the relationship between Margaret Mead and Ruth Benedict. I have had many careers, most notably, teaching Women's Studies and consulting in Quality Management. I once chaired the San Diego County Commission for Women.

Janille became a nurse for the County of San Diego. Together, we planned our fiftieth high school reunion.

My friend Monica remained in Monterrey for five years after I left. She and Lois Lowell began a preschool. Monica now lives in San Diego, fifteen minutes away. We go to movies together and sometimes reminisce.

Camille, who was a friend to me in Mexico, was written about in Elizabeth Borton Trevino's book, *My Heart Lies South.*

Father John Cavanaugh died in 1979. He never stopped promoting the idea that Notre Dame was a great and glorious institution.

Leonard joined the Veterans Administration. He married a nurse who adored him. Over the years, he had at least two operations on his heart, but he died of lung cancer in 1999.

On my grandfather's birthday, March 7, 1971, I met Anton Dimitroff. He was a young attorney practicing with an American Law firm in Paris. We married and have remained so for thirty-two years. We have one daughter, Katherine, and live in San Diego.